I0804972

British Women Amateur Filmmakers

British Women Amateur Filmmakers

National Memories and Global Identities

Annamaria Motrescu-Mayes and
Heather Norris Nicholson

EDINBURGH
University Press

Edinburgh University Press is one of the leading university presses in the UK. We publish academic books and journals in our selected subject areas across the humanities and social sciences, combining cutting-edge scholarship with high editorial and production values to produce academic works of lasting importance. For more information visit our website: edinburghuniversitypress.com

Edinburgh University Press Ltd
The Tun – Holyrood Road
12 (2f) Jackson's Entry
Edinburgh EH8 8PJ

First published in hardback by Edinburgh University Press 2018

Typeset in 11/13 Ehrhardt MT by
IDSUK (DataConnection) Ltd

A CIP record for this book is available from the British Library

ISBN 978 1 4744 2073 0 (hardback)
ISBN 978 1 4744 7433 7 (paperback)
ISBN 978 1 4744 2074 7 (webready PDF)
ISBN 978 1 4744 2075 4 (epub)

Contents

Figures

Sources and Abbreviations

Alpine Club, London
Amateur Cinematographers' Association (ACA)
Amateur Cine World (ACW)
Bristol Archives, UK
British Empire & Commonwealth Museum (BECM)
British Film Institute (BFI)
British International Amateur Film Festival (BIAFF)
British Pathé Ltd
Centre of South Asian Studies, University of Cambridge (CSAS)
Digital Film Archive, Northern Ireland Screen (DFA)
East Anglian Film Archive (EAFA)
Edinburgh Cine and Video Society (ECVS) (aka Edinburgh Cine Society)
Fédération Internationale des Archives de Télévision – International Federation of Television Archives (FIAF/IFTA)
Getty Images
Glasgow School of Art Kinecraft Society (GSAKS)
Imperial War Museum (IWM)
Institute of Amateur Cinematographers (IAC)
Leeds Animation Workshop (LAW)
Media Archive for Central England (MACE)
Moving Image Archive, National Library of Scotland (NLS)
National Film Theatre (NFT)
National Science and Media Museum (NSMM)
North East Film Archive (NEFA)
North West Film Archive (NWFA)
Rivers Video Project (Professor Alan MacFarlane, University of Cambridge)
Scottish Amateur Film Festival (SAFF)
Screen Archive South East (SASE)
The Alexander Film Archive, Valley Stream Media Developments
The British Entertainment History Project (BEHP)

Union internationale du cinéma (aka Union internationale du cinéma (non professionel) and Union internationale du cinéma d'amateur) (UNICA)
Video Home System (VHS)
Women's Film and Television History Network UK/Ireland (WFTHN)
Yorkshire Film Archive (YFA)
YouTube

Private Collections and Contributors

Beryl Armstrong
Christine Collins
Phillip Collins
Brian Dunckley
Brenda Granshaw
Angela Heywood
Holmfirth Camera Club (Edmund Spavin)
Betty Jennings
Jill Lampert
Leeds Animation Workshop (Terry Wragg)
Penny Love
Lucy Fairbank Legacy Archive, West Yorkshire, England (Ian Baxter)
John Shearsmith (*Amateur Cine Enthusiast*)
Diana Mary Thubron
Gillian Wagner

For reasons of confidentiality, full private details of contributors and amateur film collections are not listed but their access for research purposes is gratefully acknowledged separately.

Film Title Conventions

Title details observe archival practice in cataloguing, as set out by the Fédération Internationale des Archives de Télévision – International Federation of Television Archives (FIAF/IFTA). Square brackets [ ] indicate an attributed title for cataloguing purposes, where there is no evidence of a prior existing title; an asterisk * or hyphenated dates indicate the approximate date of the filmstock, and may represent a date earlier than when the film was made.

Acknowledgements

Most books are a labour of love. Ours demanded more: a leap of faith, monastic perseverance and a cathartic sense of humour when our lives, independently and simultaneously, presented us with non-negotiable urgencies. It was the help of many people that made our journey through various stages of writing this book pleasurable, possible and rewarding.

We owe our vote of gratitude to Gillian Leslie for taking on a project at a time when words such as pioneering, niche or avant-garde were not even at the adjective horizon for the type of research and methodology proposed by us. Her decision was not an exercise in supporting feminist scholarship, but the expression of an astute editorial sense for topics that break the mould, challenge comfortable interpretative frameworks and demand, all risks assumed, a dialogue with future generations of international scholars. Gillian and her colleagues, Richard Strachan, Eddie Clark and Rebecca Mackenzie, have helped us navigate the production of the book with the type of generosity and diplomacy that qualifies professional collaborations.

The book relies on considerable archival research and we wish to thank the staff at different archives and acknowledge their generous help, and the use of their materials, particularly Phillip Collins (IAC), Jane Fish (IWM), Jayne Pucknell (Bristol Archives), Nigel Buckley and Glyn Hughes (Alpine Club Library), Kevin Greenbank (CSAS), Shona Gonnella, Stephanie Ashcroft and Lois Langmead (NLS), Megan McCooley (YFA), Jane King (SASE), Sue Malden and Angela Martin (BEHP) Angela Graham and Jane Alvey (EAFA), Richard Shenton (MACE), David Parsons (NEFA) and Marion Hewitt, Will McTaggart and Mark Boden (NWFA).

To our British women amateur filmmakers, we also owe a special thanks as their interest in this film genre, and the stories we have discovered, lie at the heart of this book. There are also a number of individuals who have been extremely generous with their time and advice. We are particularly grateful to Tim Healey, John Bridcut, Ciara Chambers, Karen Lury, Kevin Brownlow, Katherine Prior, Ian Baxter and Brian Dunckley. To Michael Turner, Stephen Herbert and John Shearsmith we offer thanks for their timely contributions.

The courage and faith we had in completing our book manuscript on time has drawn strength from the friendship offered by Anna, Melanie and others, and, in particular, has been sustained by our families' patience, understanding and encouragement. This book belongs to them as much as it is our project: Steve Nicholson, Eric L. Mayes, Dorothy Norris and Adrian Ilie Motrescu supported us, laughed with us and believed in us even when our stories about the book resembled surreal monologues. For their love and comedic disruptions, our non-verbal thanks to Pushkin, Schmitz, Squidz-Yamaneko, Toby, Shinobu and Olya.

Finally, if we were to dedicate our book, we will opt again for inspiring, courageous and visionary women: Doina Constanta Motrescu, and Katya and Vikka Nicholson.

Foreword

This volume, exploring the diversity of women's amateur filmmaking from the cine camera's early days to the digital and online present, is highly welcome. Not only do its authors, Annamaria Motrescu-Mayes and Heather Norris Nicholson, bring into public view a whole body of little-known and rarely considered films by British women, in addressing the status of the amateur and the nature of their work, they open new channels between women and cinema, enlarging understanding of film as a way of gendered, class and colonial imagining, and offering a new lens through which to investigate the interactions between media use and the lived experience of social change. Hopefully, disseminating knowledge of women's past and present amateur filmmaking will encourage archives to preserve such work and exhibition venues to make it more accessible to wider audiences.

Central to the book's project is the light it throws on the nature of the amateur space. While often relegated as the naïve hobby of home-movie making, the authors reveal a potentially freer space, less bound by industry know-how and conventional ways of doing things. Some of the women investigated took up the camera at a time when filmmaking itself was still a new form and developing its own professional protocols. Equally, during the interwar years Britain was undergoing huge changes, not only in terms of gender and class relations, but, as the authors emphasise, through the incipient dissolution of empire and the rise of anti-colonial struggles. While cost meant that early women amateurs usually came from the middle classes, their position as women on the margins of key administrative, political and industrial arenas, whether abroad or at home, gave their status as amateurs a degree of openness and flexibility not available to professional documentarists – answerable to funding agencies – or to feature film producers, driven by economic constraints, competition with Hollywood or subject to censorship.

This does not, however, mean that British women amateurs occupied an empty space of free expression. Along with perceptions derived from their own class and familial positions, their approach to the evolving languages of film necessarily drew on practices of mainstream movie making, and, as the authors find, the British Empire movie could haunt their filmmakers' imaginations. But these women's films also suggest how their experiences of, and responses to, changing gender, class and colonial relationships, as well as their different motivations in picking up the movie camera – to create personal records, send filmed documents home or preserve family memories – enabled them, whether consciously or not, to diverge from the official colonial or patriarchal view. In making these films visible and offering nuanced analyses of their diversity of methods and meanings, the authors suggest how the amateur space registers contingent, fleeting, non-conforming perceptions, giving us access to subjective histories and cultural imaginaries mediated through filmmaking and enabling the cultural or film historian to observe processes of social change at work. For women's film history, such amateur uses of the cine camera and its successors reveal the interchange between how women have seen the world in particular historical and cultural contexts and their mainstream cinema-going experiences, providing important insights into reception history. In turn, unorthodox practices developed to record personal experiences and cine memories offer strategies for women's professional documentary or fiction filmmaking, both then and now. We thus approach past and still practising amateur women filmmakers not to measure their work against current criteria, but to encounter shifting gender, class and colonial relationships in process, along with the differences of the amateur's tangential uses of cinematography – all the better to see what is at stake for us today, as women, both amateur and professional, to take up digital tools and online media.

Christine Gledhill
May 2018

CHAPTER 1

Amateur Women Filmmakers as Producers of Cultural Meaning

> What beats me Helen is how you became such an expert film producer? Shall I let you into a secret? With Ciné-Kodak everybody becomes an expert first go off. It's even easier than snap-shotting because there's no worrying about keeping your subjects in order. (Anon. 1929a: 4)

An image of a family watching a home movie about a child and a dog playing accompanies these lines in Kodak's promotion of lightweight cine equipment to British audiences in early 1929. With her bobbed hair and a low-necked printed dress, the eponymous Helen epitomises the young, modern female cine user. She embodies the ambivalence of womanhood in a new age of consumerism and represents the ambiguities of inter-war middle class femininity. Kodak's advertising strategy promises the transformative power of consumption; evolving visual technologies make filming possible – even for women. Helen side-steps male incredulity and the challenges of childcare without nanny or governess support to invite *Punch*'s readers into a domestic world where movie-making routinely helps 'to keep the family together' (Anon. 1929b) and safeguard 'youth, colour, frolic, movement – stolen intact from time' (Anon. 1931a: 3).

Helen, like other fictive women amateur filmmakers, recurs in Kodak's outreach to an early female amateur market: 'Simply to hold this beautiful instrument – elegant as a jewel case, compact as a novel, is to begin to feel the thrill of making movie pictures' (ibid.). Language and imagery construct prospective users and target purchasers, emphasising the equipment's apparent feminised suitability and appeal via jargon-free terms ('the hidden motor [that] begins to purr') and 'wonderfully easy' operation (of 'the little trigger') that is stress-free and 'thrilling' (ibid.). Fortunately for Kodak's sales, camera use expanded beyond the drawing-room world evoked by these colour advertisements, and cine film's visual novelty attracted broader female interest. This book examines how that outreach occurred; where and how women made and showed their films; and what those experiences reveal about the women holding the cameras and the profoundly changing twentieth-century world they captured on screen. As taboos and patriarchal structures receded, societal and geo-political changes enabled and necessitated women to live, work and behave differently from their predecessors. At home and abroad, their self-expression and social purpose found fresh outlets via amateur filmmaking, the newest branch of photography. Access to cine equipment, via family, friends and interest groups, enabled women to engage with film production in and away from where they lived and worked (Figure 1.1). As opportunities for recreational cine use grew, so did the involvement of women drawn by friendships and their own recognition of where capturing occasions and encounters on film seemed appropriate. This book identifies those early British filmmakers' experiences within national and late colonial settings; and how, from these 'reel' pioneers, still an often under-represented and undifferentiated presence within amateur film studies literature, it is possible to trace activity through the twentieth century to their successors, the digital amateur image and media makers of today.

Through the prism of amateur cine/media practice, defined as the recreational making and interpretation of films for personal and wider non-commercial use, we explore the impact of social, cultural and technological change upon women's lives. We base this study upon archival

Figure 1.1 Still frame from *Films from Miss Fairbank*. Portrait of Lucy Fairbank (*c.*1936). © Lucy Fairbank Legacy archive / Ian Baxter.

evidence of women's own capacity to film and the subject matter captured by their cinematic gaze. Their non-fiction footage is the main focus here, although their involvement in other genres, particularly animation is also considered. Their non-fictional films, in particular, represent how they negotiated and documented change as they narrated their own lives, and those of others through their cameras. Recovering these neglected endeavours augments our understanding of women's amateur visual practice during decades that also saw production opportunities slowly opening for women within the commercial film industry and broadcasting. Most importantly, these cine women filmed during years in which national boundaries and identities were transformed by war and independence movements. Their footage coincides with when self-assurance about Britain's identity at home and in the wider world gave way to new national uncertainties and domestic preoccupations. Our analysis therefore goes beyond interrogating the visible: in different parts of Britain, during international travel or in a post-imperial/postcolonial world order, women's films testify to their own creativity and agency, to what they valued in their surroundings and how they sought to share their beliefs with others. As this book shows, their legacy lives on.

Media Making: A Century of Gendered Practice

Amateur filmmaking came into existence as early as 1895 with Auguste and Louis Lumière's first recordings of family life in their short film, *Le Repas de Bébé* (*Feeding the Baby*). Women's early cine use is harder to pinpoint: the woman holding innovative equipment for taking still and moving imagery from an early Biokam manual catalogue (Figure 1.2) may have been a marketing ploy and none of the early Edwardian sequences of children recorded in monochrome and on colour film is yet attributable to women filmmakers.[1] Indeed some media historians trace the official date for the birth of women's amateur filmmaking to 1921, the year when Marion Norris Gleason used a 16mm Cine-Kodak prototype camera to film her ten-month-old son playing in the garden (Swanson 2003). Six years later, Frances Lascot was hailed as Britain's first woman amateur director (Anon. 1929c: 101; Norris Nicholson 2012a: 20). Female interest in amateur filmmaking proliferated between the First and Second World Wars, as media technologies and societal opportunities developed. As cameras evolved technologically, prices gradually dropped and amateur filmmakers started to experiment with different film formats including 9.5mm, 17.5mm, and 70mm. Standard 8mm (1932) and Super 8mm (1965) became the most popular formats of the amateur cine era. Video

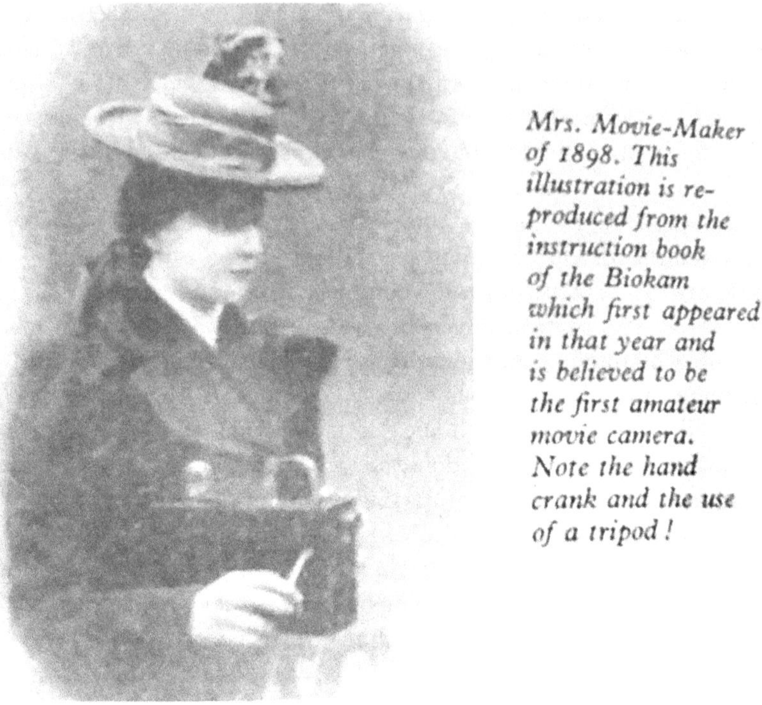

Figure 1.2 Photograph from an early Biokam manual (*c.*1899). Reproduced from *Amateur Movie Maker* (1961). © *Amateur Cine Enthusiast.*

Home System (VHS) later emerged as the dominant format in the video home recording age, although Betamax gained short-lived popularity prior to the proliferation from the late 1990s of increasingly affordable pocket-sized digital recording devices.

Surviving footage attests to how overall visual interests grew, standards varied and how people became involved in amateur filmmaking on their own or with others. Many amateur films were personalised records of private and public events, although some enthusiasts experimented with small-gauge fiction productions, social issue and commissioned training films. In time, much amateur filmmaking gravitated around a set of production guidelines and themes. These included often unscripted narratives, a seemingly spontaneous recording of events and activities, direct interaction with the people filmed, and the use of the film camera with rapid and abrupt variations of speed, focus and perspective. Owing to the prohibitive film stock prices and high laboratory costs, amateur film practice in Britain and across the British Empire remained for most of the first half of the twentieth century the privilege of the affluent classes, although cine's novelty sometimes crossed conventional class boundaries, as shown by early club minutes and biographies for some early cine users (Norris Nicholson 2012a: 44–51).

In interwar Britain, financial hardship hit amateur filmmakers and reportedly some men gave up smoking to save for a few extra film reels.[2] For instance, in the mid-1930s a two-minute reel of black and white or colour film was £24 and £35 respectively, while the average yearly salary reached barely £2,000. From the 1950s onwards, second-hand equipment also made the hobby more affordable and as Super 8mm film equipment became relatively cheaper in the post-war era, more middle and working class amateur filmmakers started to join amateur film societies and clubs. Rising levels of disposable income helped home movie-making to gain a popularity that was perpetuated by the widening availability of successive video technologies and the emergence of competitively priced recording equipment for different digital devices. A once privileged pastime thus became mainstream.

Women responded swiftly to these changing visual technologies. Just as digital formats attracted female use during the 1990s, and VHS found favour among some women filmmakers during the later 1970s and the 1980s, competing photographic companies targeted lightweight handheld cine equipment for the British market by the mid-1920s.[3] For some women, early filmmaking interests meant new theatrical opportunities to perform in plays that were filmed by local male amateur filmmakers, eager to attract audiences with a combination of entertainment, visual novelty and familiar figures on-screen (Norris Nicholson 2012a: 39–42). For some married women, film production became a creative partnership that brought shared recognition and pleasure over many years, as shown through the records of the Institute of Amateur Cinematographers (IAC) and regional clubs. For single women, cine equipment offered opportunities to direct and make their own stories in moving image (Norris Nicholson 2013).[4]

For many women, amateur film took emerging interests in cinema, identity and self-expression in new and practical directions, beyond film appreciation. Yet some of the pioneering women who joined in with the frenzy of forming early clubs gradually found themselves marginalised within the semi-formal structures that developed to support and promote amateur cinematography. Their activities were under-acknowledged in the hobby press. Newly available records and IAC material offer fresh opportunities to reappraise the involvement and achievement of those early practitioners who were named on club trophies or took part in events at regional, national and even international level. As we identify some of these early enthusiasts, we acknowledge their varied contributions to the history of informal and organised amateur media practice. Analysis of individual filmmakers is therefore considered alongside filmmakers who produced film with a partner or with other club members.

Of particular importance are the films made by British women who lived overseas during the late colonial era. The study of their films contributes to the re-examination of imperial gender politics and of colonial women's histories that are not necessarily evident in governmental or commercial productions such as documentaries, newsreels and feature films. It is from this perspective that this book presents a comparative analysis of selected colonial amateur films made by British women living, travelling and working in India, Africa, Papua New Guinea and the Middle East between the 1920s and 1960s. Either born into the privileged expatriate lifestyles of diplomatic families, or marrying or moving into such circles, these women's colonial amateur films of domesticity abroad, public service and imperial ceremony offer remarkable informal insights into the workings of late British colonialism. Their amateur films trace their surveillance upon childcare and domestic life, servants, child-minders, gardeners and drivers, as well as informing their proximity to influential colonial figures and their semi-informal gaze upon state occasions, imperial educational programmes, medical organisations and missionary work.

While functioning as first-person visual narratives of specific gendered hierarchies, domesticity, racial and cultural authority and imperial history, these films also illustrate the migration of British imperial female agency across diverse colonial and early postcolonial contexts. Investigating British imperial identities across colonial amateur films generally centres on the identification and analysis of three major thematic strands: social, political and ethnographic. The former theme, with family-related topics, is generally the canvas for the other two; the political theme covers official events and ceremonies; while the ethnographic theme becomes apparent in scenes that show directly or tangentially indigenous peoples and cultures. Most interwar colonial amateur films offer images of what one was expected to be, of how individuals had to behave according to their imperial networks. Although it is impossible to define a prescribed gender-based thematic framework, there is nevertheless a distinctive set of topics that appears to have been preferred by women within various colonial settings. This thematic schism was typically determined by their given social contexts rather than by their gender-based preferences.

At first glance, it could be argued that women filmed predominantly their domestic and leisure activities, children, pets, servants, travels, flowers, birds, picnics, weddings, birthday parties and their network of British expatriates, while men preferred to film their governmental work, entrepreneurial and military drills and parades, club events, hunting and exploratory expeditions, tours of duty, horse racing, sailing, sport competitions, safaris, motorcars, dams, railways, plantations, workers, and industrial and agricultural infrastructures. These thematic differences would indicate that there was a marked as well as expected division of gender-prescribed (primed) thematic sets that linked domestic topics to the colonial feminine domain, and the public topics to the masculine domain respectively.[5] However, when analysing, for example, the over 1,900 films-strong collection of British colonial amateur films previously held by the British Empire and Commonwealth Museum (Bristol, UK),[6] the initial assessment of themes-per-gender division becomes problematic: men also filmed in great detail their homes and immediate surroundings, gardens, pets, their families, friends, social gatherings, weddings, domestic servants, Christmas parties and travels. Often, these were the only topics covered by their collections as is the case with Major K. C. Tait (1950s) or Brigadier Cecil Leonard Basil Duke's (1930s and 1950s) amateur films.[7] Moreover, some women had access to and filmed social and cultural networks that would not have been accessible to their male counterparts. For instance, Dame Eleanor Dalyell recorded extensively her travels across the North-West Frontier Province, her husband's meetings with frontier tribal leaders, Indian itinerant communities, military parades, governmental and official gatherings, as well as traditional Muslim and Hindu religious ceremonies.[8] It is from this perspective, and within the dynamic of interchangeable thematic preferences, that British women's amateur filmmaking should be explored for its role in highlighting the porous social fabric of prescribed colonial gender-ghettoised networks (Motrescu-Mayes 2010).

Interwar British colonial amateur film practice evolved within the framework of the imperial popular film culture represented by the empire cinema genre, which consisted mostly of feature films, *topicals*, documentaries, (ethno-)travelogues and instructional films about either general themes or specific topics defining the British Empire. These films benefited from an international distribution and were an integral part of the British governmental agenda, imperial immigration schemes and war propaganda films. Most colonial amateur filmmakers had thus been exposed to, and often emulated, themes and filming styles borrowed from imperial fiction and non-fiction productions. The empire cinema promoted dominant British attitudes and popular cultural tendencies, and it had a significant role in confirming and strengthening British people's support of the imperial enterprise. Empire cinema incorporates all films, irrespective of the country of production, about the British Empire including pioneering cinematographic work such as *Savage South Africa. Savage Attack and Repulse* (Warwick Trading Company, UK, 1899) and *Attack of a China*

Mission – Bluejackets to the Rescue (James Williamson, UK, 1900). This film genre gained momentum during the interwar period, owing to the films produced in the UK by Alexander and Zoltan Korda such as *Sanders of the River* (1935), *Elephant Boy* (1937), *The Drum* (1938) and *The Four Feathers* (1939). Other empire films portraying British colonials as 'heaven born' with a civilising mission include, for instance, *Lives of a Bengal Lancer* (dir. Henry Hathaway, USA, 1935), *The Charge of the Light Brigade* (dir. Michael Curtiz, USA, 1936), *Gunga Din* (dir. George Stevens, USA, 1939) and *Black Narcissus* (dir. Michael Powell, Emeric Pressburger, UK, 1947).[9] A similar ideological rhetoric is present across most type of colonial testimonies, from diaries, letters, home movies, fiction films and, most recently, documentaries, as in the case of *The British Empire in Colour* (dir. Stewart Binns, UK, 2002).

Throughout the 1930s, the empire cinema films produced on both sides of the Atlantic shared a range of thematic templates relying on the Western European white man's conquest of new territories and his allegedly civilising and philanthropic governing of indigenous peoples. The empire cinema promoted an iconography of British imperial identities centred on dominant tropes of patriotic, self-sacrificial and unfaltering masculinity. The core topics addressed in these films were imperial expansionism, the 'white man's burden' of perpetual civilising duty, martyrdom and messianic destiny often shared with colonial women in a joint effort to illustrate the triumph of the English character. British colonial amateur films include clear references to this pervasive ideological framework and the cultural politics of empire albeit locked in images of gratifying past-time activities that were almost exclusively available to those living in the colonies, or the habitual tourist gaze surveying imperial exoticism (Urry 1990). The illustration of British identity and imperial endeavour are also present in non-fiction films made from as early as 1911 when the Topical Budget newsreels were first produced with the sole aim to show 'traditionalist Britain what it wanted to be shown of its Empire' (McKernan 1992). The British monarchy, imperial exploratory traditions and popular colonial histories were among favourite topics covered by these newsreels showing royal visits, marching troops, Empire Day celebrations, imperial exhibitions and princely tours of the Dominions. These films promoted British imperial identity worldwide on the grounds of British national pride and its civilising pre-eminence. Importantly, the newsreels preserved a Britain-centralised colonial perspective and promoted the ideological lineage of Victorian imperial credos, a visual and thematic rhetoric that was challenged only after the Second World War when the disintegration of the British Empire started through a rapid and widespread decolonisation process. Recent film and TV productions inspired by the history of the British Empire rely on stereotypical treatment of historic facts, imperial literature, testimonials, manuscripts, or oral history such as *Echoes of the Raj* (dir. Catherine Clay, UK, 2000), *Empire: How Britain made the Modern World* (Channel 4, UK, 2003) or *Lost World of the Raj* (dir. Marion Milne, UK, 2007) often used excerpts from colonial amateur films as (tautological) illustrations for cliché-ridden statements on British colonialists and settlers. Most often, their identities appear in formulaic terms, lacking social and cultural introspection, and defined outside the historic relevance of their colonial framework. In light of this, British peoples' identities remain to be (re)discovered across amateur films and photographs, all valuable for their documentary merit and authenticity. It is in this context that British women's amateur films about life in the colonies function as a memory currency exchanged between imperial outposts and Britain, especially when copies of a film reel were sent as a cine letter or journal – visual records in which the titles 'illustrated' the broad meaning found in the images (Motrescu-Mayes 2011a).[10]

Themes and Approaches

Women's emerging involvement with amateur media making was always much more than simply a hobby. It now offers a rich multifaceted and nuanced visual legacy of twentieth-century life inflected with meaning and intermeshed with other narratives of change. From the outset, women's visual practice was an expression of their complex and changing roles in post-war society, self-identity and their place in the world. While the video generation documented the diverse concerns and lifestyles of 1980s Britain and elsewhere, early amateur women filmmakers took to directing, shooting and screening amateur films about their private and public spheres, from local to distant colonial locations. Collectively they have left a wealth of little known stories about their experiences, their understanding of the world around them, and how they negotiated the complexities of age, generation, status, convention and phases of modernity. In reclaiming these narratives of changing visual practice, we identify amateur women filmmakers as producers of cultural meaning and show how their films offer unofficial perspectives on aspects of twentieth century experience.

Gendered approaches to film histories have developed diversely over the past forty years,[11] and the Women's Film and Television History Network (UK/Ireland, set up in 2009) has been instrumental in coordinating attempts to promote widening research into women's filmmaking and television history.[12] In comparison to their pioneering professional equivalents during the early decades of the twentieth century, women amateur filmmakers still remain neglected (Norris Nicholson 2015a). We thus offer visibility to non-professional women film practitioners at a time when the professional/amateur divide was malleable. As Rachael Low reminds us, many professionals started as amateurs in the early years of filmmaking (Low 1979). Cross-over inevitably occurred: the two worlds of visual production and consumption were more interconnected than the labels imply and sometimes there were opportunities for women to become directors, scriptwriters, designers and cinematographers because there were no alternatives. They were in the right place at the right time; they had access to equipment and jobs needed doing.

In keeping with widening opportunities throughout society during and after the First World War, due to wartime absence and loss of life, it is unsurprising that some women found that out of their amateur interests grew professional opportunities and experiences even if long-term career development was often thwarted by discrimination and social attitudes (Krasilovsky 1997; Lant and Periz 2006; Foster et al. 1998). Most of the early women considered here, however, were recreational filmmakers and, although covering well-trodden ground, Garber's (2001) distinction of the amateur professional/professional amateur binary seems apt. At their best, they were adept professional amateurs, proficient in their film production and well regarded within their immediate circle, rather than amateurs aspiring to be professionals. As research on women's past professional contributions enhances our understanding of media history, reclaiming pioneering women amateur filmmakers from obscurity ensures their own visibility within a broader understanding of changing visual practice.

As part of wider trajectories of media history and amateur creativity, countless women's stories about every day and other experiences are captured on amateur footage that have remained largely neglected and forgotten in Britain's public archives and private collections. This study positions women's evolving amateur filmic endeavours within longer narratives of gender history, social and cultural change, and economic emancipation. Gendered visual practice is set against a background of changing technologies, attitudes towards sexual and racial identities, and the geo-politics of the shift from Britain and Empire, through late colonialism to postcolonial sensibilities. In viewing amateur media making as gendered social practice, at home and overseas, then and now, we also identify patterns of continuity and change that open ways to further explore developments within other national and societal contexts. These non-professional antecedents to more equitable forms of filmmaking associated with the well-documented period of flourishing women's activity in the 1970s and early 1980s also invite comparison with recent and emergent spaces internationally in which women strive to gain voice and visibility via current media formats.

If amateur cinema may be a forerunner to today's personalised and permissive record-making, by modern standards of political probity, its past practitioners were also uncensored and remarkably free-ranging over content and location. Their unfettered analogue gaze upon the world across so many decades offers illuminating and sideways glances upon events both centre-stage and in the wings. Although profoundly different, those cine users that documented what went on around them espoused a sense of personal duty and the value of being publicly active, inherited from their Victorian and Edwardian forebears. With their cameras in hand to record moments of private, civic and voluntary significance, these often untroubled chroniclers of the everyday and memorable exceptions have their equivalents – increasingly circumscribed by rules of privacy and security – in today's digitised taking and mobilised sharing of visual imagery.

Despite the record-making impulse that threads through the lives and films considered here, we do not trace a seamless evolution of gendered amateur visual practice over time. Obstacles, prejudices and social conventions limited many opportunities: male smoking culture[13] or being the 'continuity girl' rather than behind the cameras deterred some single women from club life for years (Chapter 2). Family responsibilities eclipsed personal leisure time for many married women too. Like any attempt at a historical overview, our picture ultimately is incomplete, selective and partial. Able-bodied, middle class white women tend to predominate, simply because of underlying economic, social, geographical and political inequalities that have continued to affect who is likely to have access to cameras, technical knowledge and the confidence needed to film other people. Time has reduced such barriers but not brought parity and Britain's archive record still reflects the legacy of past patterns of class and racial privilege although internationally differences occur. While the focus here is on British women, activities may be set against the achievements of Zora Neale Hurston whilst studying with the anthropologist Franz Boas,[14] and Eloyce King Patrick Gist whose films reached to the African American community in the 1920s and early 1930s.[15] Elsewhere, scholarship is also revealing examples of amateur filmmakers with different sexual, ethnic, cultural and disabled identities that help to broaden our understanding of past amateur activity (Dudding 2007; 2010; Thompson 2009).

Gender politics recur as we seek to answer the questions of who, how, what, where, when and why women were filming in different ways and settings. Issues of cultural politics and representation resonate through the following pages. Nothing is neutral about how people have opportunities (or not) to shape visual stories and share memories of themselves and others. Nor are the power relations and assumptions about superiority of those framed by the cine lens and those holding the camera straightforward whether captured in a family group, school, public, institutional, travel or colonial locations. Each and every instance is a fragment of interaction imbricated with values, expectations, hidden meanings and associations which we can sometimes only begin to unravel through a combination of close visual scrutiny and interdisciplinary contextual analysis. Archival records similarly reflect gaps, omissions and silences that result from policy and practice at different times and we welcome the sensibility and cooperation of archivists and others who facilitate gendered interrogation as new cataloguing and digitisation projects widen access and approaches to materials (Aasman 2014; Norris Nicholson 2012b; 2013).

For instance, most British colonial women recorded portraits of local communities, cultural traditions and landscapes, whether in writing, or by film and photography. Primed by the imperial popular culture and encouraged to take 'an intelligent interest in the country, in the natives, and in . . . immediate surroundings' (Procida 2002:105), their understanding and representations of colonised people and societies subscribed to a tourist-gaze agenda that endorsed illustrations of exoticised behaviour (Urry 1990). However, some of the amateur films made by women revealed new political and ethnographic dimensions of their hobbyist practice as they documented the British Empire and the Commonwealth between the 1920s and the 1960s (Motrescu-Mayes 2015). Although the British cine women's amateur ethnographic gaze remained the driving force behind most of their films, there was a fundamental shift in their visual literacy. This shift was informed by fissures in conventional imperial ideologies of race, gender and identity such that their amateur ethnographic gaze focusing on, for example, Indian bazaars or Arab traditional dances started to target instances of post-war manhood, death-defying expeditions, and the racial and political unity of South Asian and African newly acquired national identities. Thus, whether living in, or travelling to, the British colonies and dominions at the time of national turmoil and ongoing struggles for independence, women amateur filmmakers transcended traditional historical discourses through their recordings of visual first-person narratives and, consequently, highlight across their unofficial visual narratives, social, racial and gender insurgencies defining various times in the history of the British Empire and the Commonwealth (Burghin et al. 1986). Scenes of domestic duties, private and public education, labour networks, parenthood (mostly instances of motherhood), journeys to and from colonies and Britain, and of official engagements, support the study of several first-person colonial visual narratives such as, for instance, amateur films and home movies that highlight new perspectives on the visual historiography of the British Empire. Most colonial amateur films offer valuable insights into British imperial ideologies and mores, and propose credible representations of British imperial typologies which challenge the egocentric, doctrinaire or mythologised typologies promoted by empire cinema films. In this context, films made by colonial women amateur filmmakers offer visual portraits of specific times and communities across amateur records of 'instances of self-observation' and 'spontaneous performances' (Neumann, 2001) – unique historical counter-narratives able to challenge popular imperial visual culture by providing authentic records of significant historical and cultural relevance.

Changing technologies impact upon many lives and films considered here: their influences upon the everyday experiences, opportunities, expectations and surroundings of women filmmakers weave through different chapters (Buckingham et al. 2009). Developments in technologies of travel and leisure, the home and workplace, and consumer culture are implicit in much of the imagery under discussion: while colonial footage exposes anachronistic lifestyles reliant on racially hierarchical social and gender politics, material hardship in interwar or post-war upland rural Britain is also made visible among clues to everyday life amidst the uneven outreach of modernisation. Evolving camera/projection equipment are foregrounded only where relevant to individual filmmakers and detailed focus on changing design and model is omitted as it is well covered by other writers (Enticknap 2005; Katelle 2000). Similarly, limited attention is given to the still imagery that preceded and sometimes accompanied cine use, even though some filmmakers considered here gained a reputation for using different formats. We thus foreground aesthetic considerations only where they contribute to an understanding of subject. Arguably the influences of immobility, monotone and pictorialism upon early women practitioners (and advertisers) merit appraisal within a fuller assessment of amateur visual aesthetics than space here permits (Hölzl 2010; Howe 2014; Thompson 2010).

This book explores Britain's shift from national strength based upon visions of imperial unity – despite the colossal losses in the First World War – through the reactions to archaic racial privilege and the aftermath of independence from colonial rule, to postcolonial reconfiguring of allegiances and identities amidst global insecurity. Our filmmakers may be understood against this background: as imperialist ideals became submerged under the strains of nationalism and domestic politics, and the end of the Empire loomed overseas, filming opportunities changed. Some filmmakers remained active and documented years of upheaval wherever they were. Others journeyed into unrest, as wives, and recorded what they found. Still others turned their cameras to more immediate subject matter: community life, public duty, younger generations, friendships and the natural world became key foci around which they made and shared their films. Their stories validated local experience and filled in details still absent from limited airtime offered by regional and local television provision. Over time their early films acquired fresh significance as windows upon the past.

The timeframe ranges from the analogue to digital cross-over and discusses different practitioners who were familiar with particular ways of working. Some women only used cine film, and sometimes they kept the same gauge and camera equipment throughout their lives. Other women adapted to different film gauges and over time they replaced worn out or outdated equipment and transferred from film to later technologies including the video recorder. Still others closer to the present have only ever used digital formats/devices as they edit, enhance, mix and rework found or family-related analogue materials. Contemporary amateur women filmmakers, like many other creative practitioners, occupy a blurred and overlapping realm of amateur/unpaid professional cultural activity with porous boundaries (Rascaroli et al. 2014). They often have unimaginable opportunities to control their productions and determine their own patterns of involvement compared to the activities of their predecessors. Yet their relative freedom as independent no/low-budget filmmakers combines with the burden of other societal expectations. Being parents (and grandparents), partners, publicists, project managers and fund-raisers often combines with the need to show and share their creative output in increasingly competitive and critical arenas. They have greater responsibility and accountability too compared with their film and video-using predecessors. Earlier acts of visual trespass, appropriation and exploitation had limited circulation and were often protected by a sense of assumed legitimacy and authority to be beyond reproach.

In comparison, today's amateur filmmakers are able to share their visual story-telling online but their wider audiences can now respond. The ubiquity yet disposability of the digital image, like other encoded data, links to survival and memory-related issues (Ernst 2013; Yzer and Southwell 2008). What will be the future archival footprint of modern reliance upon digital communication? Even as archive users gain from digitised recovery of past visual memories, interdisciplinary speculation rises on what present-day records will be available to tomorrow's scholars: how much is saved from the constant image making of contemporary life? Janus-like, digital issues permeate amateur cinema studies as we look forwards and backwards: undoubtedly, more evidence of past filmmaking by women continues to become available. Yet costs put limits upon archival transfer of amateur footage so selection occurs and deposited collections may be only partially digitised according to perceived relevance and topicality thus distorting the viewable output by an individual filmmaker. Not unique to women filmmakers, this problem has direct relevance to the study of material by women since many practitioners concentrated their activity within domestic settings. Although such material may lack the novelty appeal of more unusual subjects, it has cultural and historical significance through its replication and, in colonial settings, the recreation of the familiar in diverse ways.

Amateur-generated imagery, and its subsequent journeys into and beyond archival care, shape how and what is remembered and forgotten at a private and public level. Informality recurs through many of the films discussed here. As unofficial versions of events, or records of informal occasions, there is often a freedom to look around that captures incidental and unexpected moments. This may result simply from physical position or status, standing off-centre and filming from the sidelines or from having a camera in hand as a partner rather than being on duty shaking hands. When an expatriate wife's footage is screened decades later within a different setting, in which the ethics and politics of past imperialism may be to the fore, the colonial occasion is understood differently.[16] Colonial women's amateur footage is part of highly contested memories and subjectivities about legacies of empire but should not be seen isolated from the hierarchies of privilege and internal colonialism that also shaped relations within Britain's own national borders.[17] Films by women may also depict events not often recorded by male amateur filmmakers, either as shown by the intimate gaiety of garden scenes, or by interactions with colonised peoples thereby broadening overall historical memory of local, regional, national and global social networks (Motrescu-Mayes 2009b).

Exploring memories extends beyond issues of archival afterlife and delves further into making visual meanings. Key corporate advertising strategies from the 1920s to the latest iPhone reflect not only a century of gender/visual technology relations but also the continuing contradictions in public and private life over remembering and forgetting (Zimmermann 2008; Hunter et al. 2013). Kodak's recurring early appeal to 'everlasting joy' and 'keeping youth always young' is doubled-edged in its underlying poignancy for generations that witnessed wartime casualties and lost eligible marriage partners (Anon. 1929a: 4; Anon. 1929b: 4–5). Although a few pioneer amateur filmmakers had already used 35mm film in the early 1900s, 16mm amateur equipment entered the market too late to preserve, in moving image, those lost in the First World War.[18] Its subsequent capacity to evoke 'the years when youth has gone' (Anon. 1931b: 8) soon surfaced in amateur records of Armistice Days and commemorative battlefield pilgrimages by veterans well enough to travel (Norris Nicholson 2006a; 2006b). Within this study, oral histories have recovered other complementary and contextual aspects of later amateur visual practice: how filmmakers documented events and showed their films at different venues; their relationship with the material on screen and their audience; and their own enthusiasms, dedication and sense of purpose. Such recollections disclose wider cultural meanings associated with women's past involvement in making and screening amateur material in different settings.

Women's recreational filmmaking contributes to the growing interest on amateurism and the role of the non-professional in cultural production now and in the past. Mindful of Johnston's (1975) caution against particularising woman's creativity, we place visual endeavour firmly within evolving sociocultural contexts. For decades, some women remained active within and away from local cine clubs, festivals and competitions even though they were persistently under-represented within the hobby press. Some women achieved notability within the organised networks of amateur filmmaking while others did not. These neglected early visual practices inscribe wider cultural histories and disclose the micro-ecologies of creative endeavour that occur in the gendered interstices of home and beyond. We trace how cine users, whether at home or abroad, used their cameras as tools of expression for family, friends and different local groups.

Different reasons prompted women's amateur involvement yet, for different individuals, it became part of their social persona and of how they contributed via, what Burgess (2006) calls, 'vernacular creativity', to local entertainment, civic engagement, informal learning and local identity. For instance, although traditionally seen as a predominantly male hobby, amateur filmmaking across the British Empire has also been a pastime preferred by women almost on par with their male counterparts. Colonial women's interest in amateur filmmaking was an expression of their changing role in society, selfhood awareness and their place in the imperial world. Often, they would make 'British home-made' films during their short visits to Britain, usually when joining their husbands on home leave. Most of such films function today as visual journals compiled by estranged parents visiting their children who, according to the imperial childrearing protocol, were sent home to Britain at an early age to allegedly receive a proper education. When subsequently viewed in a colonial context such scenes would provide across repetitive projections a form of tourist-like parenting, a perpetual family reunion of an otherwise unachievable imperial familial nucleus (Buettner 2004). By directing, shooting, and screening their amateur films about personal and public spheres, from home–Britain to distant colonial locations, amateur women filmmakers have created a unique, transnational and cross-cultural visual archive informing their experiences, understanding and representation codes of their social milieus, and their negotiations of class, gender, race and historical events. Their cine practice and ensuing visual literacy had to be negotiated within the written tradition of imperial gender dynamics that stereotyped British colonial women as leading a life of leisure, 'confined . . . in cages like the feathered race' with the sole duty 'to plume themselves' (from Wollstonecraft's 'A vindication of the rights of Woman' (1792) quoted in Donovan 2012: 8), as guarantors of their husbands' social status and public image, and as caretakers of the 'little empire-builders of the future' (MacMillan 1996: 14). Imperial popular culture portrayed British colonial women as archetypal leaders of miniature versions of the empire itself – their homes away from home were vital to the imperial propaganda and to certifying their role as builders of a strong, reliable and peerless empire (Motrescu-Mayes 2014). In the imperial context where British 'men were very suspicious of their women moving out of th[is] particular groove, out of their particular role' lest they threaten the long-established stability of gender roles,[19] most women amateur filmmakers experienced, by default, a new freedom of expression and the opportunity to re-present their lives in dialogue rather than aligned to imperial patriarchal and gender-bound narratives (Zimmermann 1995; 1996). Lady Kendall and Lady Dalyell's amateur films, for instance, allow us to understand how they avoided straightforwardly, or involuntarily, some of the thematic and aesthetic subordinations to the imperial popular narratives of gender and colonial life.

Lone women filmmakers developed informal networks that were part of the social cohesion and identity of belonging to particular moments in time and place. These micro-geographies of past analogue visual practice, evidenced via subject matter, screenings and club activities, contrast with the networking and cross-platform patterns of use available to digital networkers. But temporal and spatial comparisons are not always straightforward: filming wild flowers and garden birds adapted socially approved feminine pursuits of observing seasonal change and local nature occurred in different settings. The natural world remains a subject of aesthetic pleasure and ideological concern for many later women amateur filmmakers. Tracing continuities is complex: just as early activity reveals how mass-produced material objects could memorialise fleeting experiences and delights of pre-modernity, the unproven longevity of digital formats prompts unprecedented levels of record-making that seek to snapshot moments in time for immediate consumption and circulation. Combining breadth, depth and juxtaposition, we show how the untapped potential of privately produced visual data by women over the past century increasingly finds recognition within and relevance for interdisciplinary scholarship, creative outreach and memory work. Such revaluation of these varied visual histories and practices of past amateurs thus contributes to ongoing reappraisals of everyday culture.

Sources and Structure

We explore the contribution and legacy of pioneer amateur women cine filmmakers within the wider evolution of amateur media making and against a context of historical change at national and international level. British imperial and late colonial interests offer contrasting settings for women's film-related activity overseas, and reflect how postings overseas were from all parts of Britain. Closer to home, discussion covers a geographical range of practitioners although many women come from England. Indeed, the selective inclusion of filmmakers from Wales, Scotland, Ireland and Northern Ireland indicates the need for a more systematic gendered search of national archival collections.

Sources from public, private and specialist film archives underpin this study and we draw upon personal papers, cine club records, oral histories, marketing materials and the hobby press.[20] Discussion of women's formal film practice makes use of the IAC's collections at the East Anglian Film Archive. Independent filmmakers' activities selectively use private materials and films held at Valley Stream Cultural Media and Archives, Conwy, North Wales, the Alpine Club, Bristol Archives, The Digital Film Archive, Northern Ireland Screen, Leeds Animation Workshop and the Moving Image Archive, National Library of Scotland as well as English regional public archives. Digitised archival footage held by the Centre for South Asian Studies at the University of Cambridge,[21] and accompanying collections of published and documentary material, as well as detailed knowledge of colonial, military and travel-related footage available at the Imperial War Museum,[22] the British Film Institute[23] and the unique and almost entirely digitised film collection of the former British Empire & Commonwealth Museum provide specialist contexts for interrogating issues of imperial history, visual politics, race, gender, status and identity. Our cross-archival approach helps to contextualise the making and screening of films, to identify similarities and to clarify subjectivities, camera work and issues that are germane to individual filmmakers (Figure 1.3).

The book offers a series of complementary linked discussions and approaches that focus upon different aspects of women's amateur visual

Figure 1.3 Photograph of Newcastle ACA Club members (*c*.1929). © Newcastle ACA Film and Video Makers.

practice. Each chapter reviews key literature and projects pertinent to the theme under consideration. Empirical details combine with a broadly chronological order that traces women's evolving amateur visual practice through to contemporary digital technologies. These opening remarks introduce key ideas, themes and theoretical perspectives that are central to the study. Our source materials contribute to the book's underlying interdisciplinary approaches and methodologies. Although we position our research and questions broadly within existing literatures, detailed references in later chapters identify the key texts that have informed specific aspects of our thinking and interpretation. This structure avoids repetition and directs readers to discrete but interconnected literatures on amateur film interpretation, exhibition and archival outreach, histories of imperialism/colonialism and postcolonialism, gender studies, histories of leisure and sociocultural historical change.

Chapter 2, 'Webs of Production and Practice', sets gendered practice in historical context. Women's shift beyond home projection, film appreciation and performance to practical production started with the launch of lightweight, portable equipment by Kodak and Pathé in the early 1920s. By 1927, the embryonic hobby literature featured writings by and about female directors and women critics. From the beginning, women acted in amateur fiction films, often prompting trenchant criticism of 'would be screen aspirants' in the hobby press. Club records soon referred to women scriptwriters, producers and photographers and over the next decade films by women, and all-women productions, featured in competitions, including one early contest that required each competitor to demonstrate 'a series of emotions'. The early emancipatory fervour had become marginalised by 1939 and by the 1950s women were less visible in the specialist hobby literature and apparently less involved. But had they disappeared or assumed different roles? Women's gradual concentration into non-filmmaking aspects of club life resembles the gendered nature of opportunities available at the professional level and identify how attitudes on post-war childcare and domestic roles affected female patterns of participation. Many of those women filmmakers who established themselves within amateur cinema's formal structures – or remained outside it – often enjoyed leisure time that was uncompromised by family responsibilities.

Evidence from the hobby press points to an undeniable relegation of women to supportive roles at club level, yet newly available IAC materials also invite a reappraisal of women's under-representation as amateur filmmakers. Elsewhere within regional archival film holdings and club records, details suggest that some women were much more actively involved in film production than formerly signalled by a hobby press that often ignored women's agency. Such material sheds fresh insights into women's past cine practice and it is apparent that many single and married women were dedicated and in some cases highly innovative practitioners at club level.

Club archives, printed and private papers, and oral testimonies enrich this discussion. Wherever possible, interviews with the filmmaker, or people who knew her, supplement other source materials. Women's emerging visibility as filmmakers and in allied roles enable us to set their visual practice alongside other histories of British women's twentieth-century experience. Their activities criss-cross boundaries of gender, marital status and being at and away from home. The material poses questions about changing roles in and beyond the home, community affiliation, tradition and modernity in pre- and post-war Britain. It highlights women's changing voluntary relation to technologies not associated with either paid work or domestic duties. Women's cine-related practice raises issues about education, opportunity and broader societal aspects of metropolitan/provincial and regional difference. Case studies detail the practices of single and married specific filmmakers whose activities gained recognition at the local level and beyond.

Chapter 3, 'Resisting Colonial Gendering While Domesticating the Empire', examines how colonial women amateur filmmakers often documented in detail their overseas travel and settlement experiences, jobs, sports, and private or official events in the early and mid-twentieth century. This discussion draws upon cross-archival primary sources, specialised literature, amateur films and interviews.[24] It explores the historical discourse present across several colonial amateur films made by British women in South Asia (Figure 1.4), Africa, Papua New Guinea and the Middle East between the 1920s and 1940s. Moreover, it discusses the filmmakers' simultaneous roles as vectors of colonising credos and commodified subalterns of imperial paternalism, and considers gender and racial hierarchies as shaped by imperial rule while confirmed or challenged by the filmmakers' prevailing perceptions of cinematic vocabulary and practice.

The British women amateur filmmakers selected for this study include Lady Isabella Kendall, Lady Eleanor Dalyell, Wilma Gladstone, Ursula Graham Bower and Beatrice Blackwood – the latter two filmmakers went on to become distinguished visual anthropologists. Their amateur filmmaking covers a wide range of visual imperial and gender-empowered records, from rare scenes of wedding rituals in Bahrain, interwar political

Figure 1.4 Still frame from Kendall Collection (1931–5). Film 4. © CSAS, University of Cambridge.

unrest, to anthropological fieldwork in Nagaland and Papua New Guinea. Also, their films – as well as those made by other women amateur filmmakers across the Empire such as, for instance, the members of the Australian Grail Film Group – represented the Empire from a marginalised and yet crucially critical perspective that often challenged official imperial narratives while encouraging British women amateur filmmakers to understand their visual practices as acts of gender liberation and steps toward modern times (O'Sullivan, 2000).

Several critical perspectives are employed in this chapter in an attempt to understand how the selected British women amateur filmmakers avoided straightforwardly, or involuntarily, the thematic and aesthetic subordination to the predominantly male amateur filmmaking practice and the imperial popular visual culture. Their films are analysed in relation to questions of authorship – a legal and creative attribute usually assigned to the filmmaker's husband or father, unless clearly specified and documented. Also discussed are issues of distribution protocols, especially when their amateur films were either shipped across the Empire as visual 'letters', or became the main attraction of special film screenings, as in the case of Lady Dalyell's *ciné-soirées* organised for the Shaikh of Bahrain and his royal family in the early 1930s. Additionally, three themes are considered in this chapter owing to their relevance to gender, imperial and visual studies: colonial domesticity, ghettoised imperial networks and gendered visual ethnographies. A flexible comparative methodology is employed here to allow the identification of a common gender-based nationally and racially distinctive visual language created and developed by colonial women amateur filmmakers. The chapter concludes with an exploration of issues of belonging to different social, class, ethnic and racial contexts and how particular amateur film sequences or scenes prompt valid thematic and theoretic comparative frameworks, thus allowing the identification of various gender-based visual constructions of national and imperial identities.

Chapter 4, 'Cameras Not Handbags: The Essential Accessory', focuses upon a selection of women who pursued their filmmaking interests away from the club scene and hobby press. Some experimented with fiction and animation; others concentrated on non-fiction. While some crafted their material for specific audiences, others did no more than shoot, send off their reels to developers and show their unedited reels to family and friends. Often but not always from similar backgrounds and with shared working interests in teaching, health and welfare, and other public sector jobs, for various reasons, these women had little or no contact with organised aspects of amateur cinema. During decades when many camera-owning women were not in paid employment, they often used their cameras in locations and situations not of their own making. As astute observers, their visual records include but often extend beyond recording family and friends, aspects of everyday life, celebrations, special events and travel. The discussion captures the character and defining features of the films, and contextualises their visual practice against broader societal and international shifts. Again the single woman filmmaker emerges. Among these spinsters, born at a time when marriage was still an expectation for most young women from all social backgrounds, were those women with the time and money to indulge both travel and filmmaking. Highlighting the variety of women's independent cine practice, these subjective versions of the worlds are partial, selective and incomplete, like any filmmaking, but they define identities, interests, sense of place and status in and beyond Britain during critical years of late imperialism and societal transformation.

Chapter 5, 'Through Women's Lens: Imperial and Postcolonial Class and Gender Hierarchies', charts how changing geo-political relations during late colonialism influenced conventional imperial ideologies of race, gender and identity, and brought about a fundamental shift in women's visual literacy. Through their unofficial, un-commissioned and private visual records of early postcolonial history, women were often able to promote new understandings of political, racial and gender transformations specific to crucial times for the British Empire and the Commonwealth. The case studies included in this chapter offer exceptional instances of gendered visual constructions of British and Indian manhood based on the women amateur filmmakers' choice to film them in certain contexts. This framework locates gendered identities as determined by the new postcolonial adjustments to understandings of race, ethnicity, nation and class. The chapter centres on the analysis of particular sequences filmed by Queen Elizabeth II, Audrey Lewis, and by two of Maharaja Vijaysinhji of Rajpipla's British cine women guests who, willingly or involuntarily, cine portrayed manhood within new, post-war and early postcolonial gender dynamics. Consequently, their films prompt a new perspective on how and why British women amateur filmmakers chose to record men as possible agents of national and imperial postcolonial identity. The cine women discussed in this chapter witnessed and filmed radical shifts in representations of gender-driven, post-imperial roles within specific cultural norms and opportunities. As a result, questions of gender and visual appropriation are considered in relation to feminist and postcolonial theories while acknowledging that the interpretation of British women's amateur visual practice often requires new methodologies and interdisciplinary approaches.

Chapter 6, 'Teacher Filmmakers', focuses on examples of women teacher filmmakers and their self-expression through visual practice. As a sub-group of employed single and married women that stretches to the earliest years of amateur cinema, their interests in making and showing films in and away from the classroom offer insight into how their own identities, interests and subjectivities intermesh with broader national and international changes. As classroom practitioners, their pupils of different ages and scenes of school life routinely featured as subjects, in ways that may be distinguished from the long tradition of school-related films made by many male teachers and fathers that often depicted competitive whole school events and celebratory occasions. For many women cine users, aspects of everyday playground and routine classroom scenes, with attention on individuals and groups of children filmed at their own level, predominate in their visual memory-making. Several women's films about educational visits also provide opportunities to consider the informality of staff–pupil relations and camera work away from the school environment.

Teachers' filming opportunities and practice link to wider and changing narratives about gender, work and identity during the twentieth century. Women's access into teaching, particularly with younger children, drew upon societal expectations about maternalism, welfare and public duty. Paid work beyond the home with young children, like nursing and social welfare employment, was an extension of socially sanctioned roles even though employment practice continued to exclude qualified women from teaching after marriage in many local authorities across England until after the Second World War. Better paid than in other areas of professional work available to women, teachers had both time and money to enjoy amateur filmmaking and for some teachers, this extended into sharing their passion for filmmaking with their pupils and other enthusiasts via clubs and the IAC.

Chapter 7, 'British Women's Media Narratives of Gender and Collective Memory', engages with theoretical and historical perspectives on gender in relation to amateur films of the last days of the British Raj, Britain during World War II, and pioneering alpinist expeditions with the aim to trace the visual literacy defined by several key examples of British women amateur film and media practice. This literacy appears to inform new understandings of amateur filmmaking and to elucidate how gender-driven visual narratives of gender, race and national identities function today within global online (free access) networks. The chapter has two sections. The first section includes an analysis of the amateur film made by Eileen Healey of the all-women mountaineering expedition up the Cho Oyu summit in 1959. The second section discusses several exceptional scenes filmed by Rosie Newman during a trip to India in 1935. The chapter explores issues of belonging, home-and-abroad mind frames, and of colonial and postcolonial identity-building. It also explores the ways in which documentary filmmakers and visual anthropologists have incorporated the archival footage either as visual 'fillers' for new historical perspectives on the history of the British Empire, or as 'resurrected' cinematic documents relevant to new practices in visual anthropology studies. Finally, it considers the ways in which British women amateur filmmakers confirmed their role *as* gender in documenting particular instances of historical consciousness, while ensuring an ongoing dialogue between their autobiographical memories and collective memories in general.

Chapter 8, 'Reimagining Boundaries: Amateur Animations', examines women's changing approaches to animated filmmaking. Although animation never attracted more than a minority of women filmmakers, it offers more instances of cross-over between amateur and professional film production than elsewhere within amateur visual practice. Some amateurs experimented only with animating titles and opening sequences, during the analogue era, for reasons of time, access to dedicated space, and confidence in use of line drawing and colour, and fewer overall filmmakers specialised in animation than in fiction or non-fiction genres. Animation's appeal to women amateur filmmakers is discussed as are some of the changing ways animated imagery reached out to female audiences and middle class homes. Links between story-telling and detailed observation of reality provide impetus for alternative approaches to 'real world' subjects so, within a book that largely focuses upon non-fiction filmmaking, different animated styles offer intriguing sideways routes into exploring the links between visual practice and memory, self-expression and social context.

This chapter uses IAC records that trace over eighty years of women's animation, supplemented by interviews with key practitioners, including Sheila Graber (now professional) and other amateurs, including Jill Lampert, who remain active in making animated films. Film, printed sources and reminiscence provide insight into a highly gendered area of amateur activity that crosses analogue/digital formats and invites discussion of the challenges and opportunities offered by telling visual stories by non-realistic means. Discussion explores how women's involvement in producing animation took different forms: some worked with their husbands; some worked with fellow members within a club setting; and others worked independently. Questions arise including the marginalisation of women within histories of animation and the invisibility of women within professional and amateur activities, the popularisation of animation and its targeting of women, and why there seems to have been no equivalent interest among the filmmakers in late colonial settings. Using a broadly chronological framework, cross-archival work and specific examples of practitioners, this chapter shows how film and reminiscence provide insight into an enduring area of women's amateur activity.

Our 'Afterword' highlights areas for further enquiry that arise from the preceding discussions of women's combined role as private citizens and unofficial producers of cultural and visual practice. We believe that this study of women's changing unpaid involvement with evolving film technologies brings new visibility and deepens understanding. We advocate a broader understanding of the amateur film genre's still untapped historical relevance in addressing understanding of national, imperial and gendered identities and illuminating how identity, ideology and values are embedded in the imagery produced by women. We position amateur activity within emerging discussions on creativity, acknowledge the porous boundary between amateur and professional practitioners within writing on women's media history and reflect upon the lineage of still/moving image-making within gendered visual practice. We consider changing memory-making practices within global and online frameworks. Moreover, we consider how digitisation changes and challenges notions of authority that in turn affect archival and creative practice and exhibition opportunities as online opportunities for amateur media making proliferate. In so doing we encourage readers to see women amateur filmmakers as producers of cultural meaning that have enduring significance.

Finally, we argue that *British Women Amateur Filmmakers* contributes the first in-depth analysis of British women's amateur practice to the rapidly growing specialist field of amateur film studies and to broader trajectories of cinematic and media history. Popular interest prompted by broadcast use of amateur footage, greater visibility of material made by women due to archival acquisition and cataloguing strategies, the age of this pioneering generation, and the ongoing archival digitisation of their films make this an ideal opportunity to offer fresh perspectives on women's changing use of film, video and media technologies. Our book locates women's recreational visual practice within a century of profound societal, technological and ideological change within and beyond national borders. Their film-related activities disclose how women negotiated aspects of changing lifestyles, attitudes and opportunities through first-person visual narratives about themselves and the world around them.

Notes

1. David Cleveland and Michael Harvey in conversation, *The First Colour Moving Pictures at the National Media Museum*, available at <http://www.nationalmediamuseum.org.uk/PlanAVisit/Exhibitions/LeeAndTurner.aspx> (last accessed 31 January 2018).
2. See Adrian Wood's interview, the Archive Producer for *The British Empire in Colour TV* series (Carlton Television, TWI, 2002), in the 'making of' section of the DVD.
3. For comparable US and European marketing, refer to discussion of Bell and Howell and Pathé in Zimmermann (1995: 61–2); see also Schneider (2013).
4. For example, *Sally Sallies Forth* (dir. Frances Lascot and Ivy A. Low, 1928), EAFA, no. 3823.
5. There is a substantial body of works addressing similar topics while discussing the lives of British colonial women, gender identities and power dynamics. See Woollacott (2006), Levine (2004), Procida (2002) and Buettner (2004) – all chiefly concerned with written documents and oral history.
6. Collections currently held by the Bristol Archives, UK.
7. Tait Collection, nos. 1–8 (BECM Accession number 1999/180/001; 008) and Duke Collection (BECM Accession number 2000/029/001-4 and 2001/029/003; 004-007).
8. Dame Eleanor Isabel 'Nora' Dalyell is known as one of the few women amateur filmmakers who experimented with Kodachrome (lenticular colour film camera and projector). Lenticular film was manufactured by Kodak as 'an unusual type of 16mm black-and-white film that projects as a colour image when shown through a customized projector with a three-colour lens' (National Film Preservation Foundation 2004: 11). Among other British women amateur filmmakers discussed in this book who used colour footage (Kodakcolour and Kodachrome) are Rosie Newman, Eileen Healey, Wilma Gladstone and Barbara Donaldson.
9. A selection of other significant films employing the thematic and stylistic canons of the empire cinema genre includes, for example, *Palaver* (dir. Geoffrey Barkas, UK, 1926), *The King Solomon Mines* (dir. Robert Stevenson, UK, 1937), *Old Bones of the River* (dir. Marcel Varnel, UK, 1938), *Men of Two Worlds* (dir. Thorold Dickinson, UK, 1946), *Kim* (dir. Victor Saville, USA, 1950), *Simba* (dir. Brian Desmond Hurst, UK, 1955), *Bridge on the River Kwai* (dir. David Lean, UK/USA, 1957), *North West Frontier* (dir. J. Lee Thompson, UK, 1959), *Carry on up the Khyber* (dir. Gerald Thomas, UK, 1968), *Staying On* (dir. Silvio Narizzano, UK, 1979), *Gallipoli* (dir. Peter Weir, AU, 1981), *Heat and Dust* (dir. James Ivory, UK, 1983), *Gandhi* (dir. Richard Attenborough, UK/India, 1982), *A Passage to India* (dir. David Lean, UK/USA, 1984), *The Jewel in the Crown* (dir. Christopher Morahan, Jim O'Brien, UK, 1984), *My Beautiful Launderette* (dir. Stephen Frears, UK, 1985), *Partition* (dir. Ken McMullen, UK, 1987), *Mountbatten: Last Viceroy* (dir. Tom Clegg, UK, 1986), *White Mischief* (dir. Michael Radford, UK, 1988), *Mountains of the Moon* (dir. Bob Rafelson,

USA, 1990), *Mister Johnson* (dir. Bruce Beresford, USA, 1991), *Britannia* (dir. Joanna Quinn, UK, 1993) and *Jinnah* (dir. Jamil Dehlavi, UK, 1998).

10. Amateur cine clubs and societies were founded as early as the mid-1920s (Dyson, 2012) although the existence of Croydon Cine Club by 1899 is suggested online at Grahame N's Web Pages (<http://www.pathefilm.uk/seventeen/175hist.htm>, last accessed 6 February 2018). However, it was only from the 1980s onwards that amateur cinema gained sustained academic recognition for its social and historical documentary merit, and has received extensive public exposure through national and international events, competitions, festivals and more recently dedicated websites, for example Amateur Cinema Studies Network (<http://amateurcinemastudies.org>, last accessed 3 January 2017). A list of such events includes, for example, the National Film and Television's 'The 20th century remembered: your home movies at NFT' (2001); The Association of Moving Image Archivists several 'Small Gauge Symposiums', and the annual meetings of Small Gauge/Amateur Film interest groups and related panels; the Fédération Internationale des Archives de Télévision – International Federation of Television Archives (FIAF/IFTA) Conference in Cartagena, Colombia, on issues regarding the storage of amateur films at various international film institutes (2001); Northeast Historic Film summer symposiums (2000–18) and the Orphan Film Symposiums that have been ongoing since 1999. The Home Movie Day (<http://www.homemovieday.com>, last accessed 3 January 2017) remains one of the key worldwide public events that addresses amateur filmmakers, scholars of amateur cinema, media journalism and visual artists.
11. An extensive scholarship may be traced arguably to Laura Mulvey (1975). Although not historical per se, it stimulated a succession of writings that have sought to explore issues of women's history, feminist history, and aspects of film and cinema history in and away from Hollywood. Callahan (2010) brings together significant contributors to the field and also broadens the geographical scope of film history. Bell and Williams (2009) enrich our historical understanding of women's films as does Christine J. Gledhill (2012).
12. The Women's Film & Television History Network – UK/Ireland (<https://womensfilmandtelevisionhistory.wordpress.com/about-us/history/>, last accessed 2 December 2017).
13. Pauline Harrison, recalled the smoky nature of meetings when she joined Preston Cine Club (now Preston Movie Makers) in 1975 and that the controversial decision to introduce a smoking ban prompted some members to leave, in conversation with the author, on 30 June 2007.
14. Zora Neale Hurston's films include *Children's Games* (1928), *Logging* (1928) and *Baptism* (1929) (<https://wfpp.cdrs.columbia.edu/resources/key-to-abbreviations/archival-film-print-key/#USW>, last accessed 31 January 2018).
15. Eloyce King Patrick Gist was screenwriter/editor on *Verdict Not Guilty* (dir. James Gist (1930–3) and co-producer/director/screenwriter on *Hell Bound*

Train (with James Gist, 1929–30), available at <https://wfpp.cdrs.columbia.edu/pioneer/eloyce-king-patrick-gist-2/> (last accessed 31 January 2018).

16. See, for instance, Annamaria Motrescu-Mayes (2007; 2011a; 2011b; 2013; 2014a; 2015).
17. See, for instance, Annamaria Motrescu-Mayes (2009a; 2010a; 2010b; 2012a).
18. During active service in the First World War, Ronald Gow left his 35mm camera with a school friend, Edward Horley, who shot short family films (discussed in Norris Nicholson, 2014).
19. Iris Mcfarlane, V091, BECM.
20. Kodak Collection (National Media Museum, Bradford, UK), <http://www.nationalmediamuseum.org.uk/> (last accessed 13 April 2018).
21. Centre of South Asian Studies, University of Cambridge, http://www.s-asian.cam.ac.uk/films.htm (last accessed 13 April 2018).
22. Imperial War Museum, <https://film.iwmcollections.org.uk/?_ga=2.70589840.1452448376.1525543792-275779160.1525543792> (last accessed 15 May 2018).
23. British Film Institute, <http://www.screenonline.org.uk/> (last accessed 13 April 2018).
24. H. Bowen, interview transcript, *Voices & Echoes* (research paper No.5, Roll 10, V047, BECM); I. Macfarlane, interview transcript, *Voices & Echoes* (research paper No.5, Roll 61 and 62, V090 and V091, BECM); N. Vernede, interview recorded by Annamaria Motrescu-Mayes on 8 October 2004.

CHAPTER 2

Webs of Production and Practice

> The involvement of women was absolutely vital. I don't think the IAC or any club would have survived without women's involvement, whether or not they were filmmakers.[1]

Phillip Collins' assessment of women's marginalisation within Britain's amateur visual practice draws upon almost fifty years of being involved with the IAC. Reclaiming these neglected roles reappraises the IAC's own development as it brought visibility and coherence to twentieth-century recreational filmmaking. Testimonies from current long-serving IAC members produce a picture of single and married women who gained reputations as dedicated club members and innovative filmmakers.[2] Newer archival acquisitions also point to more women making films than suggested by a hobby press that long downplayed women's agency (Norris Nicholson 2012a: 62–91). Previously untold stories drawn from its own practitioners and paperwork thus reinvigorate the contradictions, skewed gender politics and rather inward-looking nature of past amateur film activity.

Tony Rose (1971: 153) admitted 'Amateur filmmaking is a notoriously male-dominated pursuit' and under his editorship, *Movie Maker* featured cover-girls and pin-ups and advertisements for filming nudity. While the hobby literature's tone possibly alienated some would-be practitioners for years, it also indicates that women remained an active minority within organised filmmaking circles even if focusing solely on their known film output. Another narrative emerges, however, from interviews with filmmakers or people who knew them, other printed matter and identifiable films made by women. These additional sources reveal how gendered visual practices and supportive roles developed across cine networks, inflected by geographical, sociopolitical and cultural differences. They augment our understanding of the part played by formal filmmaking groups in women's lives and their varied contributions to evolving amateur visual practices.

Women's emerging visibility within a more broadly conceived amateur film practice may be set alongside emerging histories of British women's professional involvement in visual media and broadcasting (Hockenhull 2017; Gledhill and Knight 2015; Foster et al. 1998).[3] Like their paid contemporaries, amateur practitioners assumed overlooked roles and responsibilities that have often been credited solely to men. Apart from their hidden contributions to scriptwriting, editing, sound, titling, continuity and other practical aspects of location and post-production work, women were often key to keeping clubs going. Their levels of voluntary commitment and service resemble gendered patterns of activity in other associational networks and settings (Hinton 2002: 213–30). Women's versatility as IAC members and club officers evidences arenas of unsalaried and under-recognised professionalism that lasted for decades and extended internationally.

Club and IAC life became complex realms of creative and social practice in which women found niches for self-expression away from domestic duties and paid employment. Importantly, these webs of production and cultural exchange emerge as being fluid, self-sustaining and inventive. Their narrative threads criss-cross boundaries of gender, age, occupation, education, lifecycle change, marital status and responsibilities of care. They also reflect how club life sometimes acted as a mirror upon wider societal values, goals and prejudices and perhaps offered a retreat from wider uncertainties facing Britain and the world. These stories contrast with the agency now available to women who now have the freedom of digital and social media as platforms for visual story-telling.

Shaping an Identity

By the time the IAC was set up in 1932, several short-lived attempts to create different national organisations had already taken place.[4] Success, for the new breakaway group, meant reflecting the hybrid social character and aspirations of amateur film's early appeal. The fledgling IAC had to balance tradition and innovation so that establishment thinking and social conventions could strengthen rather than hinder people's interest in recreational filmmaking. Appealing to lone cine users and groups of enthusiasts was important. Balancing amateur, professional and commercial interests was another priority: hobbyists were not to be dismissed as substandard imitators or left at the mercy of rival marketing campaigns. Creating a shared identity via membership required offering a clear sense of purpose and benefits including access to advice and audiences. The IAC had therefore to create a role, identity and appeal that would enable membership to grow. Numerically, if for no other reason initially, women were too important to leave out.

From the outset, the IAC's self-styled remit as a national organisation with international outreach was built upon activities designed to consolidate its position. Networking developed its social capital: film directors, press contacts and titled patrons secured visibility and attracted sponsored trophies and media coverage. Elaborate banquets and film premieres reflected the prevailing formality in society (Anon. 1982: 6) but their popularity as social occasions continued.[5] Professional and social leverage, self-promotion via high profile occasions and ambitious goals established the IAC's credentials. Collins recalls Leslie Froude's reflections as a former IAC president and a founder member on these social strategies: 'He suspected many of the people listed as patrons on the letterhead weren't even in agreement. Their letters of invitation were never replied to so their names were just added.'[6]

Competitions, familiar from amateur still photography, attracted public interest and practical involvement. The *IAC Bulletin* circulated comment, advice and success stories to build a loyal readership. Long before the IAC developed an effective regional network of club and inter-club activity in the early 1960s, filmmaking gained a competitive culture that acknowledged women (Stevenson 1982: 31–2). 'Ladies' prizes gradually went out of use along with the replacement of reduced subscriptions (for 'ladies' and 'juniors') by non-gendered categories of membership. Women's earliest involvement in judging IAC competitions came from professional circles. Dilys Powell (1950: 33–4), film reviewer for *The Sunday Times*, was an early judge and advocate of amateurs' importance 'because they are not merely passive and receptive . . . [but also as] adventurous critics travelling far in different directions'. Margaret Hinxman (1982: 6), film critic of the *Daily Mail*, also championed 'the imaginative flair, originality and versatility' of amateur output. Women drawn from film and television were judges too until more IAC women members became adjudicators during the 1960s and 1970s (Bayne 1982: 32–3).

The IAC's first international film competition (1933) awarded Ruth Stuart's debut film, *Egypt and Back with Imperial Airways*, both equal first place and best general interest prize (Grimaldi 1934b: 29). Praise from the *Manchester Guardian* boosted the *IAC Bulletin*'s own endorsement (Grimaldi 1934a: 28).[7] Comments highlighted the 'almost irreproachable' compositional quality and 'unconventional' film work. Her 'studies of Egyptian types' exhibited a 'rare feeling for character'. This film launched the IAC's library collection, a scheme designed to sustain films' availability for viewing. Stuart (1934: 7, 9) (later Rodger) received subsequent international recognition for *Doomsday* (1935), an expressionist apocalyptic fantasy with exterior crowd scenes, dramatic indoor lighting and strong visual effects, before she disappeared, like so many women, from historical records.[8]

Her Second Birthday (1932–3), an example of live action and stop motion filming, was made and discussed by K. Agnes Thubron (1934: 12–14), another pioneer recognised by the IAC.[9] The Hampshire-based

Thubrons also made films together including a thematic project possibly shot during a visit to relations in India.[10] Their films indicate how lone workers competed without becoming drawn more closely into the IAC. Other filmmaking couples gained IAC recognition too, although who did what is often elusive, unless evident from the credits or from who was in charge of the camera. Eunice and Eustace Alliott filmed extensively in and around their home in Buckinghamshire and abroad during the 1930s. They filmed each other and Eunice's agency may be evident in choice and framing of subject matter, as well as elaborate filmed title cards in water colour on different occasions.[11]

The New Zealand born, British raised and Royal Academy of Dramatic Art (RADA)-trained cine pioneer, Laurie Abbott Bruce Jones (Dyson 2015: 7) took a 16mm camera to Oberammergau in 1930.[12] Following her marriage to Stuart Day, their commitment to amateur visual practice as co-founders of the Stoke Cine Club (1935) spanned over thirty years. Against the background of worsening European tensions, they re-edited colour footage of everyday life and family enjoyment that soon gained an elegiac quality for former happier times.[13] Successive IAC trophies acknowledged their imaginative approaches. Day's early theatre background perhaps informed how she scripted sound prologues and epilogues for their travelogues. These acted sequences were usually shot at home and edited onto live action film about places and peoples.[14] Amateur dramatics involving other club members featured in later comedy and other films.[15] The couple reportedly critiqued each other's work, developed thematic films from material shot during a world cruise, and they became lifelong IAC members (Anon. 1954: 11–12).[16]

Films by other couples feature among the IAC's library's pre-war acquisitions too. Many typify promotional advertising as they share home-made entertainment featuring themselves with family members and friends. Much of the material displays an eclectic mix of fictional and non-fictional approaches that relied upon the immediacy of domesticity or local interest as subject and setting. For instance, John Martin, also from Stoke Cine Club, involved his wife at the centre of a film about family life.[17] One of the earliest films made by the prolific Scottish filmmaker, Frank Marshall, was family focused too as children tease a maid in what Lury (2013: 260) identifies as a distinct genre of domestic comedies.[18] His wife's involvement in a hobby where Marshall long dominated and their children's participation remains more shadowy.

The embryonic club system attracted diverse membership in this formative period before 1939. Groups where people could share equipment, and make and show films grew swiftly from the later 1920s. Innovation merged with inherited political certainties, social conventions and local circumstances to shape each new club's character. Typically enthusiasts bought or borrowed cameras for personal use, attempted story-films with friends, or attempted to document the changing world around them. Students launched early university cine clubs for fiction films at Cambridge (1923) and Oxford (1924) (Norris Nicholson 2012a: 29).[19] Olga Shore's aims for the London-based Metropolitan Amateur Cinematographers' Association included her wish 'to foster a vigorous film Empire spirit' within the wider study and practice of amateur film (Anon. 1928: 22). Women gained prominence in ambitious fiction films in London, Newcastle, Finchley, Edinburgh, Manchester and elsewhere (Norris Nicholson 2012a: 31; Anon. 1932: 11).[20] They were essential to the acting, costumes, make-up, set design and often integral to film production too. Frances Lascot's *Sally Sallies Forth* (1928) had an all-women cast whose members featured in several subsequent films also made in Middlesex.[21] Women filmed, titled and performed in an espionage thriller and a romantic comedy with other members of Newcastle & District Amateur Cinematographers' Association (ACA).[22] Boosted by modest social reforms, and part of modern femininity's emphasis on active and healthy lifestyles, newly encouraged by magazines including *Woman*, *Home*, *Britannia* and *Eve* these young women captured club outings on camera too.[23] They remained active in fiction and non-fictional production for years, probably disappearing from the records due more to entrenched conventions of marriage and home life than Britain's worsening socioeconomic concerns during the later 1930s (Figure 2.1).

Figure 2.1 Photograph of club members during a Sunday morning quayside shoot for *Bon Aventure* (1929). © Newcastle ACA Film and Video Makers.

Administrative club roles soon emerged for women too. In Edinburgh, the 'industrious' Miss E. H. Kemp 'started the ball rolling' at film shows (although not identified as a projectionist), reported the earliest showing of a club newsreel and appeared in a film about club life.[24] Nothing now indicates women's other involvement at early meetings and reminiscences from founding IAC members and early filmmakers elsewhere also confirm that club activity was often predominantly male.[25] Estimated figures for pre-war clubs vary from fifty registered clubs as members of the newly formed Federation of Cine Societies (1937), to a list of one hundred groups compiled by the *World Film Encyclopedia* and even two hundred (Anon. 1936), so the sketchy nature of female club membership before 1939 now seems unsurprising (Walden 1982: 29–30).[26]

Sustaining Mid-century Momentum

Women were essential to keeping some clubs active during the Second War World. Although film shortage, restricted camera use, limits on evening meetings and military call-up reduced cine activity between 1939 and the later 1940s, there were exceptions. Kathleen Lockwood, a Yorkshire village teacher, was a co-founder of Holmfirth Camera Club in 1940 where her film shows raised wartime funds and remained in repertoire for years.[27] Where clubs ceased altogether, membership may have been predominantly male. Clubs with mixed membership were more like to thrive, as acknowledged by *The Evening News*: 'thanks to the initiative of women members and the wives of members, the Edinburgh organisation was kept in being' (Anon. 1957a).[28]

Edinburgh Cine Society drew upon wartime's lexicon of camaraderie: 'Active filming of course had to cease but the enterprising women did good work by holding period shows, promoting whist drives to provide comforts for members on service and knitting articles in demand on chilly stations' (Anon. 1957a). Women-led schemes sprang up to organise and mobilise in response to wartime needs. They re-orientated existing activities including amateur film that was put onto 'a different footing'. Members hosted film shows to raise funds for troops, people affected by bombing, and other charities and the IAC exhibited a familiar sentiment: 'cinematography may be a luxury hobby, but by Golly, it's doing a good job of work'. [29] In Stoke, Laurie and Stuart Day exemplified relief work too, raising ten guineas (£10.50) in a single day by hosting up to three film screenings of *Day Dreams* in their own home.[30]

Resilience and friendship fuelled voluntary cine endeavours that sought to combat loneliness and anxiety. Diligent and now forgotten women sustained initiatives that were rooted in the IAC's own sense of identity: its films went overseas by arrangement with the Ministry of Information, HM Customs and The British Board of Film Censors.[31] Members' holiday footage and travel films contributed government intelligence services with visual and topographical evidence of occupied countries and unwanted reels and cans were collected allegedly to be melted down for the war effort (Dunkley 1982: 16). Loss of advertising revenue led to the *IAC Bulletin*'s non-appearance in September 1939 but a month later, a hand-typed newsletter emerged in a format that continued until peacetime returned. Although many IAC records were destroyed, surviving newsletters echo sentiments and suggestions elsewhere that 'running national service war film shows' would boost national morale.[32] Public commendation acknowledged effort: the Rowes were thanked for 'the really splendid way they're carrying on. Long may they continue to dodge the lumps.'[33] Sometime later, Mrs Rowe became an elected IAC fellow 'in recognition of long and valued service'.[34] Reduced IAC subscriptions maintained a modest income and retained some members posted overseas. The revenue helped to rebalance the organisation's overspending in the late 1930s and boost its post-war revival when serving council officers resumed their IAC roles. Arguably this freezing of posts also delayed women's rise to greater prominence, despite their varied wartime contributions.

Post-war cine club numbers reportedly rose to between 250 and 300 by 1957 (Anon. 1957b: 6). Some groups relaunched themselves with publicity and new premises. Some fledging groups soon floundered but others outgrew initial home-based meetings and sought licensed premises suited to public screening and filmmaking workshops. Individual circumstances shaped inventive solutions, particularly where clubs had limited funds and attitudes affected opportunities for women's participation. In North London, the Fourfold Film Society gained praise for women's involvement in directing, camerawork in colour, continuity and stylish film show presentations that included 'lady members in evening dress [as] usherettes and programme sellers' (Fayde 1952a: 63).

Women's greater wartime autonomy was compromised by subsequent governmental emphasis on returning to domesticity (Webster 1998: x). Home-building, family and motherhood were touted as part of coping with post-war austerity and shaping a forward-looking nation (Kynaston 2007). Club subscriptions varied: Warrington Cine Society, Lancashire, reopened in 1947 with rates of 21 shillings (£1.05) for men and 'half price for ladies and juniors'. Elsewhere, subscriptions reflected continuing ambivalence to women's status within clubs. At Bury, Lancashire, wives were still half the price of junior members in the 1960s, but introducing a family rate caused dissent in at least one southern club.[35] Choice of meeting venue affected participation too: when Wolverhampton Film Makers (Wolverhampton Cine Club, founded 1948) moved its meetings into a public house some early women members allegedly felt awkward attending the new venue and left the group (see also Fayde 1952c: 160–1).[36]

Lingering conservatism offset women's opportunities for greater parity despite social and political changes introduced by the post-war Labour government. Guests of honour at the IAC's 1949 amateur film annual convention included the actress Lana Morris but the write-up noted only her garments and that she was 'rather overwhelmed by the scale of the *Daily Mail* Challenge Trophy' while presenting prizes.[37] The sole female member of the judging panel was the wife of William Vallon, the IAC's wartime chairman, although recorded only by her husband's initials. Such contributions as partners to long-serving IAC officers brought recognition that was rooted in duty and support but often confined to providing refreshments, costumes, publicity and administration (Wood 1950: 886). Caring for the filmmaking family conformed to new national emphasis (and *Daily Mail* perspective) on women's primary roles as housewives and mothers.

'Not getting a fair chance' and 'lack of opportunity' complained Iris Fayde (1951b: 636–8), the incognito advocate of greater female participation as the post-war ebb of women's practical interest in film production appeared to continue. Invitations for projectionists 'to charm away the monotony for those in hospitals and institutions' or the beneficial 'feminine touch at the filmshow' outnumbered pleas for more women filmmakers (Fayde 1951a: 805–6; 1952b: 909–11). Gendered language permeated amateur discourse: while Marie Partridge's documentary, *Whither Shall She Wander*, won at Union internationale du cinéma's (UNICA's) international film festival in 1958, another British film entry was disqualified as it had already been screened at another festival, thus, wrote Tony Rose (1958: 615) 'violating something that is quaintly known as a "virginity clause"'. Mild sexism abounded in cartoons and characterisation, as seen in contrasting responses to advice offered to a fictional young couple making their first film: Dennis (electrician, DIY enthusiast, 31) concentrates and 'frowns thoughtfully' while Jill (secretary, with a 'tremendous zest for life', 26) questions, shares horror, disappointment and ultimately delight as they learn to edit: 'Marvellous! . . . Who would have a thought that a pair of scissors could make such a difference?' (Townsend 1961: 563). It seems that provocative and patronising hobby press articles coexisted with reliance upon female activity (Shone 1961: 787).

Interviews have revealed that women's participation in amateur filmmaking grew during the 1950s. Productive as well as reproductive lives were increasingly important to some women despite obstacles of unequal wages, limited childcare and societal expectations. Individuality and leisure were part of the new Britain evoked by cinema, Ideal Home exhibitions and the contradictory messages of women's burgeoning magazines. Women's opinions were also more visible in the letters' pages of the hobby press, during the 1950s, than twenty years later, when it seems that the magazines were produced by and for men even if they featured an occasional article by a woman author. Women's varied club contributions to amateur practice throughout the decade have been overlooked too. Margaret Manvell was IAC president (1952–4), admittedly following on from her husband, Roger Manvell.[38] Joyce Skinner, as a young secondary school teacher, co-founded the South Birmingham Cine Society in the early 1950s (see Chapter 6) and Dundee Cine Society (founded early 1930s) was chaired by Margaret C. Muir in 1950, possibly the same Dr Muir who was an active local public speaker in the pre-war years.[39]

Women's opportunities for filmmaking and other roles varied. Wives, drawn into club activities, so that they were not left as 'cine wives' at home, remained widespread. Typically their involvement focused on areas of perceived skill and labour: refreshments, ticket sales, correspondence and minute-taking. Club news and photographs were often sent in by women acting as publicity officers and secretaries. Reported productions involved women as scriptwriters, camera and backstage crew, and in continuity, even if they were absent from the final credits. Such activities sustained club life and visibility even as women's voices were often absent from the article pages of the hobby press. Undoubtedly, time constraints limited women's club input and intermeshed with their own changing responsibilities of domestic and family care. Group dynamics, personalities and local circumstances affected women's opportunities where most club members were men. Club participation often lessened after there were children, despite the ubiquity of family films or home movies, but some award-winning couples including Lois and Lewis Weobly involved their children too.[40] Betty and Ian Lauder's daughters feature, 'lending colour and movement to landscape shots', within such 'serious' film projects as *Eyam* (Lauder and Lauder 1962: 470). Childless couples made films together and as part of group productions. Betty and Cyril Ramsden, two award-winning members at Leeds Cine Circle (renamed Leeds Movie Makers) started filmmaking with a friend who dropped out due to her own childcare duties. Over twenty years, they made more than fifty films together, in addition to club productions. Holidays often focused around making a documentary. Contrasting with their commissioned and local interest films was more informal cine use. Within footage of New Year domestic merry-making a playful stop motion sequence shows how hungry guests help themselves to party food that disappears rapidly from laden plates. Betty had studied art during her teacher training but her career stopped when she married. She redirected her visual awareness and sense of composition into their hobby once she became receptionist at her husband's dental practice. As competent filmmakers, their camera work stretched visual possibilities, whether filming a master craftsman, sea storm or village gymkhana or when swapping cine cameras to record frivolity in the intimacy and conviviality of a middle class home.[41]

New Kinds of Independence

Many societal changes affected women's amateur visual practice during the 1960s. Paid employment, labour-saving household appliances, modernising lifestyles and changing attitudes enabled more women to participate in organised leisure activities. As cheaper equipment became available within an increasingly competitive international market, cine camera use rose and, as in the interwar years, women became a target audience for lighter and simpler technologies. Advertising that featured women holding cameras reflected wider marketing trends rather than a significant narrowing of the hobby's gender gap. Certainly correspondence and cine literature content suggests a predominantly male readership even though one source claims that by 1969, of a million movie makers, a quarter were women.[42]

Women filmmakers gradually gained more visibility within magazine publishing. *Amateur Movie Maker* profiled filmmakers including Marie Partridge in its *Shooting Star* series whilst acknowledging that 'amateur cinematography is still very much a man's world' (Rose 1957: 30–1). By the early 1960s Patricia Hadlow was in charge of advertising at *Cine Camera*, a magazine for users of 8mm equipment and Kathleen Pengelly contributed occasional articles on making films with her husband. A new section, 'For Women', was launched in September 1961 to explore 'the world of women' and 'projects near to feminine hearts'. In 'an expedition among the hairdryers' based on her daughter's first perm, Pengelly stressed simplicity and how shooting 'followed the natural sequence of events, cutting, shampooing, curling, drying and the final comb out' (1961a: 9). She offered tips on filming pets and babies in the next issue that promised a 'kitten and kiddy colour cover to make all the girls flip'. Guidance on filming fireworks warned about noise and safety and acknowledged 'it's difficult, balancing a child in one hand and a camera in the other but it can be done'. By the fourth issue, sexist flippancy accompanied conversational tips for 'wives and girl friends' overcoming the 'ordeal' and 'the plight of going to a cine club film show' (Pengelly 1961b: 14–15; Anon. 1961: 42).

Here, as elsewhere, the hobby press was ambivalent in reaching out to women practitioners (Shone 1961: 787; 1962: 8; Smith 1961: 956). Although often defended by editors and authors as humour being taken the wrong way, antipathy towards women filmmakers grew harder to sustain (Rose 1962: 11). Women's cine practice attracted support from such professionals as Hazel Swift who drew on film industry experience when adjudicating amateur materials or writing for cine publications. The 'indispensable' role of the 'continuity girl' ('who is not necessarily female'), Swift wrote, had a special job in a filmmaking team that was similar to that of a good club secretary (1961a: 174–5, 200; 1961b: 294–5; 1961c: 482–3). If recognition of women's increasingly active role in amateur circles only dawned slowly in those shaping cine literature, at an organisational level, new identities and patterns of participation were gaining influence.

From 1962, the IAC's new regional networks created geographically based settings in which women could participate as active filmmakers. Newsletters, committees and competitions proliferated. So did the need for speakers, organisers, hosts, judges, publicity officers, treasurers, projectionists, workshop leaders and event coordinators. Women found outlets away from domestic responsibilities and paid work where greater autonomy, decision-making and activity brought satisfaction. Situations varied. Some non-smoking women found smoke-filled meetings still male dominated.[43] Others encountered hostility as some members felt their authority usurped by newcomers. Wives reportedly sometimes felt threatened by the arrival of younger women. Notwithstanding these concerns, many women flourished in Britain's amateur film circles during the 1960s. Clubs recruited well. People enjoyed making and watching each other's films and film shows attracted large audiences too as television had not yet diminished the appetite for attending big screen events and public talks. Women's varied roles helped to expand amateur activity and in some cases their own lives became increasingly defined by cine interests either shared with a partner or on their own.

Betty Jennings' memories traced such changes over almost half a century.[44] She and her husband Jack bought their first cine camera in 1962 to record their daughter's wedding. They made a holiday documentary and joined a local club in 1963.[45] At first Betty carried equipment when Jack recorded sound. 'You had to get involved or you'd become a cine widow', she recalled. They joined the IAC in *c.*1969 and Jennings soon chaired a regional meeting as the only woman present: 'I'd always been on committees even at school so I could keep order.' The expansion of committee roles filled by women reflects how the IAC required skills, time and commitment that some male members felt were distractions away from their main interests. Women found themselves drawn into activities, possibly regarded by some men as domestic housekeeping and of secondary concern, that combined practical filmmaking knowledge with administrative astuteness and intellectual acumen. For Betty, and other women, the boundaries were fluid and fresh opportunities were available.

'What I liked about the cine clubs and the IAC was the camaraderie. Everyone was very helpful and friendly. If you needed anything you could borrow something and ask for help. People liked being able to offer advice.' Jennings acknowledged the supportive atmosphere where 'you could try things out' – a freedom for experimentation, including taking on different roles, more available to amateurs than professionals in any context. 'Making better films was important. Learning from others. Going to clubs was important because people saw each other's films and could comment on them. The criticism was positive – about how to improve and what worked.'

Jennings never won anything, although her husband occasionally did. 'We made fictional films, together, and with other club members. I'd get an idea and try it out – never very long about four to five minutes at the most.' Taking part was more important than winning although competition successes were independent hallmarks of quality and sources of pride. Being a judge acknowledged expertise, conferred esteem and brought enjoyment:

> A lot of work was involved and it was very time-consuming. I'd watch the films at home first and then as a judge, I'd watch them being screened to an audience. It was so different having an audience. I'd take notes and then the notes would all have be written up . . . I'd judge at the international competitions too. Encouraging others was what was so enjoyable.

Implicit in this voluntary mentoring was freedom and service to others.

IAC activity brought friendship: 'It was sociable going out, meeting people you knew and sharing films about different subjects.' Jennings' words evoke the internationalism of the Lions Club and Rotary Club and women-only voluntary organisations. Being the IAC's international officer sustained wider links: 'I'd make contact with a cine club in a place I was visiting and there'd always be a welcome, interesting people willing to talk and share ideas.' There was a broadly middle class, middle income and middle brow political inclusivity that fostered conviviality between expatriates from post-war migration and English-speaking nations within the young Commonwealth. International competitions promoted links too: 'I went representing IAC to UNICA. The IAC was out for many years but rejoined. It was like a League of Nations.' Such sentiments acknowledge the personal and broader benefits of cultural exchanges through filmmaking, now recognised by the United Nations Educational, Scientific and Cultural Organization (UNESCO). They evoke the short-lived internationalism of the interwar years when she was young, which perhaps resonates more positively than the post-war transmutation of empire into Commonwealth. The world within the amateur-making community was a safer, friendlier place than real world politics. Jennings received a UNICA medal in recognition of her own contribution to international cooperation and understanding in 2015.[46]

Falling membership levels within the IAC, as within other clubs and voluntary organisations, reflect broader changes in lifestyles and participation in paid labour. Jennings suggested that 'In the past, women would go out in the evening if they'd been at home all day.' Within IAC and club life, she identified an ageing membership with more mobile lives and a generational shift from public to more autonomous forms of filmmaking and reflexivity:

> Young people don't seem to want the feedback. They make a film on their phones but they're not interested in talking about how they made it . . . it's easier to make a film now but not necessarily of the same technical quality.

Once the IAC logo conferred pride and legitimacy and membership brought 'a sense of family'. Affiliation to something larger, independent of overt ideologies, offered reassurance and continuity. She regretted the loss of younger audiences although acknowledged many annual film shows still attract large numbers. After her husband died, Jennings left the IAC briefly but returned for another three decades and contributes to current discussions about the IAC's future. For her, change has always been integral to amateur visual practice and contemporary challenges are just the latest in the hobby's history of reinvention.

Comparable stories of commitment recur through IAC networks across Britain. Naming risks omissions and is indicative only of the upsurge of interest from the 1960s that brought renewed impetus to amateur visual practice. Dorothy and Norman Speirs gained considerable recognition for their shared lifelong service to amateur film. Dorothy was involved with her husband's work furthering amateur practice in Scotland, promoting clubs, competitions and documenting a cultural history of amateur activity. She took part in some club productions too. Alison and John Coleman co-founded Lanark Cine Club during the 1960s and became part of a vibrant club scene that included a documentary on local Vietnamese refugee provision and resettlement in the early 1980s (Duguid 2013: 2).[47] Elise Phimister, Elise Lornie and Margaret Richardson were active Scottish club members too, and more independently, Margaret Tait also attests to the prominence of women in the nation's diverse history of non-commercial film production (see Chapter 8). South of the border independent filmmakers and husband and wife teams also occurred: Edith and Francis Williams gained recognition from *Movie Maker* as 'lone workers . . . that do everything themselves . . .' (Rose 1968: 597; 1969a: 508). Linda and Michael Gough's significant IAC careers started as young teachers in Newcastle during the early 1970s; in north-west England, Peter and Daphne (Dee) Copestake traced their filmmaking activities to the 1960s.[48] Mary Stevenson's role in regional workshops, training weekends and club life predated the IAC's plans for restructuring in 1962. Stevenson (1982: 31–2) became vice president and a fellow, in recognition of her work as a filmmaker and other varied contributions. Regional newsletters supplemented the more nationally focused *IAC News* and trace many individual evolving stories of involvement (Bayne 1982: 31–2). *Tripod*, for example covers the north-west where many women filmmakers flourished in the post-war years.[49] IAC awards and honour lists also trace the growing presence of women members given recognition since records began.

Mixing with Professionals

Decades before Leadbeater and Miller (2004) coined the term Pro-Am, some amateurs benefited from contact between paid and unpaid participation in media-related industries. Critics and filmmakers – particularly within animation – also used smaller gauge equipment in their leisure time. Christine Collins traced her interests to working in post-production on the BBC's *On Safari* African wildlife series (*c.*1957–66) and then at Gateway Film Productions, close to where she lived.[50] She bought Standard 8mm equipment and joined Potters Bar Cine Society where there were other enthusiastic women filmmakers, including Gay Ashby, who 'outshone everyone' with her award-winning films.[51] She recalled that 'we felt no discrimination' and that she 'went on to film anything and everything . . . holidays . . . weddings . . . films to a [vinyl] record . . . the usual. The films were mainly short as film was expensive.' A new projector allowed her to add soundtracks although she still edited 'on the dining table using cement splices'. Impetus came from club membership, competitions and screenings where 'you had to provide all your own equipment for these shows, projector, tape recorder, loudspeaker and a stand' (Figures 2.2–2.5).

Professional work offered opportunities for personal projects including award-winning films about London's old Covent Garden Market and the Whitehall Cenotaph. Working with hired VHS video equipment allowed Collins to record sound in sync with the picture and made interviewing possible.

Figure 2.2 Photograph of Christine Collins using a 16mm mixing desk. © Gateway Film Productions.

Figure 2.3 Photograph of Christine Collins on location during *Sound Talk* with a Sennheiser rifle microphone. © Christine Collins.

Figure 2.4 Photograph of Christine Collins using her Canon Hi8 camera. © Christine Collins.

Figure 2.5 Photograph of Christine Collins on location with other amateur filmmakers. © Christine Collins.

> I persuaded my mother to allow me to make a film of the story of her wedding day which had unfortunately been on Sunday 3rd September 1939, the day the Second World War was declared, so she had a story to tell . . .

Workplace skills and evening access to professional equipment helped with the editing. VHS brought flexibility too:

> I never really enjoyed film editing but when I progressed to video production I was able to work quickly as well as being able to change my mind during editing . . . which had not been possible with film as once you have cut your master film that's it, the shot can never go back to its original length.

Innovation brought further possibilities:

> Spurred on by the excitement of video I bought the large Hi8 Canon video camera . . . a wonderful camera . . . I could only edit by transfer from camera to Super VHS, a long and complicated job especially if you wanted a sophisticated soundtrack. I guess that my experience in the business helped me to overcome some of these frustrating barriers.

Collins joined the IAC in the late 1960s after helping with the London Amateur Film Festival. Seeing prize-winning films at national level inspired her own development and over fifty years later, she now films and edits in digital video. She became an IAC fellow in the late 1970s and, after years of making documentaries, by 2016 she was directing short, mainly comedy, club films. Collins reflected upon the interplay between her professional and amateur activity and her sensitivity to 'the "magic" that happens when sound and picture come together':

> I put great store on the importance of the soundtrack and have experienced all sorts over my working life: *On Safari*, for example, was subtle sounds of nature as well as music, whereas at Gateway it could be anything from heavy industrial backgrounds, overseas lifestyles to simple films for education . . .

She admitted that although not unique, 'her links with professional and amateur sides of filmmaking' affected how her early interests in photography matured.

Penny Love, a member at Potters Bar Cine Society since 1975, also highlighted the club's progressive attitudes and professional links with London's film and media industries: '[It] has always been a very "go ahead" club and all members equal, especially in making films. Even when we used to have to make our own tea in the interval . . . the chaps took their turns.'[52] She acknowledged that people's interests still vary: 'Some of the ladies . . . can use the projector when needed. Not all want to and not all want to make films but they all have as much interest as the chaps, though subject matter can be quite different.' Love's comment invokes Bloomfield's (2015) questioning of assumed gender bias being attributable when the identity of an image-maker is known (see Chapter 3) but remains unanswered. Gender-role assumptions persist as found when taking a film show to an outside audience: 'When we arrived . . . we both laughed when they "assumed" that I would be doing the "chat" and he would be working the equipment. Wrong! It's the other way round . . .'[53]

Love stressed how her responsibilities and opportunities changed over time, including being club president and secretary and increasingly active at IAC regional level. Assuming administrative roles sustained club vitality but filmmaking was Love's primary focus. She began by 'trial and error' using manuals and other people's tips. Wishing to record her brother's wedding in 1969, she bought a '£50.00 Kodak starter pack comprising a basic camera, projector, couple of reels of film, bottle of cement for splicing, manual and a lever-operated splicing machine.' Editing initially meant joining together silent holiday films and 'cutting out the worst bits'. Feedback improved technique and brought confidence to experiment:

> a very good family owned and run company in Radlett . . . 'striped' the film for us to add our own sound. It looked like a sort of very thin recording tape 'glued' to the both edges of the film and we could put speech on one edge and other sounds on the other.

Love acknowledged technical constraints:

> I never had a 'sound' camera but managed okay, though lip sync could be a bit hit and miss when trying to match separately recorded sound to the picture. A lot of very close up watching lips and instant pressing of the transferring button to the stripe was needed.

Editing became easier too when she

> changed to 'Wurker' splices, more like Sellotape, in a special machine and no messy cement to use. I also bought a machine to view editing as I went along and not have to keep putting the film though the projector to see if it was okay. Less chance of it getting scratched too.

Further adjustments occurred:

> Cameras got smaller and video was invented so [I bought] another camera and [began] an entirely different editing system and sound recording. This time I needed to use a VHS recorder to put my film into, edit it as I did so, then recording the speech and any music, having already transferred the original sound to a separate tape, and put the whole lot back onto the film via a mixer for all the sounds sources.

She enjoyed being self-sufficient at home:

> Now I use an Avio for editing, like a computer but with my TV as the monitor and a very easy and straightforward system. I have never edited on a normal computer but, apart from a lot of fancy special effects that a modern computerised system has, you need to put good stuff in to get good stuff out . . . Sometimes too many special effects can spoil the actual content of the film.

Animals recur through Love's films that include award-winning documentaries about using pets in therapy and training guide dogs for the visually impaired. Her mother's sight loss and local opportunities enabled her to produce a 'film (that) helped to win many competitions for the club'. She admitted that she likes 'to make films about things people know of, but not about' as seen in her documentary about a local woman's care for injured hedgehogs.[54] Such items become popular in club programmes but also have personal significance as seen in *Wow*, a filmed encounter with tigers made with friends: 'I had a "special" birthday and hand-fed two full size, live tigers.' Live action becomes a means to simultaneously record, relive and share an experience: a form of selfing or public talk through visual stories about oneself.

Other women acknowledge how professional input affected their film-making too. Although Beryl Armstrong (b.1927) shot her earliest cine films while in India, advice from a BBC employee, encountered after her return to England, shaped her own critical practice.[55] She used 8mm film for almost thirty years and coordinated family outings that also suited her husband's interest in colour transparencies. We were 'united by photography' she recalled. 'We went out as a family to film, to gather sounds . . . By letting them (her sons) take part, they could take an interest from early on.' Film-making brought pleasure and pride but also friction within club settings where the boys' independent successes along with her own sometimes generated ill feeling: 'Three years in a row, a woman and two young boys had taken the coveted club's annual cup. Phew! A few sparks flew.' Armstrong's sense of unjust criticism prompted her to film her sons making their own films. She taught them stop motion animation, involving alien invasions and the use of rice grains in Cold War style sci-fi germ warfare. She devised reel to reel sound accompaniments from field recordings and licensed music before adding sound as magnetic tape. Her published articles included technical and practical topics (Armstrong 1971: 446–8; 1972: 711, 714; Armstrong and Walden 1972: 870–1). She featured her son's own cine practice too as they gained awards and appeared on children's television. Memories of different clubs were mixed and eventually, although she had found friendship, inspiration and encouragement among other 8mm cine users, she also felt that she was still very much 'a woman in a man's world'.

Armstrong directed short comedies with her teenage sons but preferred making documentaries as revealed while watching her films together in 2016.[56] Her widely acclaimed year-long cinematic focus on her father as beekeeper brought personal pleasure and still satisfied her critical scrutiny as did her reflections upon recording children at play in a training film for preschool leaders and making an anniversary film about Greenline buses. Films about local issues and scouting activities reflected the concerns and constraints of family life within the suburban anonymity of a post-war new town. Shared interests prompted films on model railway making and the closure of steam railways. Documentaries on large working horses and farming rare breeds revealed her own quest for new knowledge and self-improvement. Voluntary involvement changed over time and a film about restoring countryside footpaths gained recognition from the Ramblers' Association. Her articles and output of over eighty films reflected how circumstance, place and time shaped her changing roles and identities as a wife and mother, mentor and filmmaker.

Combining Passions

Digitisation attracted newcomers into organised filmmaking. Britain's war years and post-war baby boom generation brought different kinds of technical literacy and life experiences to their films. Jill Lampert acknowledged her own commitment: 'Film making is my passion. When I'm not making films or learning about making films, I like to be out and about watching wildlife.'[57] The former infant school teacher took up filmmaking as a creative outlet after becoming a child protection solicitor. She joined Sutton Coldfield Movie Makers (formed as Vesey Amateur Cine Society) in 2008 because she needed 'to have people to "talk film" to' and soon gained a reputation for high quality work and also her insightful feedback as a competition judge, a role that grew rapidly within the IAC. Competitions offered her incentive for completing a project, and invaluable learning opportunities. The club's mission to share knowledge and enthusiasm suited Lampert's needs and enabled her to experiment. Since owning her first video camera in 2002, her productions have included holidays, local events, music, wedding and instructional videos, animations and wildlife. Working digitally allows her to re-edit and shorten earlier work, including a film on drug addiction recovery, and her 'first love' for documentary remains unchanged.[58]

Family interests thread through some films, now involving grandchildren as actors, subject matter or prop-makers and she identifies her longest and most ambitious project as a documentary about growing up with nine siblings.

> There were ten of us. I interviewed all of them (with the help of one of my brothers) on video and collected family photographs and newspaper cuttings from family and friends and then edited all this together as best I could.

Collectively their childhoods spanned three decades, two continents and the Second World War, during which their family home was 'let out to nuns as a school'. Family history intermeshes with the politics of war and its aftermath, decolonisation and postcolonial self-determination.

> In 1948 my parents and my siblings (the oldest being then 16) and I emigrated to what was [then called] Rhodesia and lived on a farm. More siblings were born, the last being born in 1954. My parents and a few siblings moved to Swaziland in about 1966. So it is an interesting trajectory.

Lampert defined the project's scope: 'only things that happened during someone's childhood could be mentioned. So the last memories were . . . when my youngest sibling turned 18'. Made before she joined a club and for family interest the film is not online unlike much of Lampert's other material.

Lampert's fascination for natural history follows a well-established genre of film production that traces to early cinema and pioneering cine activity by both men and women. Evolving technologies have brought successive benefits to amateur wildlife filmmakers, as shown by the changing sophistication of colour, sound, magnification, compact camera size, relative production costs and ease of editing. Amateur productions typically now share many of the high production values of their television counterparts: they too are 'beautifully photographed, filmed and edited' and offer 'an unmediated, and apparently authentic experience of nature' (Davies 1998: 16). Digitally produced natural history films feature regularly in IAC competitions and Lampert's wildlife projects find audiences at screenings and online.[59] Some projects take over a year. *The Patient Fisherman* involved visits to different heronries, extensive research and gaining critical response from filmmaking friends via YouTube. Her self-critique considers each film's visual and audio character, narrative tone and balance between factual, contextual and anecdotal details. Memories recall compromises and risks taken, her use of zoom lenses, tripods, soundtrack and when to seek permission (or not) to film in specific locations.

Lampert's nature films share the contemplative pleasure of solitary unobtrusive field observation with others, including perhaps less mobile older film enthusiasts. Her soundtracks mix quiet narration, natural sounds and music. Wildlife behaviour shot in real time combine telescopic intimacy with wide angle landscape views. Each visual story unfolds gently without fast paced cutaways or heightened dramatic content intended for visual impact and audience retention. Her research, detailed observations of male and female interactions and speculative commentary produces seasonal portraits of animal and bird behaviour that combine information and aesthetic charm. Undoubtedly pictorial these films combine an appreciation of learning and conservation message about sustaining wildlife havens in Britain's unexpected places. Quietly celebratory, their embedded cultural values highlight the enduring place of nature in personal and national identity.

Conclusion

Highlighting women's experiences within IAC and cine circles and its accompanying hobby literature over nearly ninety years uncovers varied webs of production and cultural practice. Women's personal circumstances shaped film-related activity and organised networks gave access to audiences beyond families and friends. From the outset, the IAC included women in its promotion of amateur film production through competitions, screenings, publication and discussion. The IAC encouraged good practice, regardless of gender, and wished to be taken seriously by amateurs and professionals as the public face of Britain's amateur visual practice at home and abroad. Ambitiously founded by a handful of male cine enthusiasts, during a decade of international economic depression, unemployment and social unrest that spiralled into rearmament and global conflict, the IAC now seems an unlikely candidate for encouraging women's filmmaking, let alone surviving into the twentieth-first century.

This chapter suggests that it has been successful. Set up at a point when amateur colour and sound still seemed unattainable for all but the very wealthy, successive adaptations enabled the IAC to modernise. Women's practice and participation were central to how it matured and became internationally recognised for its promotion of non-commercial filmmaking. Like any institution, the IAC is best understood as an amalgam of external and internal constraints and opportunities operating over time. Yet, as a product of societal and cultural influences it unwittingly reflects and reproduces mainstream attitudes and values. Although the IAC offers a significant arena for women's participation in amateur visual cultural production, this chapter's testimonies also disclose how individuals had to negotiate differently those evolving opportunities.

This sharing of women's experiences as disclosed through text, recollection and surviving film is selective, condensed and an incomplete record of those who involved themselves with amateur filmmaking. These reminiscences reveal women's growing autonomy as they gained recognition, offered a voice and expressed themselves creatively through film. Repeatedly, women display their commitment to film for pleasure: to take, make and share their films using available technologies and visual language effectively. They borrowed, bought or shared equipment to develop their interests and sought out skills and knowledge that were then often passed on. They learnt to film, edit, add sound and present their films. As their expertise developed they gained honours and awards from their peers. They explored different genres, recording formats, editing techniques and projection systems as they took part in events and competitions and they volunteered in different capacities from club to international level too. They contributed to the press and gave visibility to their clubs, competitions and productions as they shouldered innumerable practical, organisational and procedural tasks that supported amateur practice. Men undertook these activities too, but without having to challenge wider social conventions or patriarchal assumptions that were often embedded at grassroots club level and reinforced for years by the low level sexism of a male orientated hobby press.

In short, women became integral members of Britain's amateur filmmaking community. The housewives and homemakers who accompanied their husbands to club meetings and IAC events created niches for themselves in which their consummate skills at managing the mundane and unspectacular aspects of organisational life allowed cine activity to flourish. Such housekeeping roles did little to challenge the position of women per se although they helped to feminise amateur film culture and some partners later became involved in practical film production. More confident and secure in their identities within settings where men and women mixed more freely, women's involvement diversified. Greater participation by single and married women filmmakers from the 1960s onwards attracted other women of different ages and backgrounds. Opportunities for filmmaking, as with any other area of life, were complicated by women's responsibilities as carers and earners. Like any voluntary associational involvement, women's participation was affected by other commitments. Growing confidence and independence, linked to higher education, professional employment and changing attitudes affected women's growing visibility within the IAC and in helping clubs to keep going. Shifts in attitudes and gender perspectives occurred among men too, as broader societal questioning and reassessment of women's roles occurred.

Regardless of professional affiliation, however, women's amateur film-related activities occurred within existing economic, social and creative frameworks and expectations. Long committed to avoiding controversial topics, the IAC favoured material that did not challenge or cause distress. Through the 1970s and 1980s, independent filmmakers found other outlets for experimental work in film and later video, often supported by public funding, although some exceptions by men and women occur through the IAC's history.[60] Generally, women, like their male counterparts, used changing visual media to tell stories gently about their lives or the world around them, or make the world a better understood or appreciated place to live, as seen in films about local, social or environmental causes. Despite occasional instances of all-women productions, IAC members did not tend to use the medium to make feminist or counter-cultural statements. Rather, they offered individual and specific points of view, which might also privilege other women's activities and capture their perspectives on camera. Choice of topic, location and the logistics of shooting, post-production and subsequent screening reflected their own lived experiences, realities and sense of the possible. Women throughout the IAC's supportive environments mediated broadly progressive values and beliefs that quietly celebrated individual endeavour and achievement.

Through these networks of cultural production and creative practice, consciousness and circumstances shape women's self-expression and create more nuanced understanding of personal and collective identity. As women's history, these textures are fine-grained too, disclosing processes of adjustment and accommodation, rather than outright challenges. They reflect those women who persisted rather than left or never even joined. Successes fail to disclose the stories of those that never took part. Individual lives widen an understanding of amateur cinema commonly perceived as a male activity but, undeniably, these footprints represent only part of changing British identities and memories over the past nine decades. Like so many voluntary groups and communities of interest, the conservatism of formal associations and activities has a consensual inclusivity that may exclude others for diverse reasons. Minorities are absent, including those on the basis of colour, race or sexual orientation. In this account, amateur filmmaking does not straddle ethnic and racial divides particularly well. Social, cultural and economic factors continue to affect patterns of activity, belonging and comfort zones, as do location, mobility and other practical realities of everyday lives. Unlike the United States where recognised lesbian footage dates to the mid-twentieth century and African American cine use dates back still further, the stories of recreational filmmaking among Britain's different minorities have largely yet to be discovered and told (Dixon Anthony, 2016:35–64: see also Norris Nicholson, 2017: 73–92).[61] Perhaps some explanations exist not at home or in organised activities but in Britain's fast transforming political peripheries where women, regardless of background, were recording the world informally as they saw it, as seen in following chapters.

Notes

1. Author in conversation with Phillip Collins, IAC archivist, EAFA, 6–7 July 2016.
2. Contacts kindly supplied by Phillip Collins are supplemented by other contributors whose interest and support is gratefully acknowledged.
3. Much writing on the history, role and work of women in film has also been prompted particularly through the Women's Film and Television History Network UK/Ireland (WFTHN) and its sister organisations internationally, as well as various online databases.
4. The IAC began as a breakaway group from the British Amateur Cinematographers' Association that in turn operated separately from the Amateur Cinematographers' Association which championed local club development from *c.*1927.
5. A reproduced archive photograph captures the stylish tone of the IAC's first annual conference, banquet and presentation of the institute's inaugural national film competition awards, held at the Mayfair Hotel, London, November 1933.
6. See note 1.
7. Peter Le Neve Foster (co-founder of Cambridge University's cine club in 1923 and later founder of the Manchester Film Society *c.*1925) regularly supplied content on amateur film to the *Manchester Guardian* during the 1930s.
8. William Stull, writing in *American Cinematographer* observed that she broke an 'unwritten law' of filmmaking (see Tepperman 2014: 64). Given her youth and the rapid technical advance of amateur practice, its inclusion at a film show held by Manchester Film Society drew rather harsh criticism of her 'undisciplined imagination' (see C. R. 1938: 15).
9. K. Agnes and John B. Thubron (1932–3) *Her Second Birthday* (16mm, 5:31min, b/w, silent), EAFA no. 2684; see also Chapter 8.
10. K. Agnes and John B. Thubron (1932–4) *Transport* (10:28min, b/w, silent), EAFA no. 2685.
11. See for example, Eunice and Eustace Alliott (1931) *Picturesque People and Pleasant Places in Holland* (58:48min, b/w, silent), EAFA no. 4406; (1930) *To Oberammergau and the Alps in an Austin Sixteen* (11:57min, b/w, silent), EAFA no. 4413 (first of eight reels).
12. See for instance, Laurie and Stuart Day (1930) *Freiburg* (13:39min, b/w, silent), EAFA no. 212573.
13. Laurie and Stuart Day (1938) *Last Year of Peace* (32:36min, colour, sound), EAFA no. 2633
14. Live-action or animated preludes to travel sequences were often joined to films made by couples. A number of films featuring such openings, including

(1959) *Happy Hour* (16mm, 34:44min, colour, sound), were made by Mr and Mrs Jack and F. Wells, NWFA no. 4461.

15. Stoke Cine Society (1935) *Nancy's Garage*, EAFA old catalogue. IAC Daily Mail Trophy, 1937, also The Denham Trophy (aka Alexander Korda Gold Cup) available at <http://www.theiac.org.uk/eventsnew/biaff/iactrophies/lfpg.htm> (last accessed 21 January 2018).
16. See, for example, Laurie and Stuart Day (1953) *Dance Little Lady* (19:58min, colour, sound), EAFA no. 212566.
17. John Martin (1935) *A Day in the Life of the Young Martins* (17:27min, b/w, silent), EAFA no. 3004.
18. Frank Marshall (1937/8) *Our Angel Children* (16mm, 14:17min, b/w, silent), NLS. Id. 3805.
19. See BFI (1924) *The Witch's Fiddle* (6:24min, b/w, silent) available at <https://www.youtube.com/watch?v=dIWfr5ptzEM> (last accessed 21 January 2018).
20. Credits to Ruth Le Neve as 'Camera' and "Bob" Harper and Peter Le Neve as directors (Manchester Film Society) are cited in Anon. (1933:89, 91).
21. Sadie Andrews (1929) *The Polite Burglar* (9.04min, b/w, silent), EAFA, Cat No. 4086. Note this film was made for a club competition so that members could spot the number of errors in filmmaking; T. J. White (1929) *The Sack*, EAFA old catalogue.
22. Newcastle ACA (1929) *Bon Aventure* credits Gladys Davison for photography, Janet M. Cameron for titles and James Cameron Junior as director (9.5mm, 33:20min, b/w, silent), NEFA Id. 21330; Newcastle ACA (1930) *A Romance of the Moors* (aka *Preference*) credits Janet M. Cameron and Doris M. Graham for photography, and James Cameron Jnr as director (9.5mm, 20:50min, b/w, silent), NEFA Id. 21328.
23. Doris M. Graham (1933) *ACA Outing to Warkworth on 16 July 1933* (16mm, 5:8min, b/w, silent), NEFA Id. 21344.
24. Edinburgh Cine Society (1957) *Edinburgh Cine Society, 1936–1957* (16mm, 53:27min, b/w, colour, silent), NLS Id. 6944.
25. 2 October 1937, *Edinburgh Cine Society and then ECVS Edinburgh Cine and Video Society* (formerly the Waverley Amateur Cine Club), available at <http://www.ecvs.co.uk/> (last accessed on 21 January 2018).
26. *The World Film Encyclopedia* (Winchester 1933) list was reprinted in *Amateur Film Maker*, August 1982, p. 46. How the figures were calculated is now unknown, but one of amateur cinema's innovators and staunch advocates was Peter Le Neve Foster, secretary of the Manchester Film Society, who estimated that there were 300,000 amateur filmmakers in the country, but that only about 4,000 belong to the 200 amateur film clubs (*The Manchester Guardian*, 4 December 1936, p. 13).
27. Holmfirth Camera Club, *Minute Book I*, 1940–5. See also Chapter 6.
28. See also Edinburgh Cine Society, *Edinburgh Cine Society, 1936–1957*, NLS Id. 6944.

29. *IAC Members' Newsletter*, February 1941.
30. *IAC Members' Newsletter*, February 1941.
31. *IAC Members' Newsletter*, May 1940.
32. *IAC Members' Newsletter*, December 1939.
33. *IAC Members' Newsletter*, February 1941 (author's note: 'crump' is used elsewhere to indicate the sound of ordnance landing during the London Blitz (Vera Britten, *Testament of Experience*, 1952) so 'lump' may be a typographical error).
34. *IAC News*, December 1950, p. 20
35. Mary Stevenson, *Wide Angle*, September 1967; author in conversation with Beryl Armstrong, autumn, 2016.
36. Fayde's report of an all-women film unit, called Wulfrun Amateur Cine Club, may be compared with the history of Wolverhampton Film Makers, available at <http://www.wulfruncamcorderclub.co.uk/history.html> (last accessed 2 April 2017).
37. *IAC News*, March 1949.
38. Presidents of the IAC (list), *Amateur Film Maker*, August 1982, p. 18.
39. Joyce Skinner, British Entertainment History Project (BEHP), Interview No. 663 (interviewed by Angela Martin, 2016), available at <https://historyproject.org.uk/content/joyce-skinner> (last accessed 21 January 2018).
40. Lois and Lewis Weobley (1951) *A Dog's Life* (15:03min, colour, silent), EAFA no. 3006.
41. Betty and Cyril Ramsden (1950s) *New Years' Eve Parties* (34:23min, b/w, separate magnetic), YFA Id. 3101.
42. Kodak display, National Science and Media Museum, Bradford, autumn 2017.
43. Author in correspondence with Pauline Harrison, Preston Movie Makers, 2009–11.
44. Author in conversation with Betty Jennings, 29 September 2016.
45. Derby 854 Club was named after the address of where meetings were held.
46. UNICA's promotion of international cooperation and understanding through filmmaking since 1931 has gained UNESCO recognition and brings together different national federations of amateur filmmakers. Internal politics and personality clashes led to the IAC disassociating itself periodically from UNICA but Britain's filmmakers have long been involved independently.
47. Mr Coleman (*sic*) (1981) *Escape to Freedom* (Super 8mm, 34:24min, colour, sound), NLS Id. 7774.
48. Author in correspondence with both couples, 2008–12.
49. For other filmmakers in north-west England see Pauline Harrison (note 43 above), Barbara Lloyd (Chapter 4), Ellaline Jennings and Mary Corner (Chapter 6) and Valrie Ellis (Chapter 8); for Wyn Newton's role in the south-eastern region as writer, event organiser, judge and filmmaker see Ralph Bayne (1982: 31–2).
50. Author in correspondence with Christine Collins, summer, 2016.

51. Gay Ashby (1975) *The Girl from Willow Lane*, EAFA no. 4003; (1977) *The Match Stick Man*, EAFA no. 4060.
52. Author in correspondence with Penny Love, summer, 2016.
53. Author in correspondence with Penny Love, 16 November 2016.
54. Penny Love, *A Hand Full of Prickles* (undated).
55. Author in conversation with Beryl Armstrong, 2016; see also Chapter 8.
56. Beryl Armstrong (1968) *A Taste for Honey* (Super 8mm, 11:00min, colour, sound), SASE Id. 5912; (*c*.late 1980s) *Once upon a Farm* (Super 8mm, 15:11min, colour, sound), SASE Id. 5913. Armstrong has retained many of her other films, made on Super 8mm, in colour and with sound, including: *Look at my Hands,* (*c*.1970), *Football Special* (1972), *The Lure of Steam* (1974), *The Rally of the Giants* (1980), *Our Footpaths* (1980), *Green Line* (1980), *The Sunday Workers* (1984) and *Day after Yesterday* (undated).
57. Jill Lampert, The making of *The Patient Fisherman* (2015), available at http://www.theiac.org.uk/film/makingof/film-making9/patient-fisherman.html (last accessed 13 April 2018); *The Patient Fisherman* (2015) (10:39min), BIAFF 5 star award 2013.
58. Jill Lampert, *The Madness* (2017) (10:39mins), available at <https://www.youtube.com/watch?v=4dpgrbnrGdk> (last accessed 21 January 2018).
59. Many of Jill Lampert's films are available on YouTube including: *Who's Singing?* (2009) (1:00min); *The Ambition* (2009) (1:00min); *Coot Watching* (2009) (8:37mins); *Barbary Macaques* (2010) (10:24mins); *Parenting Styles* (2013) (4:41mins) and *The Patient Fisherman* (2015) (10:39mins).
60. As part of *Feminist Archives, Feminist Futures* (University of Leeds) 'Archiving Women in Film & TV' was set up to archive the history of feminist filmmakers and bring women's film and TV history to a broader public. The project focused on collections on women in film and TV held at Feminist Archive North, materials from Leeds Animation Workshop (LAW) and Vera Media, two Leeds-based independent feminist filmmaking collectives, and papers from the Women's Film, Television and Video Network. Together they point to the experimentalism and dynamism of video-based visual practice by independent filmmakers who used film as a tool for social engagement and raising awareness from the later 1970s.
61. For comparative films by Anna B. Harris (1896–1979), an African American resident of Manchester, Vermont, who filmed on 8mm among people of colour between 1949 and 1958 and Ruth Storm (1888–1981), a lesbian New York schoolteacher who documented her life and community at a time when most lesbian women were unable to safely live out and open lives, see 'The Woman Behind the Camera: Home Movies and Amateur Film by Women, 1925–1997', available at <http://womanbehindthecamera.org/> (last accessed 21 January 2018).

CHAPTER 3

Resisting Colonial Gendering while Domesticating the Empire

'Who, Raymond? Never. He never touched it. It was my mother and my sister who used the camera and took cine-films', said Nancy Vernede (née Kendall) in 2004 when interviewed about a collection of colonial amateur films made in India in the 1930s and 1940s, and which until then British film archivists catalogued under the title of Vernede Collection and credited it to Raymond Veveysan Vernede, Nancy's husband.[1] From 1928 until India's independence in 1947, Mr Vernede worked in the United Provinces (present-day Uttar Pradesh and Uttarakhand states) as a district officer in the Indian Colonial Service. In her interview, Nancy had fortuitously reattributed the authorship of this 240-minute colonial amateur footage and, perhaps most importantly, exposed it to new critical and theoretical interpretations.[2] Rather than having been the unitary, organic work of a male amateur filmmaker, the film collection now comprised two sets of films. The first five films, made between 1933 and 1935 on black and white 16mm, belonged to Nancy's mother, Isabella Clare Bothwell, who experimented with amateur filmmaking while living in Allahabad at the time when her husband, Sir Charles Henry Bayley Kendall, served as the Judge of the Allahabad High Court (1928–35).[3] The remaining fourteen films, made between 1933 and 1946 on black and white and on colour 8mm film, had been recorded by Nancy's sister, Mrs Barbara Donaldson (née Kendall), while living and travelling across India and England.[4] Nancy's somewhat bemused clarification regarding the authorship of the Kendall Collection pivoted the interpretation of what until then seemed to be an unexceptional set of colonial amateur films made during the final years of the British Raj. The gender-based change in authorship produced an ad hoc 'terror of method' – the need to access and verify all possible research sources and methodologies (Eliade 1988: 29). It also prompted several, urgent research questions. For instance, is it necessary or even possible to amend the critical agenda usually employed when discussing man-made colonial amateur films – the default critical perspective applied to most colonial amateur films – such that it could be equally relevant to the analysis of woman-made colonial amateur films? Also, is it possible to establish that a home movie acquires new or nuanced meanings once the gender of the amateur filmmaker is known? Furthermore, could Elaine Showalter's theory of gynocriticism, which positions women as producers rather than objects of meaning within their gender-specific critical framework of intertwined experiences, help re-code and reclaim the visual literacies, rhetoric and narratorial implications found in amateur films made by, for instance, Lady Kendall, Barbara Donaldson, Rosie Newman, Margaret Tait, Lady Dalyell, Barbara Lloyd, Wilma Gladstone, Sheila Graber or Eileen Healey (Showalter 1986)? Finally, is it possible to argue that scholars as well as private and public audiences of amateur films will always be subjected to an intrinsic gender-driven symbolism, and to a set of meanings that remain immutable irrespective of reattributed authorships? Several possible answers are explored in this chapter as well as across the present volume.[5]

British Women Kodaking the Empire on Film

One of the key visual components of British colonial culture is represented by amateur film practice, which until recently has been largely neglected in terms of its historic relevance in the construction of British imperial identity. The study of British colonial amateur films offers reliable counter-narratives to the conventional, official and commercial visual historiography of the British Empire. Most colonial amateur filmmakers documented in detail their travel and/or lives across the empire, their cultural experiences, jobs, sports, and private and official events. Moreover, recent interest in amateur cinema studies, as well as the online access to many amateur films, reinforces the importance of exploring the documentary merit of this filmmaking practice, distribution and reception patterns. Such scholarship also contributes to the examination of imperial gender politics.

Amateur film practice, generally embraced as a leisure activity, combines the ludic impulse to experiment with a specific recording technology with the filmmaker's need to preserve instances of his or her life beyond the fleeting moment. Moreover, for British amateur filmmakers living and working in colonial settings, home movie making was an important component of their social status, more so than a simple pastime. It was a necessary investment in their self-representation that confirmed their ability to be financially and culturally in touch with modern imperial times, and thus in a position of power. This was a commitment that secured their credibility within a specific social frame. The regular income secured by British colonials was not always sufficient to risk an investment in the hobby of amateur filmmaking, especially when they hoped to send their children to Britain for a 'proper' education (Buettner 2004). Across the empire, British amateur filmmakers usually belonged to the ranks of the Colonial Service, the Public Works Department, the military, or were tea planters, missionaries, aviators and businessmen – all had the means to finance, whether regularly or for special occasions, the cine equipment and the processing of the film reels. It was also customary to make copies of their films which then they sent to family and friends across the empire as cinematographic postcards – as visual snap-diaries. Importantly, missionaries in the early to mid-twentieth century experimented with amateur filmmaking such that films of their medical and educational work across the empire would secure a wider audience for their fundraising campaigns in Britain. For instance, Audrey Lewis filmed for the Methodist Missionary Society in Kenya in the 1950s, while St Joseph's Missionary Society, London Missionary Society, The Salvation Army and the Red Cross, to name just a few, had a long tradition of using visual records, from drawings, Victorian lantern slides shows, photographs and early (amateur) and later professional film productions, to promote and fundraise for their charitable works.

At the same time, women have been targeted as a profitable market for photographic and film equipment from the late nineteenth century onwards, both as consumers of high-technology leisure devices and as subjects of new social and gender networks (Figure 3.1). For instance, at the beginning of the twentieth century, *The Cosmopolitan* promoted the newly established photographic practice by announcing it as an 'appropriate physical activity for women, an incentive to good health and suitable for the feminine traits '(Hirshler 2001: 56), while in 1925 Konishi Roku produced the first Japanese all-pressed metal photographic camera – the Pearlette – and launched it with an advertisement showing a woman operating it as an indication that 'it is easy to use for [by] anyone' (Ross 2015: 44).[6] Also, George Eastman's Kodak-Girl campaign launched at the turn of the twentieth century employed slogans meant to inspire and empower women: 'Hunt with a Kodak', 'Keep Kodak Story of the Baby', 'Keep a Kodak Story of the Children', 'Modern Girls Need a Modern Kodak', 'A Vacation without a Kodak is a Vacation Wasted', 'Kodak and Brownie Cameras Help to Make the Christmas Merry', 'There is Always More Fun with a Brownie' and 'A Kodak upon a Vacation as Essential as Good

Figure 3.1 Still frame from *The Adventures of Ozzie and Harriet. David's 17th Birthday* (Season 2, episode 6, 23 October 1953). Creative Commons.

Congenial Company'. While these and other slogans acted as invitations to achieve social and geographical mobility – 'Kodak, as you go', 'Have your Kodak handy' and 'Anywhere-Everywhere Kodak', other functioned as directives to achieve the desirable status of a modern woman by becoming a new media expert, albeit one conscribed to specific social and domestic frameworks – 'At Home with a Kodak', 'Kodak on the Farm', 'The Brownie Family provides a camera for every boy and girl'. Alongside such campaigns claiming to secure women's empowerment through access to, and use of, the new photographic equipment there was the occasional slip of the pen that confirmed stricter gender hierarchies, and the old dyad of locating female identity at the junction of enchantment and sorcery – the advertisement 'The Witchery of Kodakery' from 1913 offers a case in point (West 2000).

In the early twentieth century, women experimented extensively with photographic and filming equipment, at first with 16mm and then from 1932 with 8mm – the latter being Eastman Kodak's revolutionary film stock and equipment that allowed greater freedom of movement and hence a more reliable recording proximity and detailed approach of events and places. For instance, most British colonial women amateur filmmakers living or travelling across India during the 1920s and until the late 1940s used 16mm and 8mm film (black and white, and colour) equipment. Some of them, like Eleanor Dalyell in the early 1930s, or Rosie Newman between the mid-1930s and early 1950s, also experimented with rare and expensive technologies such as Kodacolor lenticular film and shortly afterwards with Kodachrome. Others, like Wilma Gladstone, Eileen Healey and Audrey Lewis, used colour film to record exceptional events such as Ghana's independence celebrations in 1957, the international all-women expedition on Cho Oyu in the autumn of 1959, and Methodist missionary work in Kenya at the time of the Mau Mau Emergency. As discussed in Chapter 2, the use of cine cameras by women belonging to various social and cultural networks, both in Britain and across the empire, reflected the rapid technological and cultural shifts in Kodaking their biographies within specific times and changing worlds (Pasternak 2015). Their exercise in visual autobiography – the home movie-making mode and amateur photography – their intergenerational memory transfer, and their gendered visual histories of the Self require a scrupulous critical framework consisting of, at least, three investigative pathways. First, the films themselves as image-texts open to cross-disciplinary analyses. Second, a comparative discussion that takes into consideration, when available, the films' written counterparts such as the amateur filmmaker's diaries, journals, and private or official correspondence. For instance, Eileen Healey's films and expedition diary about the tragic ascent of the Cho Oyu summit in 1959, and Rosie Newman's books complementing her colour films such as *Britain at War*, *The France I Knew* or *Glimpses of India* are exceptionally rich examples of such comparative frameworks. Third, new media feminist artists' digital and ideological repurposing of colonial amateur films by British women as an attempt to raise provocative questions about post/neocolonial interpretations of British women's imperial and private visual literacies. This identity and gender dialogue between colonial/postcolonial amateur films made by British women and some of the twenty-first-century British women documentary filmmakers offers pertinent examples of past and present *lieux de mémoire* of gendered visual rhetoric – places where 'memory crystallizes and secretes itself' across several historic times and narratorial voices (Nora 1989: 7). Also relevant to this discussion are theories borrowed from social anthropology, if exploring issues of gendered subjectivity and the enunciation of experience (Moore 1994), or from cognitive psychology, when discussing the development of autobiographical memory (Howe 2015), and the creation of a storied self (McAdams 2012: 236) – all relevant, pertinent perspectives in establishing a critical framework when analysing how, and for what type of audiences, (British) women amateur filmmakers recorded their lives and social networks.

The study of women's amateur filmmaking practice aims to recover the historical discourses enabling new interpretations of gender and racial hierarchies within the framework of the filmmakers' cinematic vocabulary, and of their dependence on imperial visual culture and ideology, while paying particular attention to British interwar popular representational conventions. This is an attempt to define a possible gendered-based visual literacy across British colonial amateur filmmaking, one possibly based on, but not exclusive to, thematic choices made by women amateur filmmakers. Their implicit exercise in visual life-story-telling allows for a detailed analysis of several examples of how British colonial women constructed private and personalised life stories that needed to function as credible and acceptable narratives within their dual societies: colonial and home–Britain familial networks (McAdams 1985; Josselson and Lieblich 1993: Hermans and Kempen 1993). Their films illustrate the migration of imperial female identities across diverse colonial contexts – a gender dynamic that is not necessarily evident in British interwar governmental and commercial productions such as documentaries, newsreels and feature films. Such a theoretical framework considers women filmmakers' simultaneous roles as vectors of colonising credos and as commodified subalterns of imperial paternalism, and it explores issues of gender and racial hierarchies shaped by specific imperial rule and confirmed, or challenged, by the British women's cinematic vocabulary. Social conventions such as marital commitments, education, labour networks, motherhood, holidaying and political engagements form the framework on which the migration of female imperial identities can be located and interpreted within colonial domesticity and ghettoised imperial networks and gendered visual ethnographies. Moreover, a flexible comparative methodology allows the identification of a possible gender-based nationally and racially distinctive visual language created and developed by colonial women amateur filmmakers. Their amateur films, even when intended as meticulous (pseudo-ethnographic) records of colonised people, cover a wide range of imperial visual tributes, from rare records of weddings and religious rituals, travelogues and amateur anthropological fieldwork, to colonial governmental networks. Most films made by women amateur filmmakers would routinely represent the empire from a marginal perspective that was mostly defined by domestic or leisure activities – a standpoint defined by the women's social contexts. However, in spite of being considered an innocuous pastime activity, amateur filmmaking enabled women to bypass their immediate social network in an act of gradual gender self-liberation and a step toward modern times.

Apart from being a pastime, amateur filmmaking allowed colonial women to document their lives, activities and social networks in greater detail than letters or diaries would have permitted, and in more nuanced ways that often revealed lesser-known aspects of imperial contexts. A similar critical perspective is also applicable to colonial amateur films made by men, except that, due to their work engagements and social networks, they often had access to specific contexts and events like clubs, military operations, infrastructure networks, and railways, bridges and dam building sites. Such a cultural context seems to validate Linda Nochlin's claim that creating art or, for that matter, first-person visual narratives as in the case of amateur filmmaking, it is never an act of independent, subjectively driven expression and individualised translation of personal experience. Instead, it is a personalised language that constantly adapts and is updated according to established or temporary conventions and cultural traditions (Nochlin 1999). Consequently, analysing a text, whether visual, written or new media from the perspective of gender theories, would risk ghettoising its intrinsic meaning. Moreover, a semiotic reading of colonial amateur films would propose that the relationship between the amateur filmmakers' gender and their visual literacy and narrative symbolism, as well as issues of authorship, become superfluous since each scene (film) is the result of a continuous, diachronic process of acculturation. Such a reading would then cancel by default any methodology aspiring or claiming to deal efficiently with instances of gender-specific visual narratives, and with visual constructions of collective memory and cine-autobiographical practices. It would also revoke theoretical attempts to identify examples of gendered visuality that confirmed or challenged popular cultural canons and discourses of politics of difference among minority and marginalised social groups such as, for instance, colonial enclaves of cultural and gender affiliations. Therefore, rather than re-applying canonical theoretical frameworks to define possible (specific) visual narratives common to colonial amateur films made by the British women discussed in this volume, it would seem more efficient and relevant to consider their films from the perspective of particularly fashionable cine narrative trends, developments in film technology, and memory and perception studies. This way, the risk of a reductionist or of an overcomplicating analysis can be counteracted with factual details such as amateur filmmaking campaigns and training manuals marketed specifically to middle and upper class women hobbyists; aesthetic and thematic developments recommended to, and shared by women amateur filmmakers (see Chapters 2 and 4); empire cinema tropes commonly found in colonial home movies made by women; and a panoptical range of topics that could, ultimately, indicate a possible visual gynocriticism tradition of gender-specific colonial amateur filmmaking practice.

The core research for this chapter relies on several short sequences that invite renewed explorations of the aesthetic and ideological frameworks within which colonial female identities have been constructed, represented and misconstrued. It charts representations of women's identities across several 16mm amateur films scenes made by British women filmmakers in the 1930s in India, Africa and the Middle East.[7] It also explores issues of autobiographical memory across two thematic strands – colonial domesticity and gendered visual ethnographies – and considers these women filmmakers' involuntary portrayal of their colonial self(-image) at work when illustrating their imperial roles within specific contexts, from leisure activities to official engagements (Howe 2015: 217). Selected for the first thematic strand have been films made by Lady Kendall and Lady Dalyell in India in the 1930s. The second set of case studies explores issues of amateur and professional ethnography and the crucial role played by the filmmaker's gender in securing access to unique representations of colonised people. Once again, Lady Dalyell's collection of amateur films offers an important example of colonial visual literacy, this time with scenes filmed in Bahrain in the early 1930s. Importantly, her amateur films are discussed in comparison with (allegedly) professional ethnographic films made by Ursula Graham Bower in Nagaland, Beatrice Blackwell in Papua New Guinea during her first field trip in 1936–7, and by Wilma Gladstone at the time of Ghana's independence celebrations in 1957.

'Selfing' Gender and Colonial Hierarchies

Elizabeth A. Bloomfield has successfully argued that the gender of the viewer has a crucial impact on how an image is interpreted, and that learnt gender roles assist the viewer in 'bargaining' cultural assumptions and identity typologies (Dake 1995; Bloomfield 2015). Her thesis fits well with the wider theoretical framework claiming that peoples' reading of an image is the result of the visual priming to which they have been subjected within specific social contexts. This, in turn, perpetuates circumstantial interpretations of feminine and masculine selves and roles that are then judged as either corresponding or failing to match established canonical representations of gender within that specific context (Coles et al. 2011). Moreover, personal beliefs and values seem to drive most interpretations of visual records, whether fixed as in artworks or mobile as in peoples' body language during social interactions – that is, the framework that hosts constructions of gendered identities and narratives, all clustered in a dichotomised hierarchy of domestic versus public domains. Social settings, including colonial societies, have context-specific and well-established visual equivalents of this hierarchy with the female and the domestic counterpointing the male and the public dyads. For instance, Bloomfield (2015) has successfully assessed during an image-reading group analysis that Henri de Toulouse-Lautrec's painting *Salon de la rue des Moulins* (1894–5) was incorrectly identified by 66 per cent of the participants as having been made by a female artist simply because the core symbolism of the artwork evolves around an all-women theme. The remaining 34 per cent of the participants assumed the artist to have been a male, an assumption based on the representation of the women's scanty dresses and provocative postures –Toulouse-Lautrec had indeed found inspiration for this painting in scenes which he witnessed at several Parisian brothels (Bloomfield 2015). Similar assumptions about gender-theme biased visual narratives are equally bound to occur when viewing colonial amateur films as when viewers might expect that, for instance, films showing predominantly women in various domestic contexts and female-specific social activities would have been made by women amateur filmmakers, while films showing public, military, governmental, or science and technology related topics would have been recorded by male amateur filmmakers. As proven by Bloomfield's research, such assumptions are mostly driven by cultural and visual priming and therefore pose the risk of oversimplification – Lady Kendall's Vernede Collection of colonial amateur films being a case in point. Nevertheless, it is important to consider the ways in which gender-specific narratives, once the authorship has been confirmed, can permeate between established modes of media production and forms of expression such as when comparing letters, diaries, home movies, interviews and photographs taken by women in specific social and cultural contexts. While the ghettoised colonial domesticity illustrated across these various all-women media presents various degrees of factual credibility, it also proposes simultaneous cross-analyses of the authors' visual mapping of their explicit or mental imagery (i.e. in non-visual records) of autobiographical and collective memories across historical times and generational identities. Colonial women who made amateur films often operated, by means of their visual records' intrinsic meaning, as social vectors of British expatriate ethos, as commodified subalterns of imperial (persistent Victorian) paternalism, and as independent agents of gender emancipation and social commitment. These simultaneous gendered social roles were made possible by the new narratives of self-empowerment promoted through the act of visual self-story-telling (selfing) enabled by their amateur filmmaking practice. McAdams' hypothesis that the act of selfing is one of the key personality and identity developmental processes could support a more nuanced study of the British colonial women's visual literacy and narrative patterns found in their amateur films. The act of selfing could help to decode their implicit intent to, or fortuitous exercise in 'narrating experience to create a self' (Cohler and Cole 1996; McAdams (2012: 237) – their colonial self being in a concurrent relation with their mother-country Britain and their colonial settings, each requiring the women to abide by specific identity canons. It is also possible to argue, in McAdams' terms, that these colonial women's newly acquired modern identity by means of visual technological (and not leisure) knowledge and skills allowed them to differentiate themselves from the other women's (and colonial peers') constructions of imperial self-narratives, and so to integrate their understandings of their life stories within new and often experimental first-person visual narratives of their emerging, modern self.

The Kendall/Vernede Collection proposes an example of British women's Otherness in the context of the British Raj visual culture. The short sequence discussed here was filmed by Lady Kendall while waiting in an open-air railway lounge near the train platform – it shows her two daughters, Barbara and Nancy, and her first son-in-law, John Coote Donaldson. After a few brief general views of the group, Lady Kendall guides her daughters with indications from behind the camera about how to pose. It is the young women's behaviour and interaction with the filmmaker that confirm Lady Kendall's behind-the-camera instructions. For instance, Barbara and Nancy must take off their sola topees, stop reading the newspaper and start a lively conversation. While Barbara, the older (married) daughter, obeys her mother's indications, Nancy appears reluctant to follow her mother's suggestions to look straight at the camera, to uncover her head and so to acknowledge that she is being filmed. Nancy's refusal to perform for the camera defines indirectly Lady Kendall's amateur filmmaking as a publicly performed act of invading her daughters' privacy. Her apparently childishly rebellious behaviour and stubborn rebuffing of her mother's requests to perform simple mundane gestures could also be indicative of ongoing domestic and gendered tensions rather than of a poorly managed social awkwardness. In her interview in 2004, Nancy mentioned that her mother used to show her films to family and friends as well as to members of the Indian Colonial Service at the Club in Allahabad. Therefore, one possible interpretation could be that the sequence showing Nancy's discomfort while being filmed, and her abrasive rejection of her mother's filming, could be symptomatic of deeper reasons, well beyond her apparent capricious obstinacy. It seems reasonable then to argue that Nancy's brash response to Lady Kendall's attempt to produce her cine portrait could be seen, at least on this occasion, as an inherent response to what must have been the underlying social pressure experienced by most young unmarried British women who, like her, were still highly eligible within the compulsory social customs of the British Raj. In this under-a-minute sequence, Nancy's visual statement, negotiated through the act of filming, establishes her identity as one of gendered self-seclusion driven by a tacit revolt against specific imperial social protocols, which were ultimately symbolised by her mother's effort to visually market her youngest daughter by means of modern recording technologies and a newly acquired visual literacy. Across these images, Nancy appears to have experienced a case of dual temporarily confined womanhood: *in situ*, while waiting for a train, and visually, while being filmed by her mother. As a British colonial woman in India, Nancy secured her position at the top of the imperial and racial hierarchy. At the same time, her visual identity, as constructed by her mother's amateur filmmaking practice, was that of a gendered subaltern, of the Other within her own family and the British Raj networks (Figure 3.2). This process of othering doesn't necessarily refer to a reversed colonial–colonised hierarchy, or to a predictable gender marginalisation. It reveals a subtler alienation in which Nancy's control over her identity-image has been visually subordinated

Figure 3.2 Still frame from Kendall Collection (1931–5). Film 4. © CSAS, University of Cambridge.

to conventional social protocols and gender roles – an enduring portraiture tradition spanning from early photographic practice to new media selfing posing protocols.

This brief sequence showing a memsahib displaying signs of discomfort and rebellion when being filmed (even if by a member of her family) is one of the very few examples identified across the colonial home movie collections held by film archives in the UK. Most of the British colonial amateur film collections, with their repetitive themes and representational codes, confirm the filmmakers' predisposition to portray colonial women's life as being safe, comfortable, entertaining, and immutable in its social and racial status, and within power dynamics defined by various imperial outposts. Their life was, however, not always necessarily remarkable, easy-going, or subscribing to the 'heaven-born' – read, British Indian Colonial Service (ICS) – affluence and authority as seen in few short amateur film scenes similar to Lady Kendall's cine portrait of Nancy, or in recent TV documentaries and feature films about British colonial life such as *Echoes of the Raj* (dir. Catherine Clay, BBC, 2000) or *Indian Summers* (UK, Channel 4, 2015). In light of this, it could be argued that the study of amateur footage made by British women amateur filmmakers and showing aspects of their lives and specific imperial settings – all with their layered and interlocking imperial roles and responsibilities – often reveals surprising accounts of gendered identities, which can acquire symbolic meanings as in the case of their colonial and gendered Otherness.

Colonial home movies showing images of men playing with dogs or with their swords are rarely pertinent sources for theoretical explorations. However, two short sequences filmed by Lady Eleanor Dalyell at the Mysore Residence, India, in the early 1930s could prove useful in showing how some memsahibs have invested, though possibly involuntarily, members of the ICS with belittling identity traits – a different process of gender Othering in which colonial manhood has been visually domesticated.[8] In the first sequence, the wife of an ICS officer carefully adjusts his Wolseley helmet on his head while he straightens his back and holds his hands steady. Their gestures recall that of a mother getting her son ready for school. Under the gaze of his wife and of two other women, the officer then struggles with the hilt of his sword, especially when trying to take it out from the scabbard as if to charge forward for a mock attack on the film camera. This is nothing short of boyish playfulness. On this occasion, it is the woman amateur filmmaker's choice of topic, the wife's gestures that provoke the man's behaviour, his posture and his attempt at being funny while dressed in his ICS uniform. Although this sequence could be read either as an innocuous comical performance among friends, or as a valid source for a psychoanalytical analysis of direct and by proxy gender representation, it can nevertheless be argued that the ICS officer has been briefly the subject of a self-parodic performance, one that helped him regress to the status of a young boy playing with his dummy sword.

The second sequence filmed by Lady Dalyell was recorded during one of her husband's military inspections of the North-West Frontier, India, in 1929. Crammed between scenes of 'inspection by military officers being shown a bridge' and 'Indian troops and . . . machine gun crew',[9] this sequence also reveals nuanced visual narratives of gender as performative identity. Filmed in a large garden, it shows a British army officer holding a giant pair of scissors and pretending to cut off the tails and muzzles of two Great Dane dogs.[10] At the beginning of the sequence, he calls the dogs but since neither obeys him, he then joins them in a corner of the garden. Throughout the scenes, he struggles to add a touch of playfulness to the game while the dogs persist in ignoring him. He is ill at ease and barely manages to get the dogs interested in a possible chasse (Figure 3.3). His behaviour indicates that he might have been intimidated by the filming session. In this scene, the gag-like entertainment functions as the backdrop

Figure 3.3 Still frame from Dalyell Collection (1929). Accession number 1998/005/032. © Bristol Archives.

for Lady Dalyell's portrayal of the man's identity. If, in the beginning, he is joyfully waiting for her instruction to start the game, at the end, he puts the scissors back into their casing (with a dexterous gesture) and returns an embarrassed gaze to the camera as if to apologise for having failed to provide the necessary clownish skills required for a good cine prank.

It is possible to suggest on this occasion that Lady Dalyell's directorial suggestions translated her unwitting exercise in domesticating the conformist British ICS peerless manhood, an imperial league that defined her husband's identity too. It is also possible to interpret the scene with some added symbolism in the context of the British imperial rule in India. For instance, the man acting as a naughty boy who insistently attempts to chop off the tails and muzzles of two large dogs could be seen as indicative of the primordial desire to subordinate those weaker than him – read, colonised people in imperial popular narratives. Moreover, on a different level of contextualised playfulness, the game involves two dogs rather than two children. As in most British colonial home movies, in the absence of the family's children – usually sent back to Britain for schooling – pet dogs were filmed with the dedicated interest commonly shared by those amateur filmmakers documenting their children's first steps, games, sports achievements, school ceremonies, birthday parties and inoffensive mischiefs. At the time of filming this scene, Eleanor Dalyell had been married to Lieutenant-Colonel Gordon Loch for over a year,[11] – their only child, Thomas Dalyell, was born in 1932,[12] hence playing with the Great Danes could be seen as a family scene by proxy.

These three short amateur film sequences recorded by Lady Kendall and Lady Dalyell have fortuitously preserved nuanced narratives about imperial race and gender politics. As if 'morphing history into histories' (Ishizuka and Zimmermann 2008), they occasionally and fortuitously applied the process of visual selfing when attempting to illustrate their responsibilities or their peers' roles in colonial India. Intriguingly, most colonial women amateur filmmakers have succeeded in making complementary if not contradicting accounts of their imperial times and identities. While trying to emulate the popular visual culture promoted by empire cinema productions' stereotypical portraits of colonial women as agents of imperial ideology, and as graceful bearers of their civilising mission and imperial motherhood burdens (Ishizuka and Zimmermann 2008), they also challenged gendered hierarchies through acts of accidental humorous deprecation and informal representations of colonial woman-/manhood. Their amateur filmmaking practice often allowed them to replace the male gaze and so to reverse their female passive role into an active agency of comment and witnessing. Thus, they became 'bearers of the look' able to target the spectacle of manhood and the imperial gender and racial schisms (Mulvey 1975).

Gendered Visual Ethnographies

'The possibility that a stranger might penetrate a back region is one major source of social concern in everyday life' (MacCannell 1973: 591), and remains a cornerstone research topic for most social and visual anthropologists keen to explore issues of belonging, social intimacy and cultural authenticity. The stranger can equally be the professional or the amateur onlooker, the traveller or the tourist, the explorer or the bored holiday-maker. The strangers act in any cultural and social context as agents of intrusion by allowing their (outsider's) set of beliefs to create new narratives about unfamiliar contexts. Ultimately, the strangers are creators, as well as the audience, of what is defined as the back regions of cultural performances – a theoretical framework inspired by Erving Goffman's apt distinction of an individual's 'front' and 'back' performances of the self within and outside specific social encounters (Goffman 1956). This journey of exploration and interpretation is most often one of self-discovery too, particularly evident when comparing private collections of visual and written accounts belonging to women amateur filmmakers and visual ethnographers. This self-discovery and cultural-immersion journey is perhaps best exemplified by Ursula Graham Bower (1914–88) in her book *Naga Path* (1950) and her ethnographic films of the Nagaland and Naga people made in 1939 and 1940 when her filmmaking skills matched the amateur movie-making protocols for simple framing and editing in the camera.[13] Ursula's written account, detailed and often satirical, presents the three stages of this self- and cultural transformation. First, the original cultural setting – British colonial diaspora in Northeast India in the late 1930s, where 'life turned over pleasantly, with leisure. . . . We womenfolk idled comfortably. We shopped at the Canteen, we dined; we visited the Arts and Crafts showroom; and twice a week we went to watch the polo' (Graham Bower 1950: 5). Second, the cultural shock during her first encounter with Naga people, a shock often experienced as simultaneous bewilderment and aversion: 'Here were hillmen, tousled and nude, here were dogs, here were children, here were beggars – one jostling tide of colour on white and white on colour, streaming into the market-place in a cloud of golden dust' (Graham Bower 1950: 6). And third, the unpredictable emotional synergy with the Naga communities and her subsequent enthusiasm for documenting their cultures, albeit within an interpretative framework still marked by imperial ideology. Ursula noted the crucial moment in this about-face of colonial experience with persuasive minimalism: 'Not yet of the hills, but already divorced a fraction from my own race, I wanted nothing now but the lovely, wild reality of mountains and jungle. I had to go back' (Graham Bower 1950: 8).

One of Ursula's lengthy scenes of Naga people, whom she filmed in the late 1930s, shows a young man, left elbow resting on his left knee, pointing a rifle at a target somewhere in the distance. Attached to the riffle seems to be a label, the type used for museum objects (Figure 3.4). Filmed in colour, the scene allows the viewer to appreciate the young man's skill for properly holding (and implicitly firing) the weapon – the meeting point between a key symbol of Ursula's 'own' race's war technology and that of the Naga people's cultural adjustments to colonial influences. In this scene, the Naga man and the rifle are rhetorically presented as collectable items, both freeze-framed in a gesture charged with potential (lethal) action, and each representative of distinct albeit congruent emblems of specific civilisations. This type of visual narrative showing instances of cross-cultural identities, whether functional within specific communities, or performed for the camera, are a common and indispensable research

Figure 3.4 Still frame from *Ursula Graham Bower colour films in the Naga Hills* (1940–4). © Alan Macfarlane, 2014, University of Cambridge.

source for imperial, media and anthropological studies.[14] Post-imperial studies also relate to such images although often the focus is on twenty-first-century travelogues and I-documentaries. A pertinent example can be found, for instance, in 'Wancho Naga Tattoos of India',[15] an episode from the online ethno-adventure documentary series *Tattoo Hunter* made by Skinmodes (2013). The episode as well as the series subscribe to the rhetoric of self-discovery tourism cum anthropological exercise in which selected visualities of Otherness become a permanent mark on the film-maker's own visual representation: 'I'm on a mission to get unique tattoos from around the world cut into my skin', he claims in the introduction to the episode filmed in Arunachal Pradesh, India.

Man-wearing-a-loincloth-and-carrying-a-riffle trope is once again present (Figure 3.5) but within a richer contrasting iconography. This time, hunting trophies are displayed behind the man holding the weapon. Rather than showing a Naga man holding a new (Western) weapon, as in Ursula's film from 1939–40, the Naga man in the 2013 ethno-documentary is presented as having already used the weapon – a hypothesis confirmed by the panoply of skulls (wildlife) behind him.[16] Importantly, in contrast to

Figure 3.5 Still frame from *Wancho Naga Tattoos of India* (2013). © Skinsmods, 23 April 2013, Standard YouTube Licence.

the Naga man filmed in profile by Ursula, the Wancho Naga man is looking straight at the camera with a fixed gaze, head tilted backwards. His posing for the camera is an assumed return of the gaze. Whether filmed in 1939 or in 2013, such 'ethno-looks', to borrow Jean Rouch's term (1978), and the resulting ethno-documentaries with the relationship between the filmmaker and the indigenous population, made either as colonial travelogues or as neo-colonial docu-tourism, propose visual narratives that subscribe to the core agenda of ethno-cinema. In their implicit staging of authenticity through their choice of topics, framing and editing – the by default mode of performance of rituals or mundane activities in front of a photographic or film camera – the images recorded by Ursula Graeme Bower and Skinmodes share the same constructed rather than unmediated narrative, irrespective of their original aim to secure an 'ethno-dialogue' (Rouch 1978:8). Consequently, and unrelated to the filmmakers' gender, their tourist gaze remains unchallenged in its predetermined verdict on how best to represent Otherness. In this context, Julia Emberley's definition of ethno-documentary, albeit in relation to representations of Inuit identity, positions both the recording of 'front' and 'back' cultural performances as part of 'a range of colonial [and neo-imperial] bourgeoisie strategies of surveillance deployed to manage, govern and regulate the [Other's] body' (Emberley 2007: 79). However, a possibly different visual and ideological dynamic is found in ethno-travelogues filmed by women amateur filmmakers. There seem to be two preliminary reasons supporting this hypothesis. First, a limiting context: like most amateur filmmakers they would have not always been in the position, whether financial or social, to ask indigenous people to perform for the camera. Second, a circumstantially enabling setting: their gender allowed them access to demographic networks and cultural events which were inaccessible to men, whether colonisers or colonised.

Wilma Gladstone's (1914–2000) films made in the Gold Coast (Ghana) offer a rich example for the first type of ethno-amateur films. An educationalist from Edinburgh who joined the Gold Coast Education Department in 1945 as part of the Government Teacher Training College in Tamale, Wilma played a crucial executive role in later years when she set up a Curriculum Development Centre in Saltpond. In 1962, she left the Ghana Education Services and returned to Edinburgh where she joined the Moray House College of Education. For her services and dedication to the advancement of educational programmes, both in Ghana and Britain, Wilma Gladstone was awarded an MBE. A stalwart, principled Scottish woman, Wilma was always praised for her indefatigable work to improve access to education, always 'patiently and with much human understanding' (Forrester-Paton 2001). The 'human understanding' dimension of her social interactions is also evident in some of the scenes she filmed: people almost never posed in front of her camera. Their presence symbolised a specific craftsmanship, event or political belief as in the case of fishermen communities, Krobo chiefs and Oklemekuku Azzu Mate Kole Mate Kole II – the Kornor of the Manya-Krobo Traditional Area – attending the annual Ngmayem harvest festival, Asante boys pointing their flags at the camera, Asafo company men wearing triangular headdresses featuring the Union Jack, or several women and young girls celebrating their country's independence from Britain in March 1957 by wearing white dresses with imprints of Kwame Nkruman's portrait – Ghana's first prime minister at the time of independence and also its first president, in office from 1960 until 1966.

Most often people entered a visual dialogue with Wilma's film camera as in the case of a woman wearing a white cap inscribed with the C.P.P. initials (read, Convention People's Party) (Figure 3.6), cigarette in her month and looking straight at the filmmaker. Perhaps the most important

Figure 3.6 Still frame from Gladstone Collection (1957). Accession number 2001/083/001. © Bristol Archives.

feature of her amateur colour films of the independence celebrations was her proximity to the participants and their almost unanimous at-ease acknowledgement of her filming – Wilma was one *with* the celebrating crowd, assimilated, simultaneously at the centre and at the margins of the racial and imperial network, and yet controlling the visual identity of the events through her hobbyist practice. Wilma acted as a professional visual anthropologist per se, immersed in her subject of study while retaining the authority to document it – both 'front' and 'back' performances – according to her specific ideologically and culturally driven interests. Although always subject to cultural partisanship, her amateur films of the Ghanaian independence celebrations are the type of visual anthropological practice most valued for its least interventionist impact.

Eleanor Dalyell also had access to extraordinary and, in one particular case, unique visual records through her amateur filmmaking practice. While accompanying her husband, Lieutenant-Colonel Gordon Loch – the British Political Agent at Bahrain between 1932 and 1937 – Eleanor met with political personalities and witnessed events that were inaccessible to most Europeans. She filmed, from a close distance and without being censored or rejected by her subjects, scenes of vital relevance to historical and anthropological studies. For instance, her collection of amateur films includes scenes of emancipated African slaves dancing outside the British Agency during the Eid al-Fitr festivities in Manama, Bahrain, on 20 January 1934 and similar dances to mark Britain's recognition of Shaikh Hamad bin Isa Al Khalifa as the ruler of Bahrain on 9 February 1933;[17] the presentation by Colonel T. C. Fowle, Political Resident in the Persian Gulf, of a *kharita* – letter of congratulations – from the Viceroy of India to the Shaikh;[18] races of Hakim of Bahrain's horses at Sakhir;[19] Muharram procession on 25 April 1934; the visit of Lord Willingdon, Viceroy of India, to Bahrain on 17 May 1934;[20] Eid al-Fitr festivities in Manama, Bahrain, on 20 January 1934; the meeting between Lieutenant-Colonel Loch and Shaikh Saeed bin Maktoum al-Maktoum (Emir of Dubai, 1912–58) during the former's trip to the Trucial Coast between 17 January and 4 February 1937;[21] and scenes of 'truffle-hunting' of *Tirmania nivea*, and of 'Arab dinner' in the desert attended by Lieutenant-Colonel Loch, Shaikh Hamad bin Isa Al Khalifa, and other men of the Al Khalifa ruling family in 1937.

Eleanor's amateur films made in Bahrain before the Second World War document these special occasions from the perspective of a spectator (the 'stranger') witnessing colonial hierarchies in the Middle East while being granted specific access and recording privileges contingent to her political, racial and gender roles. This proximity to a critical time in the history

Figure 3.7 Still frame from Dalyell Collection (1934). Accession number 1998/005/001. © Bristol Archives.

of the Middle East is confirmed by her medium and close-up shots of, for instance, Lord and Lady Willingdon's welcome reception in Bahrain on 17 May 1934, and of Shaikh Hamad bin Isa Al Khalifa's presenting official gifts – a sword for the Viceroy, and a large black and white photograph of himself for the Vicereine[22] – Arab men dancing the *al ardha* (traditional sword dance), Arab women wearing full face veils (*niqabs*) or metal masks during festivities (Figure 3.7), the Shaikh's children and Sir Charles Dalrymple Belgrave's cine portrait.[23]

Importantly, Lieutenant-Colonel Loch's intelligence reports offer valuable background information about the contexts in which Eleanor filmed during their time in the Middle East. For instance, he noted on the occasion of their trip to the Trucial Coast that she succeeded in 'establishing very friendly relations with the families of the Shaikhs of Dubai, Sharjah and Ras al Khaimah' – interestingly, Eleanor's films made during that trip show mostly dhows, crowds, and ship buildings on the waterfront.[24] Also, Loch's report about the Muharram processions that took place on 25 April 1934, which they watched from the balcony of a house in Manama, highlights a shift in cultural trends to which his wife subscribed – the visual recording of almost all and every event:

> The procession in on a considerable scale and head-cutting and flagellation with chains is practiced [*sic*]. It is, however, especially noticeable to one who has known the troubles of the past, how great is the tolerations now exercised in Bahrain. The Ruler, though a Sunni and a religious man, lends horses and camels for the occasion, and some of the Shi'ahs have even been known to go so far as to *ask* for photographs to be taken. (Emphasis added.)[25]

Eleanor also filmed in great detail the wedding celebrations for Shaikh Duaij bin Hamad al Khalifa which took place in 1934. Lieutenant-Colonel Loch noted in his report that 'Shaikh Du'aij, a young and favourite son of His Excellency . . . was married at Hidd on 13th April to a daughter of Shaikh Abdullah bin Isa Al Khalifa' and commented on 'dances and display of horsemanship . . . held in Manamah and Hidd'.[26] However, he was unable to mention or describe the special festivities to which only his wife had access – the celebrations that took place in the Arab women's quarters. While no men were permitted to attend these celebrations, Eleanor had been granted the right to film at length the large group of veiled and bejewelled women, all seated, clapping their hands and moving their heads to rhythmic drum beats. Among them are several women drummers whom Eleanor filmed in medium close-up scenes in which both the filmmaker and the viewer become an integral part of this intimate space defined by the Arab women's dances, gazes back at the camera and wave-like movements of their heads in tune with the drummers' songs. Eleanor also filmed the bride while performing the *Khaliji* (*Khaleegy*) dance – a traditional dance involving delicate hand gestures, choreographed moves of her elaborately adorned *thawb*, and head moves that gradually unveiled her superb long hair (Figure 3.8). The space for these wedding ceremonies appears small, crowded, narrow and teeming with women whom Eleanor filmed most often from a high angle unless she was seated in the proximity of the bride.

It is highly possible that Eleanor's footage could be Bahrain's first visual (ethnographic) record on film of women's wedding celebrations in the early twentieth century, and also one of the early amateur, non-fiction films of a harem – the 'back space' of taboo gazes, of exploited gender roles, of Orientalist popular fiction and of politicised deviant behaviour. Implicitly, access to and becoming part of a culture's 'back region' is a dual process shaping the stranger's/intruder's sense of self: when performed, it is reversible; when assumed, it is often irreversible. While the latter instance of this self-shaping process addresses the emotional ambivalence of 'native-goers' and their respective convoluted acculturations, assimilations, and participant's observations with their implicit reactivity and biases, the former instance is often based on particular social paradigms. One of the

Figure 3.8 Still frame from Dalyell Collection (1934). Accession number 1998/005/009. © Bristol Archives.

recurrent examples of access to the 'back region' of a culture is that of cultural cross-dressing (Fowkes Tobin 1999), whether as a tourist, political activist or anthropologist – see, for instance, T. E. Lawrence's fondness for wearing Arab dress during his participation in the Sinai and Palestine Campaign and the Arab Revolt (1915–18). His cultural cross-dressing, always in Arab pristine white attire, has been thoroughly documented in the press, war reports and across several photographs including the one showing him in a rare instance of (cultural and gender) cross-dressing: wearing a *chador* and a richly embroidered full-face veil – his male shoes visible nevertheless (Lowell 1925: opposite p. 189)[27] – Lawrence claimed that this was an exercise in abandoning his 'English self, and let [himself] look at the West and its conventions with new eyes' (Lawrence, 2014: 6). This affiliation to 'constellations of others' is also echoed, at a conceptual level, by Ursula Graham Bower in her book *Naga Path* (Rock 2013: 102). In turn, by filming the short sequence of Arab women's wedding celebrations, Eleanor accessed directly the 'back space' of the Western-romanticised all-female secluded culture – the harem as the space bridging *ars erotica* with *scientia sexualis* (Foucault 1988). A gendered space that until her filming of this sequence, and long afterwards, had been almost exclusively represented by male artists in zealously detailed paintings, lithographs and drawings, all 'pitched erotically' to a predominantly male audience's 'imagined reality' of the harem (Del Plato 2002: 22). Owing to her style of amateur filmmaking – scenes recorded at shoulder and eye level, and mostly in medium shots – Eleanor witnessed as well as *became* a member of Arab women's group.[28] It was primarily her gender rather than her political affiliation, though this must have legitimated her request to film the event, that enabled Eleanor to attend and be part of these women's celebrations. In this context, Eleanor belongs to the network of British women amateur filmmakers that includes, for instance, Rosie Newman, Wilma Gladstone and Eileen Healey – women who through their amateur (and often fortuitous) ethnographic fieldwork and filmmaking fostered novel gendered visual literacies at a time when the alleged discovery of new cultures and peoples was almost exclusively a male prerogative, and the relevance of visual records such as photographs and films to anthropological studies was still to be acknowledged as a reliable research source (Mead 1953, 1970).

The gender of the filmmaker often determined his or her access to the 'front' or 'back regions' of a community – the 'front' being usually shared irrespective of gender, while the 'back' requires gender-exclusive permissions. Like Wilma, Rosie or Eileen, Eleanor was a colonial tourist with an interest in amateur filmmaking – a visual documentarist who recorded instances of invaluable cultural contexts that were rarely accessible to her contemporaries interested in accessing similar spaces of gender and racial otherness. Often, Eleanor's and the other women amateur filmmakers' visual records of similarly rich cultural contexts seem to have been spared the usual staged authenticity and mystification of local (colonial) traditions such as, for instance, indigenous people performing rituals for the camera, or acting mundane tasks based on their own expectations of what was assumed to be the filmmaker's (stranger's) expectations of their localised cultural self-representation.[29] Moreover, the gender of the amateur filmmaker often allowed for unpredictable freedom of access to 'back regions' of various cultural and social networks, and women like Eleanor Dalyell, Jenny Brown or Elizabeth Hawkins-Whitshed,[30] motivated by an astute anthropological awareness – one not necessarily prompted by their professional interests in the case of, for instance, Margaret Mead, Ursula Graham Bower, or Diana and Antoinette Powell-Cotton – succeeded in contributing through their amateur filmmaking practice to key research avenues in social and visual anthropology. However, the gender of the filmmaker could also function to the detriment of the (amateur) visual ethnographer, in which case the resulting visual narrative would be either repudiated or restaged. For instance, in the early 1930s, during her second fieldwork trip to Melanesia on behalf of Pitt Rivers Museum where she worked as University Demonstrator in Ethnology, Beatrice Blackwood filmed numerous scenes showing mundane chores and rituals performed for the camera by indigenous communities, such as making fire, carrying large logs and cooking. She occasionally framed and later edited some of these scenes to build suspense and create an element of surprise.[31] For instance, a large seemingly walking stack of hay is revealed to be just a customary load carried by a young women alongside their regular 'load', their young children. However, and in spite of her sense of assimilation within the local communities which she visited for prolonged periods, Blackwood appears to have been denied access to an important rite of passage practiced by men in Papua New Guinea – the bull-roarer initiation ceremony.[32] Her films of this ritual show only the first stage of the ceremony – the swinging of the bull-roar.[33] The subsequent elements of the ritual, for which she did not secure recording (and possibly viewing) privileges, are of considerably higher anthropological interest since, based on early ethnographic written accounts, it would have 'include[d] circumcision, homosexual abuse and /or ill-treatment' of those being initiated (van Baal 1963: 203).[34]

Owing to their gender-based unique and unexpected access to culturally and historically relevant 'back region' events, Eleanor Dalyell and Wilma Gladstone secured in their respective amateur films rare sources for anthropological research. In turn, and in spite of being a trained ethnographer, Blackwood only had access to the 'front region' of the cultures which she studied and also recorded in great detail in photographs, films and field notes. In her case, the gender of the (amateur and ethnographer) filmmaker often determined limitations rather than access to non-staged and un-mystified instances of indigenous cultural traditions. Paradoxically, it could be argued that the women amateur filmmakers acting as tourists-with-a-camera succeeded in securing authentic visual ethnographic records by accessing directly 'back regions' of some of the cultures and communities visited, while their professional counterparts researching indigenous communities – and whose filmmaking skills are judged today as on par if not lacking when compared with those perfected by, for instance, Rosie Newman, Jenny Brown or Nan Taggart[35] – remained confined to the 'front regions' of staged ethnography with its lack of cultural immersion and assimilation.

Conclusion

Amateur film practice represents one of the key components of the British Empire's visual popular culture, and of imperial history in general. This area of research has been largely neglected until recently in terms of its historic relevance to the construction of British imperial identity (Langford 2007; de Klerk 2013; Motrescu-Mayes 2011; 2013; 2014; 2015).[36] Scenes of colonial life recorded by British amateur filmmakers confirm that only a constant reassessment will save their documentary merit from critical dismissal and possible oblivion. As visual documents, these films function as primary research sources in deciphering aspects of imperial life and psyche while documenting specific colonial, racial, social and cultural dynamics. As such, and within new scholastic perspectives that challenge trends in postcolonial memory studies, amateur films act as catalysts for reinterpretations of Britain's imperial past – a discourse reinforced by half a century of postcolonial hindsight. Initially seen as problematic for its imperial narrative and visual rhetoric, colonial amateur footage offers new perspectives on the twentieth-century imperial history and deserves to be better identified, cross-examined and understood. The footage shot by British women in former colonial settings provides an unofficial yet often centre-stage view on public occasions and private moments during the final decades of colonial rule. Their films often reveal a particular insight into British imperial ideologies and mores as evident in domestic and official occasions and, consequently, propose a credible representation of a less egocentric, perfectionist or mythologised set of British imperial identities than those promoted by empire cinema or governmental productions. Moreover, their amateur films offer cinematic portraits of specific colonial times and communities in the form of constantly re-interpretable visual diaries, most of them able to challenge customary imperial narratives. Therefore, amateur film collections similar to those recorded by Lady Kendall, Lady Dalyell, Wilma Gladstone, Audrey Lewis, Rosie Newman and Barbara Donaldson, to name just a few, function as authentic records of significant historical and cultural relevance, and call for a broader understanding of the amateur film genre's historical relevance to new interpretation of national, imperial and gendered identities through renewed cross-disciplinary analyses.[37] Two possible initial theoretical frameworks consider, in the first instance, the study of distinct articulations of self-representations and self-imagining found in amateur films made by women, and secondly, the analysis of cultural constructions that legitimated specific gender-based visual narrative patterns across colonial (or British home-made) amateur films (Kuhn 1994). This possible methodology focuses on a series of narrative, stylistic and self-representational similarities and differences evident across numerous and different illustrations of social, racial and gendered self-representations that validated several indexical British national and colonial imaginings (Langford 2007). This is particularly important in the context of a larger investigation addressing amateur cinema within its self-referential visual rhetoric that has only recently been recognised by film and media scholars (among others, Zimmermann 1995; Odin 1995; Rascaroli et al. 2014) – a context also defined now by an almost ubiquitous archival online access to such films, one that facilitates their in-depth and cross-disciplinary study. This volume aims to explore several feasible interpretations of (colonial) amateur films made by women and whether such films offer a definite and definable female agent-gaze – a specific female visual aesthetic identifiable and shaped by a range of imperial, social, gendered and ethnic particularities (Erens 1991). It has also considered why films like those made by the British women amateur filmmakers discussed in this book should be explored as effective catalysts between conventional historiographic representations of the British colonial rule and emerging research methodologies and theories in imperial and gender studies. A preliminary concluding note would be that colonial amateur films made by women (whether colonials or colonised) act as unique agents for new reinterpretations of Britain's imperial past.

Notes

1. Nancy Vernede interviewed by Annamaria Motrescu-Mayes, 8 October 2004, for PhD dissertation, 'British Identities in Amateur Films from India and Australia, 1920s-1940s', and on behalf of the former British Empire & Commonwealth Museum, Bristol; the author's audio files and private correspondence with Mrs N. Vernede.
2. Recent research of prehistoric art claims that most cave paintings of hand imprints belonged to women instead of men; see 'Pictures: Prehistoric European Cave Artists Were Female', National Geographic News, 16 June, 2009, <https://news.nationalgeographic.com/news/2009/06/photogalleries/cave-handprints-actually-women-missions-pictures/index.html> (last accessed December 2016); A'ndrea Elyse Messer, 'Women leave their handprints on the cave wall', 15 October 2013, <http://news.psu.edu/story/291423/2013/10/15/research/women-leave-their-handprints-cave-wall> (last accessed December 2016).
3. The Kendall/Vernede Collection has been previously held by the British Empire & Commonwealth Film Collection and is currently at the Bristol Archives, UK. The first five 16mm black and white films have original labelling 'Lady Kendall' (accession numbers 1999/072/251–255). The remaining fourteen films in the collections (accession numbers 1999/072/256–269) include 16mm black and white films and several 8mm colour films.
4. Barbara Donaldson's husband, John Coote Donaldson, was an officer in the Indian Colonial Service. He served in the United Provinces between 1920

and 1946. Also, between 1937 and 1939, he was Secretary to Sir Harry G. Haig, Governor of the United Provinces.

5. See East Anglian Film Archive's ongoing digitisation and research project, IAC Women Filmmakers, <http://www.eafa.org.uk/highlights/42-iac-women-filmmakers> (last accessed 18 May 2017).
6. A visual rhetoric still central to Kodak's advertising campaigns, see, for instance, 'Super 8 Tips' visual – the close-up portrait of a young and smiling woman holding the new camera – included in the 'Kodak Super 8 Analog Renaissance' (2017), <https://www.kodak.com/ek/US/en/Consumer/Products/Super8/default.htm> (last accessed 3 January 2017)
7. The films discussed in this chapter have been selected from the following collections: Dalyell Collection (16mm and 8mm film, b/w/colour, India, Bahrain, 1920–30, Bristol Archives, UK), Kendall Collection (16mm film, b/w, India, Afghanistan, 1930s, CSAS, Cambridge, UK), Gladstone Collection (8mm film, colour, Ghana, 1957), *Ursula Graham Bower colour films in the Naga Hills* (16mm, colour, India, 1940–4, Cambridge Experimental Videodisc Project, University of Cambridge), *A Stone Age People in New Guinea* by Beatrice Blackwood (16mm film, b/w, Papua New Guinea, 1936–7, Pitt Rivers Museum, Oxford) and Skinmodes (YouTube channel, since 2013).
8. At that time her husband, Colonel Percy Gordon Loch, was posted to Mysore as the Secretary to Resident Sir Stuart Edmund Pearse (Resident of Mysore between 1924 and 1930).
9. Excerpt from the shot-list for Dalyell Collection (reel 61: 'Army on North West Frontier: India, 1929', Accession number 1998/005/032, British Empire & Commonwealth Museum film catalogue).
10. A similar scene is also found in one of Queen Elizabeth II's royal home movies collection – it shows the Duke of York (later King George VI) attempting to give his two young daughters, Elizabeth and Margaret, a quick haircut while using a pair of garden secateurs. The scene has been included in *Elizabeth at 90: A Family Tribute* (dir. John Bridcut, UK, Crux Productions Ltd, 2016).
11. Eleanor Isabel Dalyell married Lieutenant-Colonel Gordon Loch (later Loch-Dalyell) on 12 September 1928.
12. Thomas 'Tam' Dalyell (1932–2017) was Scotland's twentieth-century longest serving Member of Parliament. As a Scottish Labour Party member of the House of Commons (1962–2005), he represented West Lothian (1962–83) and Linlithgow (1983–2005), and also served as the Father of the House (2001–5).
13. In the late 1930s, Ursula Graham Bower undertook pioneering anthropological work in the Naga Hills District (today incorporated in Nagaland). Access to relevant information about her films, photographs and manuscripts is available at <https://www.prm.ox.ac.uk/film>, <https://sms.cam.ac.uk/collection/1810528> and <http://himalaya.socanth.cam.ac.uk/collections/

naga/coll/25/children/detail/all/index.html> (last accessed 6 August 2016).

14. See, for instance, Jimmy Nelson's art photographs of Ethiopian indigenous men of the Lower Omo Valley holding rifles and machine guns while posing for the camera (2015) <https://www.jimmynelson.com/journey/ethiopia> (last accessed October 2017).
15. <https://www.youtube.com/watch?v=G34w-YF4xz8> (23 April 2013) (last accessed 7 May 2017).
16. Following her visit to a Naga village, Ursula Graham Bower noted in her diary on 15 November 1937: 'went into headman's house & saw heads, relics of old days'. The diary excerpt is available at Cambridge Experimental Videodisc Project <http://himalaya.socanth.cam.ac.uk/collections/naga/record/r86007.html>, and a photograph of the human heads displayed in the Naga headman's house is available at Rivers Video Project (Professor Alan MacFarlane, University of Cambridge) <http://himalaya.socanth.cam.ac.uk/collections/naga/record/r86007/gallery/19.html> (last accessed 3 January 2017).
17. Dalyell Collection, film accession numbers 1998/005/001 and 1998/005/015. See Bahrain Agency file (British Library, OIOC, R/15/2/1502) in which it is mentioned that the heads of the slave parties performing on such occasions were each paid 5 rupees. Hamad bin Isa Al Khalifa reigned from 9 December 1932 until 24 February 1942.
18. Dalyell Collection, film accession number 1998/005/015. See Bahrain Agency file, 'Recognition of Shaikh Hamad as ruler of Bahrain' (British Library, OIOC, R/15/2/801).
19. Footage shot in 1933. Sakhir hosts now the Bahrain Grand Prix.
20. The Bahrain Political Agency file 'Visits of Lord and Lady Willingdon to Bahrain, 15 April 1933–7 October 1934' (British Library, OIOC R/15/2/590) details the arrangements for the visit.
21. Shaikh Saeed bin Maktoum al-Maktoum was the Emir of Dubai between 1912 and 1958.
22. Dalyell Collection, film accession number 1998/005/009. See Bahrain Political Agency file 'Visits of Lord and Lady Willingdon to Bahrain, 15 April 1933–7 October 1934' (British Library, OIOC, R/15/2/590).
23. Sir Charles Dalrymple Belgrave was the personal financial advisor and chief administrator to Shaikh Hamad ibn Isa Al Khalifa until 1942, and to Shaikh Salman ibn Hamad Al-Khalifa until 1957. Special thanks to Dr Katherine Prior for her comments and research notes about the Dalyell Collection.
24. Dalyell Collection, film accession number 1998/005/008. See Colonel Gordon Loch's Intelligence Reports, nos. 2–3, 1937 (British Library, OIOC, R/15/2/312, ff. 165, 168, 170) for his accounts of this trip to the Trucial Coast (27 January–4 February 1937).
25. Dalyell Collection, film accession number 1998/005/009. Colonel Loch's Intelligence Report, no. 2 of 1934 (British Library, OIOC, R/15/2/311, ff. 10–12).

26. Dalyell Collection, film accession number 1998/005/009. Colonel Loch's Intelligence Report, no. 1 of 1934 (British Library, OIOC, R/15/2/311, f. 3).
27. Lowell (1925). The caption for the illustration opposite page 189, and allegedly showing T. E. Lawrence, reads: 'Lawrence occasionally visited enemy territory disguised as a gypsy woman of Syria'.
28. The *Khaliji* (*Khaleegy*) dance sequence filmed by Eleanor Dalyell in 1934 shows the traditional setting, the (all-women) audience and the dance techniques specific to this folk dance. More recent versions of the dance are marketed as part of acrobatic belly dancing competitions and, importantly, aimed at mixed-gender audiences.
29. A colonial amateur filmmaker's gender, social status, and military or political rank always played a crucial role when negotiating access to indigenous cultures. For instance, Gerald Pakenham Stewart, who joined the Indian Colonial Service in 1930, served as Deputy Commissioner of the Sylhet District, Assam Province (until 1938) and later served as the Political Agent in Manipur State between 1946 and 1947, recorded the *Monkey Dance* amateur film in 1935, while travelling across the Manipur Hill Tracts, Assam. This short film shows a group of Kuki men – Tibeto-Burman indigenous people – performing a dance imitating primates having intercourse. On this occasion, like so often, it was the gender and the colonial rank of the amateur filmmaker that ensured his access to a traditional ceremony performed especially for him and for a small fee. Moreover, he has produced a dual amateur visual ethnographic record: one that informs on his film practice as aspiring amateur visual ethnographer, and one that illustrates the tradition of performed indigeneity. In his memoir, Stewart noted that he recorded this amateur film 'in a village in the Hill Tracts of Manipur State, Assam. It was a Kuki village. The Kukis normally would do this dance when drunk at night during some feast. The Chief obliged me by arranging it to be done or demonstrated by day so that I could film it. I think I gave him about 20 rupees buksheesh [*sic*]. In the dance, the Kukli tribesmen imitate monkeys so that it is somewhat lewd and suggestive in parts.' Even without access to Stewart's memoir, the visual rhetoric in this sequence is indicative of a staged performance – the returned gaze of the men while engaged in a subservient dialogue with the filmmaker, their repeated lascivious gestures in response to the filmmaker's 'stage directions', their embarrassed laughter during the performance, and the way they all posed for a group photograph at the end of their performance. While the CSAS had not made this film available online in an attempt to prevent any misuse of it only streams five of the six films in the Stewart Collection (see <http://www.s-asian.cam.ac.uk/archive/films/item/stewart-collection-film-1/>, last accessed 1 September 2017), the British Film Institute (BFI) is streaming it in its entirety while providing insufficient and somewhat misleading background information – see <https://player.bfi.org.uk/free/film/watch-monkey-dance-1935-online>, last accessed 1 September 2017).

30. Irish-born, Elizabeth Hawkins-Whitshed (1860–1934) later become known as Lizzie Le Blond among the late nineteenth century and early twentieth centuries' international network of pioneering alpinists.
31. *A Stone Age People in New Guinea* by Beatrice Blackwood (16mm film, b/w, Papua New Guinea, 1936–7, Pitt Rivers Museum, Oxford), <https://vimeo.com/88908952> (last accessed 9 June 2016).
32. It is possible that Beatrice Blackwood would have been familiar with Frank Hurley's *Pearl and Savages* ethno-documentary (Australia, Stoll Film Company, 1921) which he filmed in Papua New Guinea and Torres Strait, and with the pervasive filming protocols that allowed colonial amateur filmmakers with an interest in ethno-travelogues as well as visual ethnographers to prompt and record re-enactments of indigenous cultural traditions as a sign of well-preserved primitivism.
33. Of note, this particular phase of the ritual was supposedly meant to 'warn off (and frighten) those persons who should stay away from the rites (the women and children)' (van Baal 1963: 203).
34. Subsequently, Blackwood used a bull-roarer, which she had collected for the Pitt Rivers Museum, during demonstrations for her students. Alison Kahn, who digitised and researched Blackwood's films for the Pitt Rivers Museum, noted in an email addressed to the author on 19 December 2017: 'She was the Museum's demonstrator and she would famously take the bull-roarer out of its case and go into the carpark to show her students how it worked. The projection of her film would accompany this as an innovative teaching method which would bring the object and the people who used it to life.' Kahn also offered a different perspective on '[Beatrice Blackwood's] partial filming of the ritual [that] has to [be] pieced together in non-linear narratives that rely on a range of materials she produced such as her diaries, photographs, objects, and what would have been her spoken voice as she described the ritual to her students.' Relevant information about Beatrice Blackwood's work is found at <https://www.prm.ox.ac.uk/manuscripts/blackwoodpapers.html> (last accessed May 2017).
35. Information about Rosie Newman's amateur film collection is available at the Imperial War Museum (London), while information about Jenny Brown and Nan Taggart's amateur films is held by the Scottish National Library.
36. Various visual artists have also used colonial amateur films in their works and publications such as, for instance, Yervant Gianikian and Angela Ricci Lucchi – *Images d'Orient – Tourisme Vandale* (2001), Erika Tan – *Persistent Visions* (2005), Chambers et al. (2006), Rajkamal Kahlon – *Double Take* (2013) and Péter Forgács – *Looming Fire* (2013).
37. For instance, both Alison Louise Khan and Catherine Moore have successfully employed colonial amateur footage recorded by women when visually mapping private and publicly shared memories across historical times and generational identities (Butler 1990). Kahn directed and produced the ethno-documentary *Captured by Women* (The Oxford Academy of Documentary Film and the

Pitt Rivers Museum, 2011, <https://www.prm.ox.ac.uk/kahn.html>, last accessed June 2017) in which she used amateur ethnographic footage recorded by Ursula Graham Bower in the Naga Hills District, and by Beatrice Blackwood in Papua New Guinea. Lara Ehrenfried, a postgraduate student in Visual Arts and Culture, at the University of Durham, has also researched and promoted Beatrice Blackwood's and Ursula Graham Bower's early ethnographic films – see <http://pittrivers-photo.blogspot.co.uk/2017/09/behind-scenes-at-museum-placement-at.html> (last accessed September 2017). Finally, while working as a doctoral research associate at the Powell-Cotton Museum, Catherine Moore designed and curated the interactive digital film and exhibition *Gesture and Image: The Powell-Cotton Museum's ethnographic film archive re-exhibited* in which she used almost exclusively amateur films made by Antoinette and Diana Powell-Cotton in Angola in 1937.

CHAPTER 4

Cameras Not Handbags: The Essential Accessory

> [E]nabled by their wealth and social rank, they were citizens of just about everywhere: the private home; the public world and the reaches of empire. (Williams 2000: 185)

Unlike the ubiquitous mimetic reach of contemporary social media devices, small enough to fit into the body, let alone a pocket or a bag, early amateur cinema concerned people with relative wealth and influence: if not quite the omnipotent world citizen elite, identified by Williams (2000: 185), still confident enough to record the world as they saw it. Filmmakers abroad enjoyed a freedom to film sustained by what Bhabha (1984: 129) calls the ambivalence of colonial discourse and also the dual complicity needed to maintain the mantle of civility. If the spurious entitlement to picture others rested upon increasingly contested notions of superiority based upon race, colour and class, back in Britain, dwindling imperial authority, international influence and economic strength were impacting subtly upon women's everyday lives too, along with the gradual decline in traditional privilege. This changing national identity and role on the world stage not only affected people's lives and shaped their responses in practical and personal ways: for filmmakers, as shown in this chapter, it informed the filmmaking context, whether or not at a conscious level.

Women's visual practice, in Lerner's (1977: xvi–xvii) words, helps to validate women's experiences and the rhythms of their lives. Away from fictional or story plays and other non-fiction club productions, their filmmaking was often biographical and autobiographical. It reflected immediate circumstances and self-sustained interests. Using oral histories, correspondence, archival and printed sources, this discussion foregrounds the enthusiasm, pride and achievement associated with filmmaking. Film remains the central raw material of enquiry but filmmakers' practice and experiences feature too, reflecting interviewees' interests and pertinent historical issues. Commonalities link different stories and hold relevance for women's visual practices and literacies studied elsewhere and, given the richness of this little-mined amateur visual record, still awaiting discovery.

These filmmakers were not hobby press readers and had little or no sustained contact with organised amateur activity although occasionally they later linked with clubs. Their discovery has often been serendipitous. Some insights into past visual practice derive from where films have survived within family hands or within archival care. Attention focuses on the years between the late 1920s and early 1980s: these dates acknowledge that much of women's later amateur video material, particularly, tends to be under-represented even within public archives although more inclusive acquisition is growing. VHS video-tape of personal material was often later wiped, reused or disposed of and for years was less valued for its evidential quality or aesthetic form than earlier film gauges other than when produced within art movement or feminist contexts (Knight 2000: 261–2).

The discussion covers filmmakers of different ages, backgrounds, occupations and locations. Their visual knowledge, practice and output varied. All but two are white, a pointer to wider inequalities of race and ethnicity. Wherever possible analysis of visual meaning also considers subjects, audiences and intentionality. Typically, creative camera use was part of what Griffiths (1995: 2–3) identifies as the webs of identity that construct and constrain women's lives. Film practice complemented other interests and fitted around paid or unpaid work. It was often integral to women's roles as mothers, wives, sisters, aunts or daughters that, like their filmmaking, changed over time. While serious practitioners, defined by Tepperman (2014: 47–66) as 'advanced amateurs', became proficient and screened their films to varied audiences, other filmmakers simply shot, sent off their reels for development and showed unedited films to family and friends. Many were self-taught or received tips informally from other camera users and their practice reflects spontaneous responses to opportunities around them. Film narrated visual autobiographies and according to Rugg (2004: 4) 'authorised' their own points of view. Self-expression enabled women to represent, perform and exhibit personal identity and interact with others. Available time and resources varied and some filmmakers ceasing filming when their equipment wore out. Upgrading to new equipment occurred less than among filmmakers exposed to others using evolving camera technologies. Some women edited minimally, either in camera or through splicing film reels together, while others devised titles, scripts or accompanying sound tracks. Aesthetics, composition and choice of genre varied too, depending on a filmmaker's technical knowledge, her own equipment and awareness of wider cinematic influences.

Lives of Privilege

As Britain's social and economic landscapes reconsolidated after wartime injury and loss, death duties, taxation, land sales and the fragmentation of vast country estates, new expectations and lifestyles arose from adjusting patterns of privilege (Horn 2015). Disposable income for members of the nouveau riche as well the well-heeled remnants of Britain's aristocracy brought fresh ways for self-expression through travel, motoring, entertainment and leisure. Cine use exemplified how upper class life reasserted itself through new materialism and behaviours that interwove with political influence, privilege and patronage. Enabled by their wealth and social rank, the well-to-do became camera-carrying citizens at home, in public and through the empire. Explicit and implicit social and cultural norms embedded in their imagery bound individuals into wider power structures. Subsequent watching of their films reinforced memories and fostered collective identities. Attitudes, values and beliefs about entitlement, lifestyle, family, domesticity, relationships, travel and the relationship of private to public space were shaped and circulated through women's actions of making and exhibiting their films.

Lady Mary Douglas-Hamilton (1884–1957) highlights Britain's internal colonialism and aristocratic reach into church, government, industry, innovation, welfare and intellectual circles. Family connections produced situations where the privileged gaze of inheritance enabled her to use a hand-cranked camera with self-assurance and competence. Economically cushioned, despite facing hefty death duties and the loss of English estates after the First World War, her wartime nursing role in Glasgow and subsequent setting up of a convalescent home on the family's Isle of Aran estate widened her experiences. She accompanied her husband, the 6th Duke of Montrose, as he carried out voluntary roles and different responsibilities of land management and governance.[1] Lady Douglas-Hamilton's cine diaries repeatedly identify her observer role and confer legitimacy: during official visits to other Scottish islands and the mainland as well as deer hunts and point-to-point horse meetings. Shots of airfields and small planes highlight networked busy lives and filming bound her into narratives that helped to define and maintain social roles. Family scenes, as the children grew up, offer foci for subsequent emotional response and reflection when later viewed together, even many decades later.[2] Entertaining guests, meetings, the launch of a new lifeboat, visits to historical and archaeological excavation sites, and viewing Donald Campbell's speedboat 'Bluebird' on Loch Lomond provide markers within these cine stories (Pinder 2015).[3]

As modernity undermined the historical rationale, self-sufficiency and cohesion of hierarchical rural and island societies, Douglas-Hamilton's ethnographic gaze embraced estate workers, lifeboat volunteers and communities still reliant upon fishing, crofting and woollen industries. Visiting royalty at Holyrood Palace, clerics and other public figures filmed informally at private and official occasions sanctioned traditional roles and authority. Filmed visits to relatives and friends on country estates affirmed continuity and strengthened bonds of familiarity and identity. Her hand-held 16mm camera work was steady without additional editing. Films of family members afloat, water skiing, on beaches and at home denote a comfortable intimacy unrestricted by cost. The courteous and relaxed indifference to the camera's presence and the absence of performed responses hint at roles and selfhood, even among younger family members, accustomed to public attention. Girls and women do not predominate in footage that, despite its strong sense of geographical location and family identity is reminiscent of contemporary imagery by other wealthy women – and men – inhabiting colonial roles in and beyond Britain.

Camera use among Britain's interwar wealthy was widespread and provides variations on recurring themes. Before their relocation to a Scottish estate, Virginia (Ginie) and Stephen Courtauld created a basement darkroom and home cinema in their art deco refurbishment of Eltham Palace, south of London. Stephen's inherited wealth from textiles, his own business acumen and different roles as patron, trustee and as financial director of Ealing Studios combined with Ginie's sociability ensured a lavish lifestyle for them in Britain and later in Southern Rhodesia (Zimbabwe) where their philanthropy sought to alleviate worsening poverty under white minority rule. More privately they filmed their travels, sailing on their yacht and other hobbies and their pet ring-tailed lemur although few fragments of their material now survives (Turner 2015: 29). These were, it seems, leisured moments to amuse each other and their friends.[4] Also in the 1930s, Eunice and Eustace Alliott, two IAC lone workers based in Buckinghamshire used black and white and, more experimentally, Dufaycolour to record overseas travel, fox hunting, visits to London and domestic life.[5] Kathleen Arrowsmith documented home county life on and around a large farm estate. Enid Semple Briggs, originally from Leeds, filmed local events and family life on 16mm around Broadstairs in Kent where she lived with her mother and sister from the late 1920s.[6] Such amateur practice represents innovation and interest sometimes sustained over many years.[7]

On the English/Welsh border, affluent lives in late imperial Britain were captured on cine camera by Marjorie Alexander (1893–1983). Her family and friendship connections with royalty reflected how identities and influence were shaping new relationships between old and emerging social hierarchies. Alexander was part of a broadening upper middle class that brought together politics, business, finance and culture as the old landed gentry melded with provincial urban and industrial elites. She was born into a prosperous Liverpool family and it is believed that her fiancé was killed during the First World War. She never married but, following her sister-in-law's unexpected death in 1930, took into her own home her newly widowed brother's young family and complete household. Ample time remained for her filming which seems to have begun during the later 1920s and continued for the next forty years.[8]

Alexander's record of family, holidays and her own extensive travels epitomised upper middle class living in the last century. Cine films documented the children growing up: parties, picnics, sailing excursions, holidays in Anglesey and boarding school visits. European holidays followed familiar patterns in the interwar years: river and sea cruises, and visits to France. She recorded swastikas at a German airfield, military parades at Nuremberg and, possibly from a hotel window, Hitler passing in an open vehicle. The rise of fascism did not deter England's well-to-do from visiting Germany until the later 1930s and Alexander's causal curiosity towards Nazism reflects the opportunism of many amateur filmmakers (Norris Nicholson 2012a: 194–5). Unrestrained by the cost of film, she was able to document the unexpected and unfamiliar as generously as her sequences of family life and this continued through her later travels.[9]

Although the Second World War impacted directly upon the family, Alexander's cine practice continued unrestricted by wider film shortage as she became involved in local politics after peace returned. Occupying a position within the Wirrall's social elite, Alexander moved from a status initially based upon her father's and then her brother's position into quasi-public independent spheres of local leadership and civic activism like other upper class women between and after the wars (Thane 2010: 11–28; Williams 2000: 185; Spencer 2005: 97). Circumstances denied her roles as a wife and mother but kinship legitimised an unconventional household arrangement in which she assumed a form of socially acceptable maternalism. Her imagery is a reminder that, as Elsaesser (2009: 32–51) reveals, complex family structures and household arrangements may be hidden within benignly constructed memories on cine film. Alexander's later involvement in welfare and charity, like that of other filmmakers under discussion, reflects the gendered nature of opportunities for women in paid and unpaid work beyond the home during the twentieth century (Lewis 1984).

Alexander documented her surrogate family more assiduously than most mothers could, thanks to the support of domestic staff. Well connected, mixing within professional circles and with some high-ranking military/naval associations, she continued to make and show films until well into her seventies.[10] She seems to have been self-taught perhaps in a home where still photography was already in use or a social setting where others dabbled in cine filming. Nothing suggests that she joined a cine club although nearby groups were active. She used colour Kodak film from 1937 and she preferred the flexibility of handheld shots. Her films survived unedited on their original reels.[11] She seemed to delight in capturing the immediacy of the unexpected, whether the children's governess on a garden seesaw, a listing steamship in mist on the River Mersey or a young British queen coinciding with her own visit to New Zealand. Whether her record of *Inn of the Sixth Happiness* (Mark Robson, 1957) being filmed in North Wales was prompted by curiosity or her own social care interests in children from Liverpool's Chinese community being used as extras is unclear.[12] Generally Alexander's visual practice replicated the role of conscientious chronicler or family archivist assumed by women in many homes. However, the disruptions of wartime loss and post-war dispersal overseas meant that subjects were holidays, local places and occasions with friends rather than the birth and childhood of another generation. Circumstance and class thus invert a more familiar pattern of family-orientated home movie making and draw her closer, in her camera use, to some of the single women considered elsewhere.

Travelling with a Camera

For many amateurs travel was often the impetus to start filming (Norris Nicholson 2012a: 175–207; Kerry 2014). The interwar rise of recreational travel opportunities enabled individuals with money and time to travel further, faster and in greater comfort than ever before. Recreational sea and river cruises priced to suit different budgets broadened the travelling public. Camera use soared among the well-to-do: they filmed activities afloat including their own seated inactivity while others worked, views from deck and on shore visits during cruises, transatlantic crossings and visits to the Canaries and Azores, and journeyed along Europe's great rivers. Air travel, although in its infancy, before the 1950s, attracted British cine users too as did touring by car, caravan and later by bicycle. Women made and featured on much holiday footage shot with varying quality from the mid-1920s onwards (Norris Nicholson 2002; 2006a; 2006b; 2009a).

Some women had walk-on parts in films largely made by others. Strategic positioning in doorways, at viewpoints or interacting with children denoted their self-assurance as late imperial travellers. They posed alongside local people who often became ethnographic accessories as traders, craftworkers, porters and drivers at tourist sites or outside hotels. As Bertie

Preston travelled with her father and twin brothers, gesture, body language and expression disclosed her confidence in such manipulative poses during shore visits on holiday cruises during the 1930s (Norris Nicholson 2009b). Eunice Alliott similarly organised action caught on camera by her husband, Eustace, during their visits abroad (Dyson 2015: 5). Not all settings were conducive to outsiders' visual curiosity, as seen in local people's indifference to cine using visitors in Soviet Russia in 1932. Almost three decades later, Sir Geoffrey Haworth's 16mm travel footage at the height of Cold War tensions, and with much less apparent official restriction, recorded individuals among Moscow's May Day crowds, smiling workers at collective farms and posing groups of villagers. His wife Dorothy interacted benignly with children, young people and women on camera during their independent excursions in the former soviets, seemingly uninhibited by the lack of a common language (Norris Nicholson, 2009c; 2013).

Some filmmakers were less coercive, as seen in films by the award winning Scottish pioneer amateur couple, Nat and Nettie McGavin (sister of Frank Marshall). Nettie McGavin's well-made film, *Holidaying in Harris* (1938), combined clarity and controlled camera movement with carefully composed frames and varied focal length. Ostensibly a record of a holiday that involved taking the family car by ferry and the opportunity to visit the home of Marshall's maid, McGavin filmed many local people including Nat talking with quayside herring sellers and their daughters joining a crofter as she dyed wool with lichen (Norris Nicholson 2002). Portraits of women involved in peat-working, collecting water by bucket, washing clothes in a burn and gutting herring attest to McGavin's respect, and several women talk silently on camera possibly about their tasks and skills. Their apparent ease perhaps suggests feeling less awkward in front of a woman's gaze.[13] Other surviving documentary films sometimes include Nat briefly on camera too, although McGavin also filmed independently particularly during their visits to plantations in Kenya, Ceylon (Sri Lanka) and elsewhere as part of the family's tea business.[14]

As imperial certainties and convictions of Britons abroad diminished and sensitivities towards such visual objectification grew, staged holiday poses with local people declined but did not disappear. Arguably the amateur's impulse to document the unfamiliar and visibly different remained fundamentally unchanged: magnification made filming possible from further away and shifts to relatively cheaper video and then digital formats enabled longer sequences of recording otherness although not always of higher quality. Indeed, filmmakers' collection of visible difference as picturesque tropes possibly expanded as travel opportunities grew. Tradition, as a much-recorded condition of the colonised, survived into postcolonial encounters as testimony of an enduring absence of modernity. However, the strongly empathetic travel documentary imperative, seen in the films of Arctic explorer and botanist Isobel Wylie Hutchison and the Shetland-based teacher filmmaker Jenny Isabel Gilbertson, did sometimes surface in films made by women as personal responses to living somewhere else (Neely 2014: 303–6). Dorothea Mitchell (1877–1976) was another remarkable British-born, Indian-raised and much travelled pioneer: she is credited with the first amateur feature-length film made about her life (*A Race for Ties*, 1929) and is now part of Canada's independent filmmaking history (Beaulieu and Harpelle 2005).

Audrey Lewis (1928–*c*.2009) joined her fiancé who was already two years into a posting in Kenya with the British Methodist Missionary Society.[15] Travelling on SS *Uganda* she later recalled that 'An atmosphere of adventure with a sense of freedom and hope filled the ship.'[16] A departing missionary had equipment to pass on: 'He offered me the camera for about £30.00. I took the opportunity . . . Somehow I felt that somebody ought to record something.' Over the next three years Lewis and her husband developed the former German mission station that had been closed during the war when its Lutheran staff were interned by the British. Her close involvement with the lives and physical needs of local Kikuyu people caught on camera a people in flux.

The Lewis' outreach in the Tana River region coincided with the mounting struggles against failing British imperialism in East Africa. Their filming shifted from the adventure of bush life as newly-weds into recording the daily impact of people being caught up in the Mau Mau Emergency. As missionaries they were both imperial subjects and agents of imperialism (Ford 2015: 11). They found themselves in the midst of a civil war trying to evangelise within an increasingly untenable colonial vision of progress. They travelled with and visited their Kikuyu intermediaries who were engaged in pastoral and ministry work. While Ian visited schools, building and water projects and talked with groups of villager elders, women and children, Lewis documented rural traditions and missionary-led activities. Her camera work attests to the promotion of colonial cultural values and her own maternalist concern with the female empire (Bush 1998: 218–19): adult literacy classes, the morals, loyalties and purposeful leisure of being Girl Guides, productive handicrafts, growing vegetables and, after her husband lifted a previous Lutheran ban on dancing, opportunities to learn European folk-dancing.

Lewis did not film everywhere: as a woman she could attend women's welfare, health and educational settings; as a European missionary's wife she could film all-male gatherings albeit at a distance. Acceptance and authority were not automatic. She filmed her husband, often from behind or over the shoulders of seated male companions, as he attended rural Sunday Schools, prayer meetings and met with youth groups. She recorded the mission church and also the hospital boat that brought treatment to outpatients and transported people to the health centre. Sometimes she roamed independently and filmed more private ritual practice and sacred sites from further away. The boundaries to her colonial gaze seemed contingent rather than an entitlement conferred by gender, status and race (Stoker 2002: 42, 254). Her authority to look and the requirement to disregard were finely balanced. She was not always in the midst of action or a close spectator: she filmed village elders, young mothers attending a baby clinic, washing or gathering fuel and water. When she portrays people suffering from such diseases as malaria or Lymphatic filariasis (elephantiasis) in close-up and medium range her objectification most obviously renders them visual spectacle and denies their agency (Griffiths 2002: 320). Sometimes power relations between the image-maker and her subject are stark. Her mobility contrasts with those people who may only look back or ignore the camera. They are limited to turning away their eyes, ignoring the camera or adjusting their head covering.

Lewis highlighted diversity of faiths and ethnicities in Kenya's urban coastal areas too, where roadside filming, perhaps from a vehicle, enabled her to record passers-by, street traders, construction sites and historic buildings and the self-confidence of school children less deferential than their rural and older counterparts. With Ian's appointment as principal of a theological college near Nairobi, and the birth of their first child, filming opportunities changed but dangers for expatriates remained high. The Methodist Missionary Society recognised that Lewis' films were ideal material for fund-raising and training and paid for professional editing and the addition of a sound track. Lewis had contributed audio pieces to the BBC while working with vulnerable groups in London and drafted an accompanying script for the film, now titled *African Eden* (1955–8).

The commentary, spoken by Alvar Lidell, combined with sounds that Lewis recorded in the field on battery operated equipment, created a travelogue infused with evangelism. Judicious visual editing accompanied her message: Kenyans were 'restless to be on a march to a new and better day . . . people in towns had been 'brought to the crossroads of destiny'. Lewis filmed within a context of escalating violence, detention camps, dispossession and the forcible relocation of Kikuyu into policed settlements. Long-neglected African resentments over socio-economic inequalities rooted in racist public education, health and employment practices together with colonial policies of dispossession and eviction from ancestral lands were compounded by the racially divisive policies of land distribution to returning war veterans. Her images of missionary church, school and hospital promised hope: 'In an atmosphere of discontent, movements such as Mau

Mau are born and people are caught up in struggles . . . that express the sub-conscious resentment of the soul.' As a missionary film, faith promised comfort to those who 'perhaps knew the rigours of the Mau Mau prison camps and the struggles of rehabilitation'. Lewis acknowledged 'Race [as] the greatest problem in Kenya today' but she saw a route to harmonious coexistence via the church rather than a political solution. Like later films made with teenagers after their return home against the background of public concern about adolescent behaviour, her camera use was as much about social concerns as personal memory-making.[17]

Beryl Armstrong (b.1928) began filmmaking by chance too. After an itinerant childhood and disrupted education as her parents sought work overseas, her marriage to a civil servant brought suburban stability in one of London's post-war satellite towns.[18] When the Commonwealth Relations Office – formerly the Dominions and India Office and later absorbed into the Foreign Office – required that her husband should be posted overseas as part of routine training, Armstrong acted on advice from his colleagues and bought a Standard 8mm cine camera.[19] As part of expatriate life in Delhi, the family soon had an *ayah*, a bookable staff car and driver and she had time to film and edit. Although the family developed no lasting friendships with their neighbours, the mutuality of diplomatic compound life offered some reassurance and featured in some films.

Armstrong's camera offered symbolic protection and a rationale for being there. Filming became a means to assimilate and accommodate the contradictory identities of India that she encountered. Within the hierarchies of Commonwealth life, Armstrong sometimes felt awkward, including when the sound of her camera briefly attracted the unwelcome attention of an irritated young Queen Elizabeth on tour. However, curiosity prevailed. Poverty and the exposed intimacies of life on Delhi's streets attracted her gaze and perhaps, like many Brits abroad, was what she expected and was conditioned to see (Cannadine 2001: 135). The coexistence of colonial legacy, antiquity and tradition alongside the unfolding modernity drew her attention, whether filming from her apartment's balcony or when out and about. 'I had no editor', she recalled. 'Every reel after projection had to be rewound over the top. With a lamp underneath I was able to cut out unsuitable shots and rejoin to make the film reasonably presentable for showing on screen – the white wall.' Many of her films depict routine expatriate experience: disruption during monsoon rains, sightseeing excursions and hill station visits. In *Festive India*, she captured the pomp and pageantry of postcolonial India on Republic Day.[20]

Her husband's press ticket enabled Armstrong to film the tenth anniversary parade from a scaffolding tower erected for media coverage close to the India Gate. The inherited architecture of British imperial ambition became a vast backdrop to nationalist pride, achievement and celebration (Morris 1978: 374 –5). Military and other uniformed groups filed past as Armstrong recorded a spectacle that embodied self-confidence and an ebullient grasp of staged statecraft. She filmed in strong sunlight on Kodachrome, regretting that she 'would miss some action' as she changed films. Almost sixty years later, she recalled the urban theatricality of the Rajpath and panoply of passing people, marching bands, caparisoned elephants and glittering costumes. 'Fortunately I had the screw on telephoto lens to give variation with long and close up shots but again, scenes were lost in the changeover.' She believed she had 'achieved some spectacular shots' that she could improve by different positioning and camera orientation: 'To add variety in viewpoint we walked down Rajpath the following year and also filmed . . . the parade emerging from the other side of India Gate.'

Republic Day was part of a weeklong celebration that included hundreds of dancers performing in the National Stadium. Armstrong recalled, 'They put on a display before a select audience under floodlight. Photographers were invited to the daytime dress rehearsal and we could mingle freely.' Aesthetically satisfying, she filmed musicians and dancers as they rehearsed or waited. Cultural iconography blended with memories as she recalled the atmosphere near Rashtrapati Bhawan (the President's Palace), 'the British character of military bands' and how she sat with her husband and small sons 'on huge laid tarpaulins amongst the crowds of Indian families'. Postcolonial India's exoticism seemed even more visually choreographed at dusk: 'The ceremony is so timed that the final notes of the last post fill the square as the sun sets and the lights are switched on, outlining every dome and tower in the vicinity.' As the apogee of her Indian cine work, *Festive India* consolidated an interest that continued for almost thirty years.

Views on History

Dame Gillian Mary Wagner (b.1927) traced her filmmaking to joining the Georgian Group in London.[21] Set up in 1937 to preserve historic buildings from the influences of modernity, wartime bomb damage brought fresh urgency to its campaign. 'That was my first job and there's where I met my husband. He was on the council of the Georgian Group and when we got married it meant a lot to us . . .' Wagner's filmed visits around

Figure 4.1 Photograph of Gillian Wagner filming during the 1960s. © Gillian Wagner.

London and overseas developed her appreciation of architectural history. 'We did these expeditions which were really very interesting and involved . . . people who knew a lot about architecture which I didn't. I took my camera with me and I'd photograph them walking around.' The silent imagery became a trigger for remembering (Figure 4.1).

Wagner became adept at recording people informally. Other than helping to label boxes, Anthony was not involved in her hobby although he sometimes featured on film. Family holidays, visits to relatives and sequences of the children each Boxing Day built a personal visual record that was shaped by social and intellectual connections. Married life brought increasing contact with Britain's mid-century historical scholars and other public figures that arose from Anthony's emerging prominence at the College of Arms where he held official roles in heraldic and ceremonial duties of state. Opportunities for camera use proliferated and included access to film during preparations for the investiture of the Prince of Wales at Caernarfon Castle in 1969 and during regional royal visits.

Excavation of the Sutton Hoo ship burial site had ceased in 1939, so its post-war reopening offered Wagner another opportunity to film near their home:

> We knew the chap from the British Museum who was in charge . . . and the lady who owned the land . . . Once we'd gone without telling them and we had to drive over the fields to get there and there was a gamekeeper waiting for us . . . I climbed up something and I could zoom down and see their paintbrushes and their getting the earth off the nails . . . In this particular dig there was nothing new – all the great jewellery and treasures been already been found and removed. This was just logging the site, the length of the boat, the number of nails, and holes and all those rather boring details they needed to know. I thought this is historic and I'd like to record.

Wagner recalled that the activity seemed too far from London to make archaeological news. She recorded Aldeburgh's emerging international music festival and the building of the famous concert hall too. Pride in filming its royal opening in 1967 and its rapid rebuilding after fire damage was tinged by a disgruntled bystander:

> I had my camera and it was making a whirring noise and there was a man standing beside me and he kept turning around to stop me because of the noise he couldn't hear the Queen speaking . . . I was standing a little bit higher and the camera was right by his ear. I can remember him being very annoyed [but] I thought this is a historic moment.

Wagner rated *Suffolk in the Sixties* about these events as 'her most serious film' and regretted its loan to the National Trust and subsequent loss.

Wagner's films include the controversial politician, Enoch Powell, who later gained notoriety for what became known as his 'Rivers of Blood' anti-immigration speech:

> It's strange to think I've got pictures of picnics with the Powells when a play about them has just been put on . . . it happens to be from Wolverhampton but it could have been us. He was known for his picnics.

(See also Treneman 2016; Fisher 2016). Her picnic films date no later than the early 1960s, when Powell was Minister of Health, although he already had a reputation for his Tory radicalism, intellect and recognition for his scholarship (Heffer 2008). Anthony Wagner and Powell shared a passion for historic institutions and traditions:

> You see, my husband was a scholar too . . . They loved picnicking and exploring churches . . . He and Enoch would sit at the back [of the car] with piles of books, guide books, discussing this and that. Enoch would probably choose the place we were going to have our picnics, like a kind of route march so we could look across the country at a church spire or something like that . . . If there was something in the church that wasn't quite right, he'd tried to work out why was it there, putting it into context.

Wagner recalled: 'We never discussed politics at all. That was completely out. Politics didn't interest my husband in the least little bit.' Church interiors were too dim for much filming so her focus was on the picnic. She was unsure if she had ever shown the films to the Powells afterwards but was adamant that she had not shown them to the Georgian Group: 'I don't think there was any kind of occasions when I could have done. It was for my pleasure for me to remember what we did.' Memories, emotional reaction and reflections elided with the film itself:

> Pam [Powell] and I and Anthony [were] sitting around and Enoch was . . . standing there . . . waving his arms around and explaining to us . . . Along came some people . . . They suddenly realised who it was. We were in stitches. Enoch went on talking and suddenly he realised that there was somebody else listening. It was so funny. I don't know whether I caught it. It would have been too immediate.

Sometimes, even for the most enthusiastic filmmaker, being there was more absorbing than recording it for subsequent enjoyment. In time, Wagner's filmmaking grew less and private picnic memories and the friendships of which they were part became buried in another phase of life. Filmmaking ceased as work with Barnardo's led on to social care policy, study and historical research (Wagner 1979; 1982; *c*.2004). As lives moved on the cine films were stored away for over thirty years only to re-emerge intact in 2016 (Figure 4.2).

Figure 4.2 Photograph of film reels entitled *Investiture* and *Powell Picnic and Daddy Punting* (1963). © Gillian Wagner.

Through Artists' Eyes

While Powell saw no value in offering British citizenship to the millions of people living in the old empire, some of those citizens were reversing the gaze to record their own experiences in the final years of colonialism. Winifred Atwell (*c*.1910/1914–83), already a qualified chemist, moved from Trinidad to study music first in the USA and then later in London (Bourne 2001: 91–8; 2011). Combining her classical training and distinctive ragtime 'honky-tonk' and boogie-woogie styles, she became popular and successful through radio broadcasts and her own television shows, as well as her recordings and sheet music. Making films started during travelling on international concert tours with her husband–manager, the comedian Levi Levisohn. They created a miniature cinema in their North London home where they projected 16mm colour cine films of nature, travel and domestic scenes, as well as performances and social occasions with friends and fans. Levisohn recorded Atwell playing the piano to accompany the imagery. Their work featured in the *Shooting Star* series of profiled women filmmakers in the short-lived *Amateur Movie Maker* at the height of her celebrity status in Britain (Phythian 1958: 33–4). Patronising in tone, the piece is a rare acknowledgement of a black woman amateur filmmaker in 1950s Britain and is included here as Atwell's visual practice predated Trinidad and Tobago gaining independence in 1962 and she gained national recognition as a Trinidadian shortly later.

Little is known about Atwell's cine film work that possibly perished in a house fire shortly before she died. As with other childless couples, film production gave a shared focus and spanned years of success and financial security. It enabled Atwell to evidence 'the good life' when they visited her parents in the Caribbean, possibly mitigating family concern over her move overseas and shift from classical into popular music. The films perhaps asserted identity too, particularly as Atwell encountered racist attitudes during her 1955 visit to the USA, lived in Britain during years of open colour prejudice and after moving permanently to Australia championed Aboriginal rights. It seems likely that travel brought the couple into contact with other recreational filmmakers. Atwell possibly encountered cine using African-Americans when she went to the USA, among island visitors from cruise ships as a child and used by soldiers still based in Trinidad after the Second World War (Figure 4.3).

Wherever the impetus derived, Atwell was not unique as a Trinidadian filmmaker at this time. Richard Fung combined his mother's

Figure 4.3 Photograph of Winifred Atwell, *Shooting Star* series, *Amateur Movie Maker* (1958). © *Amateur Cine Enthusiast.*

home movies with her stories, other narratives and autobiography in *My Mother's Place* (1990).[22] He later wrote that her hobby started as a distraction for his terminally ill sister and that Rita Fung recorded what she valued: her children, weddings, Carnival, holidays, Christmas and other notable occasions. The interiors, ceiling fans, lush gardens and village streets, as well as scenes of himself playfully wearing his sister's dresses, watched afresh as an adult, captured home life during the island's final years of colonialism as seen through his mother's eyes. For Fung, her camera became a prop in her own performance of status and class mobility. Her cine use disclosed how her identity was shaped by race, gender and social aspiration. His hardworking mother emerged as a well-dressed good colonial subject, a monarchist who filmed the island's visitors selectively (Queen Elizabeth but not Léopold Senghor, Haile Selassie or Indira Gandhi), a lover of English roses and an avid reader of *Good Housekeeping* (Kim 2002).

A son's video reworking of his mother's late colonial cine footage highlights the cross-generational technological shifts that trace through the narratives of amateur cinema. As the impact of automation and mechanisation grew, new designs and techniques penetrated all aspects of life. Established tropes of filming other people at work gained more personalised significance. Mid-century cine portraits of British family businesses often concentrated on work practices and the personalities involved but Barbara Lloyd's sound film of her father's Lancashire printing works did not just record technical functionality.[23] Shot on Standard 8mm, her film paid tribute to a family firm, set up by her grandfather and still sustained by her parents, and was a visual celebration of skills and technique. Lloyd's spoken commentary and filmmaking acknowledged her father's lifelong relationship with printing. Machinery dominated the dimly lit workshop space that defined her father's world. Rough un-plastered walls and draped wires contrasted with the alchemy of liquid lead as it turned into individual characters for printing. Well-composed sequences from different angles captured the precision of gleaming mechanical parts and her father's concentration and moving hands (Figure 4.4).

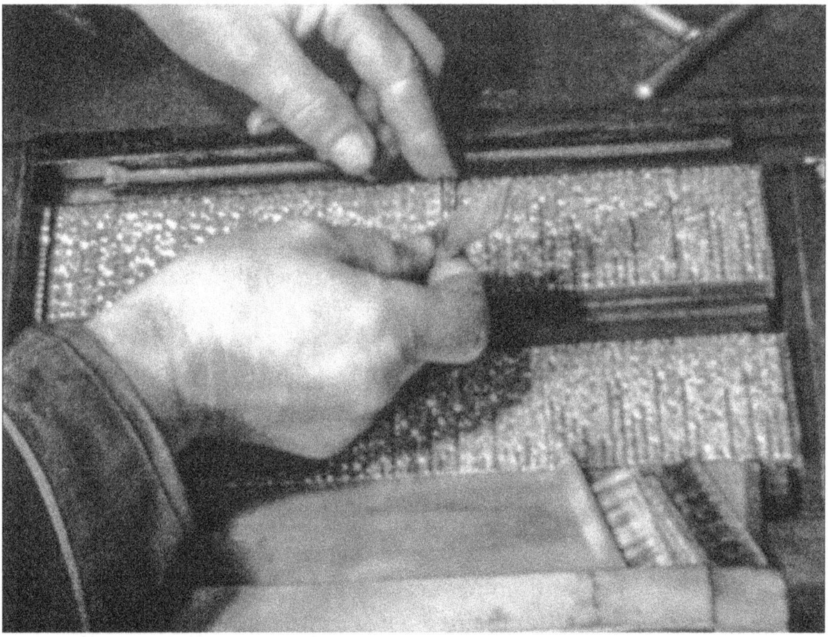

Figure 4.4 Still frame from Barbara Lloyd, *A Printing Job* (*c.* 1969). © North West Film Archive at Manchester Metropolitan University.

Lloyd's father embodied the traditional relationship between work and identity amongst letterpress printers at a point when offset printing was replacing older techniques. Three years before John Berger's *Ways of Seeing* television series brought Benjamin's cultural critique of mechanical reproduction to British audiences, Lloyd responded to societal and communication change when she showed how her father's craft and knowledge faced technical obsolescence and economic irrelevance.[24] The printing works closed when her father died a few years later, but its presence survived amid other personal films of holidays and family. *A Printing Job* contrasts qualitatively with Lloyd's other work but, perhaps like her short film of a woman sculpting a head in clay made over ten years earlier, it reveals how opportunities and expectations shaped her visual practice. It also highlights the filmmaker's capacity to give permanence and value, and the intuitive visual ways in which many self-taught women expressed their responses to the world around them.

Conclusion

This chapter highlights the variety of women's independent cine practice. These subjective versions of the worlds were partial, selective and incomplete, like any filmmaking, but they defined identities and interests in and beyond Britain during years of late imperialism and major social change. During decades when many camera-owning women were not in paid employment, they often filmed in locations and situations not of their own making. Filmmaking offered ways of sharing memories and stories in voluntary and personally driven ways. As astute observers, their visual stories redefined women's established roles as guardians and transmitters of cultural knowledge. Their non-fictional narratives embodied self-awareness and brought distinctive perspectives to what it means be a woman in charge of a camera.

Many but not all women attracted to amateur film were motivated by similar reasons: to document and celebrate immediate experiences – their children, homes, holidays, special or festive occasions and the everyday pleasures of observing others. Much was recorded spontaneously for personal enjoyment and future reliving of particular moments. Other stories featured too: the micro-details of local events and changing lives; and continuing traditions and upheavals caused by human, political or other causes. Some women used their cameras as part of their work or during travels with friends or a partner. Evolving equipment brought successive improvements to design and operation that made filmmaking and projection more attractive to users. The shift from manual analogue to compact automatic digital formats ultimately made filming and editing simpler, brought compatibility with other home devices and technologies and streamlined the production process. As relative costs declined, access widened. So eventually did the scope for taking control of each stage through production to exhibition which reduced reliance on others and maximised flexibility. Women, in particular, benefited from the successive technological shifts that brought smaller, lightweight and portable equipment, even though video cameras briefly grew larger as the analogue and emerging digital eras overlapped. Networked technologies seemed to bring professional and amateur visual practice closer together, despite early promotional hopes for new media's democratising potential now seeming rather hollow (Taylor 2014: 2–3). More marginal to the amateur movement than the IAC's lone workers and sometimes operating entirely on their own, many women amateur filmmakers experimented with their cameras, even in their own back gardens. Films became part of how they defined themselves and were seen by others.

The changing nature of marriage, family and work formed a backdrop to women's lives and available leisure time. None of them lived as their mothers had done. Marriage brought independence for some from the parental home but set new limits to personal autonomy shaped by a husband's ambitions, achievements and uneven sharing of childcare. Filmmaking was an option only for those whose circumstances permitted time and financial means but its appeal to women, regardless of their status, prompts questioning its specific allure and place in their lives. For some amateurs, time rather than level of interest constrained what they did after their films were developed, and compromised their ultimate potential. For many women, camera use and subsequent film production enabled them to reclaim a sense of self – their way of knowing and viewing the world unavailable elsewhere in their daily lives in paid and unpaid labour. Film offered their version of events, people and places. Their vision could communicate life's complexity to others. For them, using a camera could be even more potent a symbol of identity than carrying a handbag.

Notes

1. Duchess of Montrose (1932) *Trip to Skye, Orkney and Shetland* (16mm, 15:38min, b/w, silent), NLS Id. 1928.
2. Lady Jean Fforde's collection of imagery remains in private hands (at the time of writing) although her name appears on some catalogued items within the Moving Image Archive at the NLS. Cine footage by her mother, Lady Mary Douglas-Hamilton, was included along with Lady Jean Fforde's own

photographs when BBC Scotland visited her home on Arran during the making of *Scotland's Home Movies* (broadcast 9 August 2015).

3. James Graham and Lady Mary Douglas-Hamilton (1931–1952) Fforde Collection (16mm, 34:14min, b/w, silent), NLS Id. 2123.
4. Author in conversation with Michael Turner, Historic England, October 2017. See also Turner (2015).
5. Eunice and Eustace Alliott (1933–5) *Riding and the Countryside* (16mm, 14:27min, b/w, silent), EAFA no. 4394; (1939) *Some Experiments in Dufaycolor* (15:32min, colour, silent), EAFA no. 4398.
6. Enid Briggs Collection, *c.*1927–59, SASE, Id. 1018–23 and 5245–55.
7. Kathleen Arrowsmith (*c.*1935–40s) Arrowsmith Family Collection, SASE Id. 1090.
8. Author in conversation with Stef Bate, *The Alexander Film Archive*, Valley Stream Media Developments, Betwys Coed, Wales, October 2011; see also <http://www.valleystream.co.uk/company.htm> (last accessed 20 January 2018).
9. See also Chapter 6 (Lucy Fairbank).
10. Marjorie Alexander used a 1931 Cine-Kodak BB Junior 16mm clockwork-operated camera and projected on older Kodak equipment throughout her life.
11. Author in conversation with Stef Bate, *The Alexander Film Archive*, Valley Stream Media Developments, October 2011; see also <http://www.valleystream.co.uk/company.htm> (last accessed 20 January 2018).
12. BBC News, 'Reunion for film classic's cast', BBC website 24 April 2004, available at <http://news.bbc.co.uk/1/hi/wales/north_west/3657343.stm>(last accessed 20 January 2018).
13. Nat and Nettie McGavin (1938) *Holidaying in Harris* (16mm, 12:42min, b/w, silent), NLS Id. 0136.
14. See also Nettie McGavin (1930s) *Ceylon Calling* (16mm, 11:00min, colour, silent), NLS Id. 0146.
15. Audrey Lewis Collection (1953–8) *African Eden* (16mm, 13:13min, colour, sound), YFA Id. 1896.
16. Audrey Lewis, Article ID: A5234861, *WW2 People's War*, 21 August 2005. Credit: WW2 People's War is an online archive of wartime memories contributed by members of the public and gathered by the BBC, available at <http://www.bbc.co.uk/history/ww2peopleswar/stories/61/a5234861> (last accessed 20 January 2018).
17. Audrey Lewis Collection (1961) *The Trophy* (standard 8mm, 16:40min, colour, sound), YFA Id. 3205.
18. Author's correspondence with Beryl Armstrong and an opportunity to stay with her and watch her films with her provides the basis for this section. Screen Archive South East holds some of her films.
19. Completely independent from the Colonial Film Unit, Civil Service amateur filmmakers had been well served by work-based clubs since the 1930s, including the Civil Service Cine Society (1930), and the Whitehall Photo-Cine

group (aka Westminster Cine Society and Whitehall Cine Society, 1932–late 1960s (Walden 1982: 29–30)).

20. The anniversary of when the Indian Constitution (1950) came into force to replace the colonial Government of India Act (1935) and the formal announcement of India as a sovereign, democratic country.
21. Author in correspondence with Dame Gillian Wagner and an opportunity to interview her at her home provides the basis for this section.
22. Richard Fung (1990) *My Mother's Place*, available at <http://www.richardfung.ca/index.php?/scv/my-mothers-place/> (last accessed 20 January 2018); see also Fung, 2008, p. 34.
23. Barbara Lloyd (*c.*1969), *A Printing Job* (Standard 8mm, 9:10min, colour, sound), NWFA no. 7257 and acquisition files.
24. Walter Benjamin's publication, *The Work of Art in the Age of Mechanical Reproduction* (1936), written against a background of new sound film technologies and the rise of Nazism and control over communication, prompted art critique John Berger to draw fresh parallels between technology, society and art in the late 1960s, as seen in his collaboratively produced book and television series entitled, *Ways of Seeing*.

CHAPTER 5

Through Women's Lens: Imperial and Postcolonial Class and Gender Hierarchies

> *Chaque discours y reste inégal, à lui-même inadéquat* [Each discourse remains uneven, inadequate in itself]. (Derrida 2013: 324)

Issues of authenticity in art are always urgent and often involve gender politics, making any discussion about gender-based visual expressions a worthwhile albeit convoluted challenge. Assigning, recognising and validating the intrinsic originality of a visual record as the unequivocal expression of a recognisable gendered narrative continue to be contested theoretical battlefields. For instance, could it be that a scene from a silent amateur film showing people strolling in a garden indicates through its visual indexicality the gender of the filmmaker? It is possible to prove that such a claim is more than just a precarious exercise in media and perception studies only if the starting point of analysis is not anchored, as perhaps expected, in the study of the filmmaker's choice of framing, editing or overall narrative. The starting point of analysis should then be centred on the meticulous decoding of the visual responses, on the behavioural feedback offered by the people filmed – their context-driven ways of returning the filmmaker's gaze.[1] This is particularly important since recent studies have shown that audiences are prone to appoint *ex officio* the gender of a visual artist – painter, photographer, filmmaker, sculptor etc. – based primarily on the core themes and details depicted. As noted in Chapter 3, Elizabeth A. Bloomfield has demonstrated that 'gender role stereotyping along with the gender of the participant affects the symbolism within the artwork that results in the attribution of artwork being created by a male or female artists' (Bloomfield 2015: iv). Moreover, she proved that learning about gender roles in specific cultural contexts usually leads to stereotypical thinking, and consequently to future genre-role stereotypical representations. One of Bloomfield's revealing examples, and one especially relevant to the discussion of amateur films made by women,[2] is that concerning Jan Steen's painting, *Life of Man*, made in 1665 (Bloomfield 2015: 33). This is a sumptuously detailed theatre-stage-like image of a prosperous household where each member, old and young, male or female, is busily focusing on their tasks at hand, from preparing oysters for dinner to singing, negotiating, or flirting underneath a golden birdcage and under the gaze of a boy playing with a human skull. This scene of daily life is incredibly rich in its representation of behaviour patterns and norms documenting a specific time-stamped culture. A heavy drapery hangs on the left corner of the painting as if to encapsulate the message of Steen's artwork: the world as a stage, the audience as its *de facto* voyeur. The scene can be read either as an illustration of that time and people, or as an allegory of universal human interests, hence making its narrative simultaneously complete if approached from either perspective, or uneven if the viewer cannot fully negotiate the abundance of details. It was this variant perception that led 55.2 per cent of the participants in Bloomfield's experiment to attribute *Life of Man* to a female painter. Some of the key reasons behind this conclusion included the artist's compulsive attention to detail, the opulent colours, the lavish features which were interpreted as signs of emotional exuberance, the sexual tensions symbolised by the fleshy oysters, a young woman's coquettish rejection of her pretender's bold gestures and, importantly, the predominance of women characters depicted in the painting. Notwithstanding this artwork's self-explanatory title – *Life of Man* – Jan Steen's painting was thus adjudicated as representing a woman's life and also as having been made by a woman. In this case, statistics borrowed from perception and cognitive psychology studies would make media scholars feel safe in their initial judgement when attributing amateur film scenes showing, for instance, stylish European women dancing or posing among brightly coloured rhododendrons to a woman filmmaker. Following the same logic, other amateur film scenes such as those showing a young crew at work on HMS *Berkeley* – a British Navy destroyer that took part in the Dieppe Raid on 19 August 1942 – with their upper arms tensed to breaking point, their youthful smiles framed in close-ups and their energetic precision invested in manning the naval guns or undertaking watch duty, would implicitly indicate the interest of, and special access granted to, a male amateur filmmaker. In both cases, and even in the absence of detailed archival information about the respective filmmakers, these assumptions could be completely incorrect. Once again, rather than applying the shortcut style of reading visual narratives by relying on the conventional, routine interpretation of gender-alleged stereotypical iconography, the study of such amateur film scenes requires a fine-tuned analysis of the gestural behaviours presented by those filmed. For instance, an exaggerated, almost theatrical response, or a persistent reluctance to engage candidly with the filmmaker, are not necessarily indicators of the filmmakers' gender but would most likely suggest their social class or military rank respectively. Nevertheless, the study of the return-of-the-gaze pattern identified across an amateur film collection often reveals a gender dynamic and visual literacy that overwrite the cultural priming effect mentioned by studies like Bloomfield's experiment.

The film scenes described above offer a case in point: the garden scene has been filmed by a man, and the scene showing naval manoeuvres by a woman. Moreover, both amateur filmmakers benefited from unprecedented access to specific social, racial and gender-defined contexts that would have been usually unavailable to their peers: Maharaja Vijaysinhji of Rajpipla (1890–1951) maintained a wide network of British female companions during the 1930s, and Rosie Newman (1896–1988) was allowed by the Admiralty to spend a few days in June 1941 to film in colour – a luxury in wartime Britain – the drills and life aboard HMS *Berkeley*, a Type I Hunt-class destroyer of the Royal Navy. Whether an audience is misappropriating the gender of a Baroque painter, or media scholars and film archivists straightforwardly misattribute amateur filmmakers' gender and authorship based solely on subject preferences and recurrent themes (see Kendall versus Vernede discussion in Chapter 3), such instances offer examples that confirm the role played by visual and cultural priming processes in challenging the basic criteria employed when assessing gender-alleged stereotypical iconography.

This chapter discusses examples of contradictory perception patterns prompted by recurrent thematic and representational strands found in amateur films made by British women around the world or in Britain between the 1940s and the 1960s. It examines how amateur films of seemingly mundane, personal events or of collective trauma reveal unexpected portraits of imperial and postcolonial class and gender hierarchies. It also aims to establish a theoretical framework particularly applicable to the study of amateur films; one in which priority is given to 'systems of viewing' (Lavaud 1999: 206) that allow, alongside the analysis of the amateur filmmakers' practices – a crucial methodology notwithstanding – the translation of the gazes and behaviours presented by the people filmed as in a circular, reciprocal challenge of the filmmakers' ascribed gender roles.[3] This framework permits a critical interpretation of the visual dialogue between amateur filmmakers and those whom they filmed, and also of their occasional *slip of self-image*, whether directly to the camera or when unaware of being filmed. It also considers some pertinent analytical strategies that can challenge the fixed referential framework still defining a gender-related thematic narrative – an interpretative framework in which media scholars continue to anticipate women amateur filmmakers as having recorded primarily domestic – nature and nurture related topics – and educational subjects, in contrast to men who would have filmed the more momentous topics such as political, military, economic and high-culture (public rather than private) events, and would have also experimented with technology in a sustained and competitive way. As shown across various examples in this volume, this is not a lucrative framework especially since most women amateur filmmakers simultaneously challenged and advanced amateur filmmaking practice within networks of cultural production in which their films could never function just as mere substandard copies ('fakes') of those commonly made by their male peers; nor can women amateur film practitioners be held hostage to the perpetual role of an 'amateur' emulating certified visual narratives endorsed by men cine hobbyists and non-professional filmmakers.

Despite belonging to markedly different social classes, the British women amateur filmmakers discussed in this chapter shared a coherent visual approach, language and rhetoric that reveal most of the twentieth-century British culture and historical events in rigorous terms. Their films allow for new perspectives on British and Commonwealth gender and social dynamics, while simultaneously, as in a film developing process, *revealing* the filmmakers' roles as important producers. This is possible when challenging their prejudiced dismissal (the 'negative' image) as amateurs two times over – a judgement primed by their gender and choice of film genre. It is therefore the acknowledgement of their films as resourceful social statements that grants these women the overdue recognition (the 'positive' image) as valid memory and history documentarians (Figure 5.1).

The case studies selected on this occasion belong to three distinctive amateur film collections, each defined by different social and cultural networks: home movie scenes recorded by Queen Elizabeth II in the second half of the twentieth century, very short scenes filmed by Audrey Lewis in Kenya at the time of the Mau Mau Emergency, and a few scenes made by several women guests of Maharaja Vijaysinhji of Rajpipla in the mid-1930s.[4] The latter examples relate to a few instances when the film camera 'switched' hands and possibly gender perspectives – the maharaja allowed his guests to use his 16mm film camera. Each of these case studies offers a fertile ground for examining how the returned gaze of the subjects filmed, and the visual priming at work in each respective context, can help to gauge the filmmaker's gender in more nuanced ways than those allowed

Figure 5.1 Queen Elizabeth II operates her cine camera to film a tiger and rhino hunt from a wicker basket on the back of an elephant during the Royal State Tour of Nepal (1 February 1961). © Paul Popper/Popperfoto/Getty Images.

by an analysis of their choice of topics and themes. These case studies are also meant to buttress three strands of theoretical enquiry, namely issues of analysis, issues of interpretations and issues of diasporic identity.

First, issues of analysis posed by these case studies, and implicitly other examples discussed in this volume, relate to the central research topic: the role played by the filmmaker's gender in establishing the intrinsic visual narrative of the recorded scene. This surpasses the immediate assumption that women amateur filmmakers' choice of topics was usually the result of their specific social and narrative ghettos (read, networks) informing primarily domestic, educational, nursing and charitable activities. As women, they become a category of analysis against which they constantly negotiated their representations of self and of the world as cultural and ideological composites; moreover, their *by proxy* representation of the self – through the act of filming as a means of endorsing and renewing culture – confirms them as authentic agents of a shared, gendered history, one that can challenge and resist 'the totalising imperative of age-old "legitimate" and "scientific"' hegemonic discourses (Mohanty 1984: 334).

Second, issues of interpretation are addressed from various, interrelated perspectives that evaluate both the subject matter of a scene and the wider cultural context that encouraged or permitted British woman filmmakers to present their personal visual translations of it, hence singling out their own view out of the 'many correct views' about a specific gender and power hierarchy at any particular moment (White 1978). In other words, by filming a scene – creating a visual narrative – women amateur filmmakers instantaneously became its readers too and so they assigned to it, out of the interpretative 'void', a dual meaning: their personal understanding, and the future audience's infinite and simultaneously potential interpretations, though neither incorrect nor ultimate (Eco 1994). From this perspective, British women making amateur films *inside* male-dominated imperial and postcolonial visual cultures have negotiated constructions of power from the fringes of their gendered and gender-themed otherness. They did this not as cultural impersonators, but as frontrunners for new evaluations of Britain's recent history.

Third, issues of diasporic identity can feasibly be discussed in relation to all British women amateur filmmakers. This is a pertinent approach owing in particular to their filmmaking practice that has placed them at the intersection of historically variable economic, cultural and identity re-making processes. Whether making amateur ethno-travelogues while visiting different parts of the British Empire, or risking being killed during a night air raid just to secure a few colour film scenes of the Blitz, or courageously filming an all-women tragic mountaineering expedition, or showing the ludic side of royal officialdom, the women amateur filmmakers discussed in this book *migrated* from their prescribed social identities and roles towards the empowering role as culture-markers. Here, Avtar Brah's concept of 'diasporaspace' is best applied in relation to the 'confluence of narratives' identifiable across these women's individual collections of amateur films, and to the ways in which their choice of subjects and the ensuing visual dialogues, whether as an individual gaze or a group's response, produced a continual collective re-memory process (Brah 2003: 617).

Ludic Domesticity and Royal Family Matters

The hobby of amateur filmmaking ran in the family. It is claimed that King George VI and Queen Elizabeth made home movies, and often. Their two young daughters featured in most of their home movies. Later, their oldest daughter, Queen Elizabeth II, would also be known as a keen amateur filmmaker. Their combined film collection made on 16mm, 8mm, and Super 8mm must be of a considerable size, perhaps slightly bigger than the box half-filled with film reels, which Prince Charles unveiled in 2016 to the delight of a global audience watching the BBC documentary *Elizabeth at 90: A family tribute* (dir. John Bridcut, UK, 2016). The documentary, meant as a 'celebration of Queen Elizabeth II's ninetieth birthday', was based on 'unique access to Her Majesty's complete collection of cine-films' and announced that: '[T]he Queen makes history by discussing her own memories with Prince Charles as together they view this extraordinary footage.'[5] The latter claim is distinctively elating for anyone interested in new and nuanced details about the history of the British royal family – there could be no better access to an insider's view into royal matters. Watching the documentary does offer a few such perspectives, all mildly tinted with benevolent gossip and deadpan humour served at the fringes of this family's exceptional social backstage. However, most of the home movie scenes used in this documentary had not been filmed by Queen Elizabeth II, but by Prince Philip, Her Majesty's parents and other family members, or by commissioned cinematographers as in the case of her wedding to the Duke of Edinburgh on 20 November 1947, and of her Coronation as the monarch of the United Kingdom, Canada, Australia, New Zealand, South Africa, Pakistan and Ceylon on 2 June 1953. Understandably, neither of the amateur film scenes used in the BBC documentary pose any risk of controversy as has been the case with the archival footage that littered British tabloid front pages in 2015 with images of Princess Elizabeth, then six or seven years old, giving the Nazi salute to the camera. The images belonged to what appears to have been one of her father's home movies made in 1933 or 1934 at the Balmoral Castle in Scotland.[6] Perhaps the images that made the Queen somewhat uncomfortable while 'making history' by watching and commenting on archival (royal) family films were those in which she is seen leading an indefatigable pillow fight against her mother's then private secretary, Arthur Penn. 'This is frightfully unkind', the Queen comments while watching the black and white home movie footage before adding 'I don't think the corgi is enjoying it very much', to which Prince Charles responds 'No, the corgi certainly isn't.' Following a few more similar scenes, the Queen concludes 'It really is rough stuff, isn't it?! Extraordinary.' There are many feasible interpretations of this uncanny instance of *Gogglebox*-like royal reality show,[7] in which the return-of-the-gaze is not addressed to the filmmaker, though the pillow fight was particularly fun to perform for the camera, but a gaze returned onto oneself across decades, onto a past-self at a time when gender was not yet a role.

Based on what appears to be the Queen's own home movies in *Elizabeth at 90* – filmed by her, rather than by other members of the royal family – it is possible to argue that the key narrative of her amateur filmmaking is anchored in the visual morphology evident in scenes showing her immediate personal environment – a choice for expressing ludic freedom. This hypothesis is supported, for instance, by two short, albeit rich in content, sequences. The first sequence shows Princes Andrew and Edward as young children playing in the garden at Buckingham Palace and with several corgis in attendance. These images have been filmed in colour, like most of the Queen's home movies, and include lengthy panoramic views of the estate saturated in a beautiful autumnal light, with the children picking up dead leaves, playing with the dogs and running. These scenes confirm the Queen's talent as a visual story-teller with a sharp sense of colour, light, and composition. For instance, Edward's bright red pullover and wellingtons puncture the rusted golds and greens of the landscape. On viewing these images during the making of the *Elizabeth at 90* documentary, the Queen commented that '[w]e were allowed to rake the leaves and put them in the [garden cart]'. Beside the indication of having been granted permission to rake dead leaves, this recollection would suggest at first glance nothing more than a group of people ambling and playing in a garden in late autumn. But there is a visual twist – an unexpected change in narrative that makes this home movie about family life and seasonal mundane activities function outside canonical iconography, whether compared to similar working class or royal amateur films. We see Prince Edward, the youngest boy, sucking his thumb while nestled up to his chin in dead leaves – his cradle is the garden cart. There are several close-up shots of him – a blond, blue-eyed boy diligently watching his mother's *gaze-camera* while at the edge of the frame corgis are seen patrolling around the garden cart. Then, Prince Andrew takes centre stage, burying himself underneath dead leaves until he can pose just like his younger brother. Edward remains undisturbed – 'busily sucking his thumb' – while their faces are now framed by the leaves like in a *lived-in* portrait.

A similar cine framing game designed by the Queen, and perhaps more striking in its visual effect, is found in another sequence. This time, the scenes were filmed at Holkham Beach in Norfolk, England, and show first a young Prince Charles jumping from one sand dune to another. During the viewing-cum-interview under the direction of John Bridcut, the Queen was quick to confirm to Prince Charles that '[i]n those days you didn't mind the prickly grass'. The next scenes in this sequence have recently become the poster image for most journalists mentioning the Queen's home movies: a patch of fine sand and wispy grass form the visual frame as well as the background for a three-character scene: a corgi sitting in between two children's heads. The corgi displays what dog owners would recognise as their pet's unflinchingly non-judgemental patience. The children, Prince Charles and Princess Anne, are alive with laughter but scarcely able to move their heads: they have been both firmly buried in the sand – their bodies trapped in the game. In the documentary, Prince Charles chuckles when watching this scene and says '*That* I remember. Feeling you were never going to get out' (emphasis added). The Queen continued to film them while they tried to move their shoulders, barely dislocating the sand. The images are striking and journalists should be forgiven for using this scene as a visual currency, especially when Prince Charles points at the massive plasma screen on which he and the Queen were watching the film and exclaims 'It's such a good photograph . . ., isn't it?!' The image and presumably the memory of it too. The Queen pans over his remark, not disrespectfully but rather concerned: 'He [the corgi] doesn't think that's funny at all.' A few images later, the scene hasn't changed too much: the children are still buried neck-deep in the sand, the corgi is still sitting in-between their heads until at some point, muzzle pointing slightly upwards, he senses movement from underneath. The children are finally determined to escape. 'The sand starts to move', says the Queen. 'It's revolting!' teases Prince Charles.

Princess Anne, when watching the next scenes showing her and her brother struggling, unsmilingly, to unearth themselves, concluded: 'Old jokes are the best, aren't they, really?' before adding, deadpan, 'I wonder if you'd get away with burying your children nowadays.' She pauses briefly, crosses her arms, looks at the screen again, tilts her head backwards, and then gives a discreet rhetorical smile. Leaving aside the visual and verbal details quilted in this documentary sequence, and which would support successfully a comprehensive cross-exercise in psychoanalysis and media studies, the most valuable narrative feature found in the sequences filmed by the Queen in the garden at Buckingham Palace and at Holkham Beach relates to the way in which she chose to portray her children. Her manner of filming – framing, staging, the length of each scene, unrestrained in its playfulness, even when slightly challenging the limits of prescribed safety – is unconventional, progressive even when compared with the mainstream narrative found in most home movies, whether made by men or women, and showing children at play.[8]

Paradoxically, the manner in which the Queen has staged these sequences invites a dialogue between a mother's cine gaze and her children's engagement with it; a direct communication rather than the usual children-at-play performance for the camera – her own pillow fight for King George VI's home movie being a case in point. Most parents filming their children, whether in the 1930s or in the 1960s – to keep to the timeframe relevant to the archival footage used *in Elizabeth at 90* – would have opted for orderly and ceremonial dress codes, good behaviours, and conventional social contexts such as birthday parties, holidays or school festivities, all events which would have highlighted their children's talents and validate their social suitability. The great majority of home movies from this period subscribe to this storyline code. It is in this framework that most of the Queen's home movies made in the 1950s and 1960s dislocate the narrative canon by adding a vigorous and surprising sense of nonconformity. In the case of her amateur film collection, representations of familial playfulness, whether deliberate or involuntary, contradict and humorously challenge popular expectations for stereotypical (culturally suitable?) depictions of royal childhoods.

In a chapter that aims to deal mainly with films made by women amateur filmmakers across the British Empire and the Commonwealth, and with their portrayal of imperial and postcolonial class and gender hierarchies, it could come as a surprise to read an extended analysis of some of Queen Elizabeth II's home movies showing her children in various locations across Great Britain. The reasons for this choice are threefold. First, amateur footage filmed by the Queen of imperial outposts and events is particularly hard to identify in the selection provided by John Bridcut for *Elizabeth at 90* – an exceptional source for researching amateur films belonging to the British royal family – although there are numerous allusions to their existence such as when a newsreel documenting the Queen's and the Duke of Edinburgh's first visit to India and Pakistan announces '[i]n the Fortress Stadium of the Lahore Cantonment was held Pakistan's National Horse and Cattle Show . . . Pictures of the show and much else of the royal tour will provide home movies for the Queen's children' (see the image on the front cover of this book)[9] – an indirect suggestion that the Queen could essentially *produce* for her children a home-movie-illustrated-book in the tradition of Harry Golding's *Wonder Book of Empire*. Similar public or private statements are very difficult to match with certified amateur footage taken by the Queen, especially when they are mixed in with scenes of the Queen either filming, photographing or attending various official ceremonies and events. It is also mentioned in the documentary that both the Queen and Prince Philip shared an interest in amateur filmmaking and so they must have occasionally also shared film cameras and even the odd film reel.[10] Second, the Queens' collection of amateur films is justifiably a unique research source and access to it is currently available only through validated media and research channels.[11] Third, the aim of this chapter, and of the book in general, is to identify the ways in which British women amateur filmmakers produced visual narratives about national, imperial and postcolonial identities in the twentieth and early twenty-first centuries. Therefore, issues of gender and class are interpreted in this context as the cornerstones of their visual discourses. It is from this perspective that Queen Elizabeth II's home movies are compelling visual testimonials about discourses of gender identity and class status, and which might affect (or not, as discussed here) the ways in which imperial and postcolonial autobiographical visual accounts can be historically negotiated. Importantly, in the absence of reliable access to the Queen's colonial and postcolonial footage, it becomes imperative to compare her home movies of domestic and leisure times with newsreels and other peoples' colonial amateur films showing her imperial tours and special visits.[12] And, equally important, is the comparative framework in which official visual records portraying Queen Elizabeth II and Prince Philip in a symbolic contrary-to-custom gender hierarchy (Figure 5.2) are discussed in relation to home movies made by the Queen in which this hierarchy is restored across short scenes of visual intimacy. This way, it is then possible to start deciphering how the Queen, arguably the architype of British female identity, might have used images to express or to seek 'any knew knowledge about herself', as did most other British women amateur filmmakers through their own visual records (Smith and Watson 1998: 23).

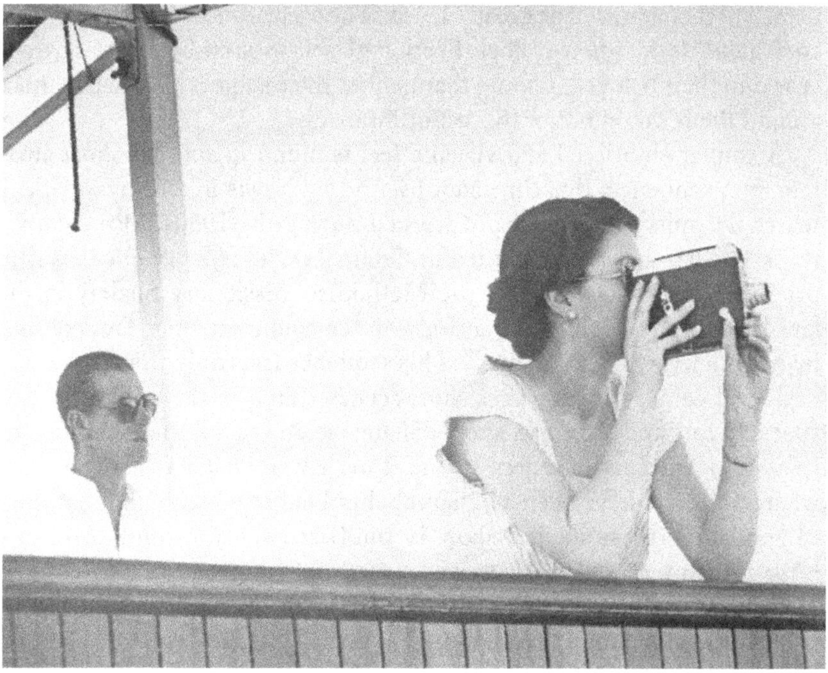

Figure 5.2 The Queen films the arrival of the escort ship HMNZS *Black Prince*, while in the South Pacific en route to Fiji, aboard the SS *Gothic* during the coronation world tour (11 December 1953). © Hulton Archive/Getty Images.

Two colour scenes, each showing men filmed from a distance and allegedly without their knowledge, offer a valid example of the visual syntax shared by the Queen and another British woman amateur filmmakers. These film scenes have been made sometime in the late 1940s and early 1950s, each lasting only a few seconds. The scene from the Queen's amateur film collection shows the Duke of Edinburgh standing in a garden some time during their South Australian tour. The Queen filmed him from a short distance, in medium shot and from profile. The Duke of Edinburgh (later Prince Philip) – sunglasses on, white shirt unbuttoned at the top and both hands dug into his grey suit trousers' pockets – is 'framed' as a glamorous, solitary, independent and deep-in-thought man. He resembles a male cinema star, a romantic one. In this case, there is no return-of-the-gaze that could confirm either their (emotional) relationship or a possible gender classification. Instead, this is confirmed by the Queen's choice in making his cine portrait – through framing and the brevity of the scene – as if it were a stolen image, and by the almost tactile emotional charge invested in this scene. This is a very short portrait of a man, whether admired or greatly loved. The scene functions as a cine gaze equivalent to the intense albeit fleeting glance speared by lovers across a crowd to their beloved, hoping that neither their subject of love nor those around them would notice this act of intimacy.

A similar emotional and visual effect is found in another short amateur film sequence, this time shot by Audrey Lewis in a Kenyan village where her missionary husband worked during the 1950s.[13] Predictably, this scene has not been included in the final cut of *African Eden* – a film produced and distributed by the Methodist Missionary Society in the late 1950s, and which relied entirely on the colour amateur footage shot by Mrs Lewis while in Kenya.[14] This sequence lasts only thirty-one seconds and comprises four very short scenes edited in the camera. It was shot in a forested area, at a short distance from several thatched huts of (possibly) Wakapomo elders in the Tana River District. Filmed from what appears to have been a hideout behind tall shrubs, though not fully camouflaged, these images show in the first twenty seconds Audrey's husband, Reverend Ian W. Lewis, sitting on the ground, shirtless and wearing a pair of khaki shorts. With his arms crossed, he first listens to the local elders and then addresses them at length – their interaction is marked by their well-matched hand gestures, hence the assumption about the dynamic of their interaction. At the end, Rev. Lewis stands up, adjusts his trousers around his hips, stretches his back and leaves the meeting. The following eleven seconds in these sequence were filmed from the same angle but from further back from the initial hideout post as if to mask even better the filmmaker's presence. It shows a similar scene in which Rev. Lewis, wearing again just his khaki shorts, sits on the ground and listens to a young African man telling him something of importance – his body language is determined and passionate. During this short sequence, the men never look in the direction of the filmmaker – a detail that, together with the distance and the angle chosen by Audrey Lewis when recording these meetings, gives the viewer a faultless sense of double voyeurism. First, by becoming an accomplice to her *stealing* – capturing, hunting – moving images of a men-only meeting. Second, by experiencing that moment instantaneously and *by proxy*, through her gaze. This four-part sequence, as well as the Queen's surreptitious portrait of the Duke of Edinburgh, exemplify what visual anthropologists define as the imbedding of time in an image such that the audiences 'see the world with the gaze of another, a past gaze', which during the viewing process 'it could also be [the audience's] present gaze' (Belting 2014: 154). In the case of these two sequences, the implicit anthropological discourse is centred not on what is shown, but on how it is shown such that the viewer learns more about the filmmakers than about the subject of their films.

This exercise in scopophilia confirms Laura Mulvey's call for a radical '[16mm, etc.] alternative cinema' but also turns the tables on her theorising of the male gaze – ultimately, still valid across the mainstream cinema – as the source of the women's 'to-be-looked-at-ness' identity (Mulvey 1975). These two examples of footage recorded by British amateur filmmakers place the male subjects at the centre of the visual narratives as their subjects of desire, whether from romantic or professional perspectives. Romantic, because of the known marital relationship between the filmmakers and the men. Professional, chiefly in Audrey Lewis' case since, although trained as a missionary like her husband, she was nevertheless denied access to contexts where evangelical agendas did not yet overwrite gender prohibitive hierarchies. In return, Audrey filmed *her* man next to *his* African male peers and thus made them all *her* subjects. A similar example of image-body cine territoriality albeit fictionalised is found in the TV drama series *The Crown* (UK, Netflix, since 2016), in a short sequence in series one, episode two – 'Hyde Park Corner'. It shows at first a newly-wedded Princess Elizabeth, and future Queen Elizabeth II, filming wildlife at night from the top of a savannah-style hut propped on stilts. The next scenes show her filming again, at dawn and aiming her camera not at elephants, hippopotamuses and giraffes drinking from a water pool, but at her husband who is seen sleeping naked on their bed, face down and head turned away. This time, poetic licence has been lavishly employed in describing a boudoir scene in which the young woman amateur filmmaker, wearing only a see-through white shirt – camera held high up as if it were her own gaze – slowly approaches the bed while *filming-hunting* images of her man within the safety of his unawareness. The erotic contemplation experienced by the fictional filmmaker alongside the audience is provoked, again, by a male body.

As in the case of the Queen's amateur footage of the Duke of Edinburgh and of Audrey Lewis' scene of her husband, the male body disrupts the popular visual (media) representations and the 'sexual imbalances' of the active/male and passive/female scopophillic hierarchies (Mulvey 1975). Moreover, the Queen and Mrs Lewis have challenged (perhaps involuntary) the visual priming at work across traditional construction of gender by briefly counteracting recurrent male representations of power through dominant, enviable and unnegotiable iconicity with clandestine snapshots of eroticised male vulnerability. This is a vulnerability implied by the men's unawareness of being exposed to, and visually *consumed* by, their wives' cine gazes. In these instances, both women amateur filmmakers – representatives of two far-apart British worlds – have made history by acting as agents of a shared exercise in reconstituting gender in two different imperial spaces – South Australia and Kenya – and identical timeframes. Both have filmed their husbands in the early years of their marriages, when their contemplation of the object of their desire defined their men's identities outside and against the normative constructions of imperial or early postcolonial masculinity.

Be a Man, Strike a Pose!

At the beginning of the twentieth century, Western women were encouraged to get 'out of the gardens, out of idleness, out of ignorance, and into wisdom, service and adventure' (Vicinus 1985: 1). Moreover, historians of colonial women's ethno-travel accounts and imperial autobiographies remark on the recurrent theme of the social freedom British (and other European) women experienced while living in colonial societies – contexts that allegedly allowed them to challenge and even escape 'some of the constraints of the British society' of their times (Mills 1996: 129). However, British colonial amateur films made between the late 1920s and early 1950s regularly showed women as symbols of a life of leisure, whether attending entertaining or ceremonial social events, riding horses, hunting and posing triumphantly next to the(ir) kill, playing with children (but mostly with dogs), visiting famous archaeological sites or dining with local nobility. Importantly, most British women appearing in colonial amateur films, unless they were missionaries, nurses or teachers, are regularly shown posing with multitudes of flowers in bloom and hence 'placed' back into the garden – back within the traditional femininity reference codes of social and gender markers: signalling beauty in themselves or by association, decorative, precious, poetically inclined, and passive par excellence. This visual protocol is found in most colonial amateur films, irrespective of whether the films were made by women or men. Lady Kendall filmed her daughters, Nancy and Barbara, in their large rose garden in Allahabad; Rosie Newman never had to worry about securing vast amounts of (expensive) colour footage used in lengthy, detailed scenes of luxuriant flowers which she filmed throughout her extensive international travels; and, ultimately, most colonial amateur filmmakers would have not denied themselves the chance to use the last few feet at the end of a film reel just to record, one more time, their gardens or potted flowers placed at the entrance of their South Asian, African or Australian homes.

Maharaja Vijaysinhji of Rajpipla also filmed women in gardens, mostly European women. He recorded innumerable garden scenes across beautifully landscaped English gardens surrounding his twenty-seven-room Victorian mansion at Old Windsor, Berkshire, or in the grounds of his princely palace in India. His visual appetite for depicting garden scenes, and his perceptive care in selecting details for his close-up shots of flowers, recalls that of Mary Moser – the famous eighteen-century English floral painter, and one of the only two women artists, alongside Angelica Kauffmann, to be a founding member of the Royal Academy in 1768. In the imperial context, commonly 'perceived as a fundamentally masculine enterprise' (Levine 2004: 137), the maharaja's fondness for highly decorative topics would have placed his artistic style within a more feminine imagery-kinship, hence granting a dual amateurship to his film-making practice. However, a particularly long sequence that he filmed in the late 1930s exempts him from this association, as discussed below, and grants him full ownership of the traditionally dominant male gaze. With only a few exceptions, all his amateur films have been shot in colour and so there is no shortage of copiously vibrant colours and of clusters of flowers in bloom across all seasons. There is also no shortage of women posing in his films either: all young and all obliging when helping him record their cine portraits, whether by standing self-consciously next to tall shrubs in bloom, dancing for him with undulating suggestive gestures bordering playful lustfulness, or point blank embarrassed – all recalling Barthes' remark on the act of 'posing' in front of a photographic (or film) camera.[15] Importantly, none of these compliant women was South Asian. They were all British, or, to be precise, Scottish, like his favourite cine subject who later become his last wife – Ella Atherton, the future H. H. Maharani Ella Devi Sahiba. The maharaja's ad hoc cinematographic garden enactments were performed by women with an almost translucent fair skin, rusty-red or platinum blonde hair, and with a pitch-perfect Hollywood-like diva presence, their cine portraits ultimately defining the iconography of a portable, cinematographic harem.

A man of superlative wealth, Maharaja Vijaysinhji of Rajpipla was also an innovator in agricultural, transport and irrigation infrastructures across Rajpipla State, a keen reformer of his state's educational infrastructure and a committed investor in innovative wealth programmes. He was also a renowned dandy, a talented polo player, a bettor envied for his flair when enlisting wining horses in competitions such as the Irish Derby in 1926 and the Epsom Derby of England in 1934, and a vocal patriot – Rajpipla State was among the first Indian princely states to join the newly created Indian sovereign state in 1948. Most official visual records of him testify to these roles, whether subscribing to tabloid or official narratives. However, his amateur films made in the 1930s reveal a man of different mores and interests. This becomes evident in his series of garden scenes, which can be divided in two sets. The first set was filmed by the maharaja himself with the precise patience of an artist making micro-sculptures: each female body is inspected with the help of medium and close-up shots, from a variety of angles; the women subjected to this visual taxidermy are often shown as unique objects of scopophilic scrutiny, surrounded by extravagantly beautiful clusters of flowers, or as part of an all-women dancing scene, flirtatiously offering their cine vignettes to the camera as when cutting curls from each other's hair, or lifting their skirts to show their undergarments while lounging in the middle of opulent gardens. Sometimes the maharaja's European guests also wore expensive saris, with one of them attempting a more dynamic engagement with the camera by performing a few vaudeville steps while draped in a beautiful yellow sari. Unsurprisingly, the peerless cine star of his films was Ella – his cinematographic 'Barbie' judging by the varied instances in which she had to pose, act, pretend to ignore the camera – allowing for his staged exercise in voyeurism – or catwalk parade in exquisite dresses, including the time when she wore a sari during their trip to Biarritz in the mid-1930s. Less frequent, but nevertheless well framed, lengthy and carefully composed, are detailed scenes recorded by the maharaja of some of the women's D-cup brassieres, or of their generous smiles framed by freshly applied bright-red lipstick. Without exception, all the European women filmed by him performed for the camera. They did not opt for the studio-photograph traditional posture as did all his Indian female guests. This rushed review of the ways in which the maharaja filmed his female companions becomes relevant when discussing the handful of his cine portraits made by some of his female guests. One of his sequences filmed in a garden acquires particular meaning – it shows at length a young British woman performing under his direction various postures while relying on a changing wardrobe. The woman is very young and somewhat overweight – at least, in comparison with his other British female guests/film subjects who could have modelled successfully for reputable fashion designers. During their filming session, she gradually gathers the courage to pose in a more sexually suggestive manner and, although not entirely at ease, she lets her outfits be changed from a simple, neat dress to a one-piece swimsuit and, finally, to beautiful veil-robes which soon become irrelevant. He filmed her from various angles and in several corners of his garden: standing, sitting, lounging, or leaning on one elbow, head tilted, gaze thrown directly at the camera, albeit somewhat bewilderedly and self-consciously. Her posing is almost mechanical, suggesting that all her gestures were the result of instructions – how to stand, how to look provocatively over the shoulder, how to stare contemplatively at some horizon line, how to move, how to perform a back stand exercise,[16] and how to show her bare breasts. The young woman performed her gender for the camera, not with complete indignity but with an assumed sexuality that, traditionally, would have been 'held to be her responsibility, her shame' (Millett 1973: 862). In sum, this long sequence offers a rare example of colonial (amateur) softcore erotica filmmaking.[17] Most often, constructions of gender are not only performative acts specific to contextualised ideological morphologies but also vectors of gender agency with individuals able to simultaneously perform and interpret their performance 'in order to insert him/herself into them' (Smith 1988: xxxiv–xxxv). In the case of this sequence, the woman's returned gaze and the maharaja's style for staging and framing her cine portraits imply a response to a predatory gaze and, within a traditional reading of twentieth-century mainstream cinema, authenticate the filmmaker's gender.[18] This sequence, however, acquires a new meaning when analysed in comparison with the very few and frustratingly brief scenes in which Maharaja Vijaysinhji of Rajpipla has been filmed by some of his British female friends. On these occasions, the return-of-the-gaze and the gender hierarchy became more nuanced and possibly equally aggressive. From visual and social anthropological perspectives, an image is 'the result of personal or collective knowledge and intention', thus leading to the hypothesis that it is always crucial to identify the subtle shifts in people's self-representations in front of a camera, especially when their visual (cine)-portraits reveal social insecurities (Belting 2014: 9–10).

Once again, Lavaud's claim that individuals, whether scholars or the general public, always deal with 'systems of viewing' (*systèmes de regard*) rather than with systems of images, ties in two points of perception and analysis. First, how did the people being filmed anticipate their visual (cinematographic) portraits and consequently staged them to fit pre-existing visual norms? Second, how does the constantly renewed audience of any visual portrait – the recipient's (*destinataire*) initiative to decode an image – whom Umberto Eco defined as the ultimate creator of historical meaning to a text/image (Eco 1994) – reconstruct gender within renewed cultural settings? Possible answers are found in the few short amateur film scenes showing the maharaja returning his gaze to the British women filming him – these scenes complete his visual and social portrait in greater detail by revealing significant details about his gender identity; details beyond his control. For instance, the longest of these scenes – it lasts almost seventeen seconds – presents him as a shy, tense and somewhat embarrassed man who ultimately chooses an abrasive exit from *under* the woman's cine gaze.

Maharaja Vijaysinhji of Rajpipla's brief and awkward cine portraits were filmed by his female companions or by his friends' wives, each scene lasting around five or six seconds. They show him, for instance, sunk up to his elbows in various armchairs while attending garden parties or taking tea with friends in England and India, sporting a cigar with perfected dandy-type allure while standing on the deck of an ocean linear, and smiling proudly next to his future Scottish wife while visiting the New York World's Fair in 1939. While most of these occasions only required him to pose briefly for the camera, three scenes filmed by his guest women amateur filmmakers indicate that occasionally he took part, somewhat willingly, in a filming game. While not entirely at ease, he appears to have indulged in this temporary reversal of dominant cine gazes and so he lent his film camera to two of the women whom he filmed in his gardens: twice to Ella and once to an unidentified British woman. The latter opted for his close-up shot cine portrait filmed against opulent clusters of red flowers – this time, the osteoma on his forehead, already visible in some previous short scenes, seems larger and so it anchors the viewer's gaze and might have possibly determined the woman's choice of framing too. In this scene, the maharaja appears to be engaging with the camera but it remains unclear whether his smile is just a squinting grimace against the blinding sun or part of a candid visual dialogue with her – at some point, he even turns his head such that she could film his profile in an involuntary exercise in anthropometric photography of a colonial and gender subject. The short sequences filmed by Ella are substantially more revealing of his behaviour in front of the camera. In the first sequence – as per the archival listing rather than what might have been the original chronology of the footage – after having posed at length for the maharaja in a rose garden, Ella was given the 16mm camera to film him in the same context: framed by a stone wall and at the top of a flight of steps. During the first seconds of this scene, the maharaja smiles affectionately at the camera while resting right hand on the stone wall and keeping his left one tucked in his trousers' pocket. To date, and based on the archival footage held by the Bristol Archives, this is the only instance in which the maharaja strikes a pose and performs, albeit briefly, for the camera. A second and a half later, he starts walking towards Ella whose grip on the camera wavers – the filming stops abruptly after recording just a few last frames of his face in close-up. When the filming resumed, the maharaja is shown standing once again at the top of the stone steps but this time displaying a fixed smile, his body trapped in a rigid pose. Moreover, following what seems to have been

Ella's directorial instructions regarding a proper pose for his cine portrait, he adjusted his crew neck sweater, especially the collar. By accepting Ella's recommendations – whether because he credited her expert opinion as a film actress, or as a result of his affection for her – he allowed her to visually construct and present his portrait. Each of the two scenes that form this sequence lasts a few seconds only, with the maharaja quickly aborting each state of his cine dialogue (game) and his candid or staged poses for Ella's film camera.

The second sequence filmed by Ella took place in a public park, possibly in Europe. Once again, the camera changed hands to secure a twin cine portrait: first Ella's, filmed by the maharaja with vertical camera movements starting at the tip of her shoes and moving slowly upwards until framing her face; then the maharaja's – a cine portrait filmed by Ella while he first sat then stood next to the same rock on which she sat minutes before. While being filmed sitting on the rock (on which Ella had left her black clutch bag), the maharaja displays signs of discomfort – he fidgets, looks ill at ease and unsure of his posture. Self-aware, he then suddenly stands up only to be even more uncomfortable, rubbing his hands between half-finished gestures, briefly digging deep into his trousers' pockets or tugging out his pocket silk handkerchief and then immediately cramming it back in. To most viewers, his discomfort is almost palpable, which makes Ella's persistent and steady-hand filming function an act of unexpected aggressive visual scrutiny.

In these two brief sequences, while centre stage and failing to make his gestures match the image of a man of the world, or at least that of a man engaged in an affectionate exchange of gazes with his lover, Maharaja Vijaysinhji of Rajpipla performed his masculinity from the margins of a new gender dynamics – one created by placing his film camera in the hands of his guest women amateur filmmakers as if it were an extension of their inquisitive identity review. Thus, he empowered their cine voyeurism at the expense of his own image. In this case, once again, it is the returned gaze of the person being filmed that indicates the gender of the filmmaker: the subject's self-image insecurities highlight the women filmmakers' prerogative to assess and reveal, through the act of recording, whether the man in front of their camera–gaze merits a to-be-looked-at-ness identity. The maharaja negotiated his constructions of power in these brief scenes from the peripheries of his temporary gendered otherness and, consequently, he became a 'function' of the self-images he created rather than an 'illustration' of his official prestige and awareness of nuanced social conventions (Flusser 2006: 10). Rather than concluding on this note, and should it be possible in terms of archival information, one last key stage in the analysis of the maharaja's cine portraits would need to consider the ways in which Maharaja Vijaysinhji of Rajpipla might have behaved in front of the camera had he been filmed by men instead of his own subjects of erotic contemplation.

Conclusion

This chapter has attempted to address the ways in which British women amateur filmmaking practice has allowed them access to a different type of freedom of expression and documentation while experiencing various colonial settings, including social contexts that remained inaccessible to men as in, for instance, the traditional wedding ceremonies filmed by Lady Dalyell (see Chapter 3) and which remain one of the rare, if not unique, cinematographic counterparts to some of the mental images proposed by female colonial travellers when describing in their diaries exceptional visits to harems. Moreover, women using their cine cameras to map the well-guarded spaces of imperial male identity re-gendered the colonial space as seen in Ella Atherton's short cine portraits of her future husband, Maharaja Vijaysinhji of Rajpipla. A fine-tuned analysis of the gestural behaviours and the return-of-the-gaze of the men whose cine portraits were made by colonial women amateur filmmakers will continue to present a rich resource and an open invitation to media scholars and historians to use such visual manuscripts as reliable tools in challenging various limits of interpretations, and to forge new lines of investigation across disciplines such as perception studies, cultural anthropology or the politics of gender representation and self-presentation. Finally, some of the British women amateur filmmakers' footage, recorded outside publicly consumed and commissioned visual records – empire cinema productions, documentaries, newsreels and so on – but inside colonial domesticity and tight social networks, often succeeded in challenging and even reversing conventional imperial gender hierarchies.

Notes

1. For a discussion of how it is possible, or not, to decode amateur filmmakers' gender based on their subjects' returned gaze in amateur/new media semi-professional production, see Erika Lust's and Holly Randall's films presented in 'Women on Top' (episode one, series one, Netflix series *Hot Girls Wanted: Turned On*, 2017).
2. See also Motrescu-Mayes (2005; 2007; 2008; 2009; 2010; 2011; 2012).
3. Original French, *systèmes de regard*.

4. The Rajpipla Collection (Accession numbers 2007/132/001–010) is currently held by the Bristol Archives. The collection has been initially donated by Princess Premila Rajpipla to the former British Empire & Commonwealth Museum in 2007.
5. *Elizabeth at 90: A family tribute, documentary film*, director John Bridcut, BBC, UK, 2016. DVD back-cover summary.
6. The incident was covered extensively by the press and prompted a wide political and ethical controversy among historians and journalists. See, for instance, Hughes (2015) and Halliday (2015).
7. *Gogglebox* is a British reality show launched in 2013 and produced by Studio Lambert for Channel 4. The format and narrative storyline offer vast – its tenth season was broadcast in 2017 – and rich research avenues for scholars exploring the simultaneous circularity of a returned gaze: the (TV/online) viewer is watching groups of people watching and commenting about various TV shows.
8. See Kay (2016). Stills and a few short clips from *Elizabeth at 90*, including the two scenes discussed here, are available at <http://www.dailymail.co.uk/news/article-3555139/Candid-footage-taken-Queen-offers-magical-insight-royals-pillow-fighting-horsing-holiday-sliding-deck-beloved-royal-yacht.html> (last accessed 3 May 2016).
9. *Queen in Lahore, 1961*, British Pathé Ltd, <https://www.britishpathe.com/video/queen-in-lahore> (last accessed 2 September 2017).
10. This invites another research project, provided there is access to the films alongside accurate background information.
11. See, for instance, Urbach (2015).
12. See Lury (2016) for a discussion of amateur filmmaking practice in relation to specific community-performance protocols (impersonations, school children parades, make-believe queens) employed in constructing visual representations of the British monarchy.
13. For additional information about Mrs Audrey Lewis' life and work in Britain and in Kenya see, for instance, 'After the War, 1946–1958', <http://www.bbc.co.uk/history/ww2peopleswar/stories/61/a5234861.shtml> (last accessed 2 March 2017).
14. The former British Empire & Commonwealth Museum held a copy of most of the amateur films made by Audrey Lewis as well as a VHS copy of *African Eden* (Accession number 2005/013/001). This material is now held by the Bristol Archives. Copies of these films are also held by the Yorkshire Film Archive. Of note, the information presented on the Colonial Film website misidentified the filmmaker/photographer of *African Eden* as Rev. Ian W. Lewis (<http://www.colonialfilm.org.uk/node/4065>, last accessed 3 June 2017).
15. 'Now, once I feel myself observed by the lens, everything changes: I constitute myself in the process of "posing", I instantly make another body for myself, I transform myself in advance into an image. This transformation is an active one: I feel that the photograph creates my body or mortifies it, according to its caprice' (Barthes 2000: 10–11).

16. A postgraduate history student, seeing this sequence during the author's lecture on 'Visual anthropological perspectives on South Asian history' (Michaelmas term 2016), commented that the slow development of the scenes, from a decorative mode to an erotic one, 'turned up the creep-factor'.
17. It is possible that the few (outdoor) nude scenes of Hedy Lamarr in Gustav Machatý's controversial *Ecstasy* (Czechoslovakia, 1933) might have been a visual prompter for the maharaja and possibly other male amateur filmmakers in the 1930s and later.
18. An uncanny contemporary counter-narrative is found in Claude Cahun's sexually rhetorical self-portraits made in the late 1930s – she posed using props ranging from live Siamese cats held in between her bare legs, spider web masks, tiger plush toys or large leaves that covered her naked body. The returned gaze in the case of her photographs is equally predatory whether subscribing to the surrealist or feminist visual literacy.

CHAPTER 6
Teacher Filmmakers

> Thirty-one children; Thirty-one chances. Thirty-one futures, our futures . . . Everything they become, I also become. And everything about me they helped to create. (Codell 2001)

Esmé Raji Codell (2001: 194) writing about her first year of teaching in a Chicago elementary school in 2001, captured her acute sense of how personal and professional subjectivities intersect. This close connection is not unique to newly qualified teachers; for many teachers it is part of classroom relationships that combine authority, agency and emotion as aptly summarised by Deborah Britzman's words, 'We are affected by the worlds we affect' (2006: xi). Such reminders sensitise us to the expectations, experience and awareness embedded within cine films made by teachers in the past. Not only did those professionals have to negotiate their own roles with their pupils and colleagues: the opinions of parents and other people, social attitudes and past stereotypes all contribute to teacher identity. From the early and middle part of the last century, whether college trained or advancing from pupil-teacher status in their own local school, being a paid woman professional challenged gender norms and expectations. For the women in this chapter – and referred to elsewhere – filmmaking was part of how they navigated their sense of selfhood in settings where the contradictions of tradition and modernity coexisted.

Throughout the history of amateur cinema, some women filmmakers have been teachers. They made films during school holidays, encouraged others to make and enjoy films, and filmed where they worked. Public fears and policy shifts on child protection have greatly reduced informal filming in schools even for parents, but for much of the last century, teachers had unrestricted access to recording their pupils.[1] Outside academia, such scenes of past school life have popular appeal as unproblematic visual connectives to aspects of childhood and growing up. Public appetite for such materials' immediacy and connections to past memories often pays scant attention to the person in charge of the camera.[2] Shifting attention to the filmmakers, however, discloses interests in recording in and away from the classroom that, for some women, became key features of their own visual practice, reputation and identity. This chapter explores how some women teachers responded to the visual opportunities offered by moving imagery and produced films sometimes discussed too narrowly as nostalgic reverie (Chalfren, 1987: 75; Ishizuka and Zimmermann 2008; Niemeyer 2014).

Although some teachers were active within IAC circles (Chapter 2) and animation also attracted some teachers (Chapter 8), other cine users thrived as they made and showed films independently. Even when they were connected with a local cine group, they were largely self-sufficient in how they made and showed their films about school and other interests. Couples with shared film and teaching interests are therefore not considered. Films made by pupils with or independently from their teachers are similarly excluded.[3] Teachers' solo filmmaking, as discussed here, reveals identities and subjectivities as well as relationships to external events and change. Varied archival sources and oral testimonies, including comments from relatives, friends and pupils who remember them, offer insights into filmmaking, working and social contexts that span over seventy years.

Filming at School

For decades Britain's state and private schools offered accessible subject matter for amateur filmmakers that found ready audiences among colleagues and parents. Validated as legitimate topics by a tradition of documentaries on educational reform, children's welfare, social policy and state provision (Low 1979) teachers' films expressed their strong affiliation with their work as well as attachment to and professional interest for the children in their care. School life was, for many, an integral part of their own lives. Sharing film imagery had an immediacy and mutuality that was rooted in ties of locality, proximity and recognition. Older pupils often enjoyed seeing each other filmed during lessons, educational visits or playing sport: for some watching themselves on screen might be a memorable moment or self-conscious spectacle; for others, there was less overt response to becoming part of a teacher's film. As when framed on family films, some younger children became so accustomed to being on camera that their apparent self-absorbed natural play became part of why showing and watching school-related cine film had such appeal.

Education was such an important arena in which aspirations about societal success played out that visual evidence of children's industriousness, ability and relationships with each other was welcomed by parents, teachers and community leaders alike (Jackson 1991: 168–238). Teachers' films of children and young people engaged in purposeful pursuits, like those made by professional production teams, helped to validate successive educational reforms that kept children at school longer, introduced different curricula and reorganised school provision (Todd 2005: 69–70). For working class parents who rarely went beyond the gates, such films gave reassurance that their children were making progress and preparing for later life. For decades, encouraged by the hobby press, teachers offered such visual proof from their record-making in the playground, during lessons, at afterschool clubs, competitive events and educational visits (Scholes 1939: 184; Rose 1981: 105–6). But what personal meaning might these films have held?

Filming Children

Teaching younger children was a respectable paid extension of domestic childcare roles in the early twentieth century and an acceptable route towards greater female independence. It brought social mobility and security, and working conditions were better than in nursing or clerical work. State subsidised teacher training and opportunities for career progression gave women access to academic recognition, professional status and greater gender equality with men than in many other occupations even if salaries were less. As Oram notes (1996: 12–13) teaching was attractive to young women as it offered male privilege, intellectual fulfilment and scope for public service without having to compromise their femininity. Indeed, professional discourse linked teaching of younger pupils specifically with mothering and care so teaching was accepted as a vocation where a childless person actively chose to work with children. Katherine Holden (2007: 188) suggests that teaching was seen as 'their legacy to the future, a material and emotional investment in the next generation' and helped to compensate for 'not having children of their own'.

Women teachers had to negotiate their life choices and selfhood in relation to social expectations. Restrictive employment practices and persistence of the marriage bar meant that in many of England's local authorities single women teachers predominated in elementary schools (junior and infant) into the post-war years (Todd 2005: 51). Others gave up teaching upon marriage. For unmarried women teachers, sometimes still living with and caring for their parents, the combination of financial means and time enabled cine interests to develop. Given the relatively small numbers of professional women between the wars, it was not surprising that women teachers' cine practice often occurred independently or among predominantly male professional camera users.

Making and exhibiting films about their young pupils acknowledged teachers' professional and creative interests, reinforced their emotional, social and cultural capital, and conformed to established tropes of feminised nurturing and social maternalism. Recording children on camera offered critical and reflective classroom practice and also turned a sympathetic lens upon the children in a teacher's care. Like their films of animals, friends or holidays, these films disclose the affective nature of teaching. If filming young children conformed with societal and professional expectations of woman teachers (and woman amateur filmmakers) as attentive observers and carers, it also fulfilled the advertisers' promises about eternal youth (Anon. 1929d: 12). Furthermore, filmmaking provided scope for drawing, painting, crafting skills and story-telling that were already assumed to be feminine attributes well suited to the infant classroom. Given such embedded social norms and despite the tensions inherent in being women and teachers, it seems unsurprising that they filmed their pupils.

However, women teachers were not the only amateurs involved in filming in educational settings and the hobby press encouraged filmmaking about children (Wain 1951:7 9; Norris Nicholson 2012a: 92–117). Parents, including those who were also teachers, documented their children's lives from infancy onwards, sometimes combining personal and pedagogical interests with new awareness in child development and psychology (Valentine 2006: 60; Giardiello 2014: 122–38). George H. Higginson's visually experimental films as a mature art-student gave way to an ethnographic focus upon his children attending nursery (Hawley 2009: 3–6).[4] Head teachers also saw the medium's wider potential. During the 1950s, Miss Long, a Lancashire head teacher, believed that films were more informative than open days. She encouraged two school parents, Ray and Eileen Norris to film lessons, seasonal festivals and a colleague's retirement party.[5] When Norris passed the material into archival care thirty years later, she recalled the mix of improvised and scripted activity and that 'the children became so accustomed to seeing them [the filmmakers] that they just proceeded naturally . . . ignoring the camera'.[6] Mary Corner, another innovative Lancashire head teacher, produced thirteen 16mm films about the value of play as well as many films made alone or with her local cine club members.[7] Her films about experiential learning within publicly funded nurseries anticipated later campaigning films in the 1970s (see Chapter 8). She filmed at the children's own height and her scenes of physical activity and creative play capture details of nursery provision, toys, fashion and regional ethnic change. Corner's sense of an inclusive and close-knit learning community also prompted her to film her kitchen staff.[8]

Teachers of younger children often became embedded into community life through contact with families that was sustained by teaching siblings and successive generations in localities where traditional employment lessened mobility. Cine films by Grace Foster and her daughter, also Grace Foster, at Mersey Street Primary School in Newtownards, East Belfast, reflected continuities over thirty years: they worked in an area where a strong sense of rootedness persisted until the rehousing of families occurred during The Troubles.[9] Their 8mm films portrayed the school as an extended family and their imagery, like that of their own children and family occasions, conferred reassurance and continuity. Amid scenes of young children playing, nonetheless, expressions and abstract mark making in khaki green and black perhaps hint at how worsening sectarianism encroached upon daily life.

For all filmmakers, time, place and status defined roles and shaped opportunities. The next two sections explore how two single filmmakers made and shared their films. Oral histories unlock third person narratives about both filmmakers and their cine practice. Interviews, undertaken with and independently from watching imagery, contribute to understanding the making and exhibition of films and their place in a filmmaker's life.[10] Their subjectivities complement the visual narratives offered by the films but provide insights mediated by hindsight. Both examples show filmmaking interests were shaped by personal, professional and political circumstances. Neither women were immune from wider shifts and the instabilities brought by war, economic and societal changes that were transforming the lives of teachers and whole communities (Lawn 1987: 60).

Chronicling a Community

Kathleen Lockwood (1908–97) was the daughter of a village head teacher and local councillor, who lived in the Holme Valley in West Yorkshire.[11] Her father considered her prospective partner 'not good enough', so she never married. Lockwood's career spanned teaching at two small village schools. She had financial independence and mobility as a self-taught car-driver. She lived with and later cared for her parents and she travelled with former college friends. Although 'incomers', the family were accepted into the Valley's hill-farming and mill communities where people were linked by marriage, school and chapel attendance. Weather, isolation and shared wartime loss, shortage and hardship shaped neighbourliness. Angela Heywood recalled stories of how her aunt and great-uncle would 'go out in the family car distributing eggs and groceries among the rural poor'. She believed that Lockwood's 'interest in photography had started with her taking pictures on these outings as she was growing up. This became part of sharing local news around the Valley.'[12]

A strong educational imperative underlay Lockwood's cine practice. For years, she filmed using a handheld windup Cine Kodak Model 20 and later on Super 8mm and claimed 'a tripod would restrict her vision'. Film captions indicated intentionality and a shot's significance: 'feeding the turkeys with corn – the last supply until after the war'.[13] Titles, like her read-out scripts, reinforced visual meaning: 'out for a nature walk carrying their gas masks always alert to rush to the air raid shelter . . . if sirens sounded'. Text gave clarity as at 'evacuees at Holme House' and heightened impact, as seen in 'a piano put out to dry' and 'beautiful cloth washed through the windows [of a mill] during devastating floods'. Captions conveyed relief, novelty and excitement too: 'coal finally arriving by horse-drawn sledge during severe snow'; or when recording a royal visit and the local drama group's 'barn-storming' Valley performance tour by wagon for the Festival of Britain. 'She always had a camera', Angela recalled or so it seemed in childhood memories: 'She took still photographs and for a while also experimented with slides', as borne out by various club successes.[14] Lockwood was usually right in front of the action for filming too.[15]

Angela's reflections upon her aunt's visual practice echo other filmmakers' comments: 'She believed it was hard being a women in a man's world of photography. She received criticism and she was critical of how much criticism she received simply because she was a woman.'[16] Entrenched attitudes, echoing Fayde's comments (1952c: 160–1) 'affected her determination to improve her work and move to new technologies'. She was 'banned from Dixons (in Huddersfield) because of how many times she returned asking for help' but she 'learnt how to use video equipment, with help from a [more local] family-owned electrical appliance shop now closed . . . [I]n later life she wiped a number of the tapes during her attempts to play them back and work with them.'[17]

For years, Lockwood was the only regular-attending woman at Holmfirth Camera Club where she held different offices and eventually became vice president. As a co-founder member along with two doctors and a barber in 1940, club records reveal that her films helped to sustain wartime meetings. Home-front life emerges too from her imagery of street scenes, fund-raising events, evacuees, children with gasmasks, farm work, a shot-down aircraft and the impact and aftermath of clearing up disastrous flooding in May 1944 when national attention was focused on the evacuation of Dunkirk. For years, she showed films made for club competitions with an accompanying spoken commentary. She filmed constantly but rarely at school. She gathered new material on holidays and locally and she documented club outings.[18] Few other women camera users ever attended and 'ladies nights' and free attendance for wives were part of club life well into the late 1970s. Angela suggested that 'Possibly she wasn't an easy [club] member . . . where she was the only member to win in every category then in existence. She was a quiet but dedicated person.' Practical self-improvement was central to club life as members exchanged tips and occasionally screened films from elsewhere. Lockwood was 'completely self-taught – no signs of any manuals etc. in her possessions. She was rigorous and learnt from her mistakes.' She never linked with the IAC. Angela called her 'a perfectionist', recalling occasions of repeated actions with her brother until their aunt was ready to film.

Community events were integral to her sense of teacher identity.[19] They allowed her to give something and share holiday experiences with others unable to travel as recalled by her niece:

> [Choppards Mission Chapel] was a place of worship . . . but also an important social centre . . . hosting teas [after Whit Walks, choral events and brass band processions] and film shows. There were never any charges . . . Whole families came to watch the films. Lots of children.

The mix of original and commercial small-gauge films attracted audiences even after the opening of Holme Moss transmitting station (Anon., 1951). For years, her film evenings had little competition; watching the Coronation (1953) on rented televisions and other local memories point to limited access to broadcast entertainment. 'There would be a mix of my aunt's films and also bought films – Disney . . . Mickey Mouse, and others.' Angela identified her aunt's self-reliance: 'She was small and slight but would set up the projector and screen.' Technical hitches were accepted as part of the occasion: 'Film shows involved watching quietly and recognising people and events apart from when the projector stopped when the film broke. Then it would become noisy while she rethreaded and started the projector again.' Evolving technologies brought their own challenges:

> Later she learnt how to match sound tapes to her films and when the film broke, the reel to reel continued so that it was chaotic until the film was repaired and the tape rewound. People would fall silent as soon as the film began again.

Lockwood used a reel to reel sound recorder and, like another local pioneering cine user, visited 'the blind taking sound tapes she had made to accompany her films' (Norris Nicholson 2015b: 25–9). Angela suggested that 'the Valley and its people became [her aunt's] extended surrogate family'. She filmed events and anniversaries 'as if they were her children'. Lockwood's familial and professional status gave her authority:

> She was well known and respected, but also recognised for her determination and commitment . . . She was strong-willed. She'd stop traffic to gain a shot. She'd shimmy up onto a wall to have a good vantage point for filming in her final years and have to be helped down again . . . it was her way of relating to the Valley and elsewhere.[20]

Lockwood filmed modernity's advance: the building of a new reservoir, supermarket and housing and loss of landscape views or country walks. She captured industrial decline too as textile mills, chimneys and chapels were demolished.[21] Sometimes 'she would record whether it was filmic or not - for instance, tree felling at Yateholme, tree-planting and river clearance'. Additional title shots, news cuttings and her own still photographs and commentaries complemented these visual diaries. As a self-appointed chronicler, she recorded moments of commemoration and celebration. Her films testified to the spirit of self-help. They became her version of the Valley's history and demonstrate attachment and a strong sense of place.

Like other women amateur filmmakers, Lockwood filmed flora and fauna close to where she lived.[22] Although modest in comparison to the fieldwork observations of the Scottish botanist and filmmaker Isobel Hutchinson, these portraits of seasonal change and animal behaviour resemble the nature diaries meticulously recorded in watercolours and ink by an earlier generation and resemble other films made at about the same period. They expanded the view offered by classroom nature tables and celebrated the continuities of the countryside. They seem to gain importance as Lockwood grew older 'just filming through the French windows' and 'were some of her personal favourites'. Angela believed that they were possibly 'some of the most revealing about what she liked and herself ' as seen also in a film about a disabled man gardening.[23] She probably showed her films at school although logbooks are no longer available.[24] From her own college days, Lockwood possibly knew about the burgeoning availability of children's educational and scientific films, and Mary Field's involvement with the pioneering natural history series *Secrets of Nature*, although evidence of using instructional films in teaching has not been traceable due to the condition of school records.[25]

Lockwood's sense of natural form and landscape aesthetics is apparent in her films about artists and craft workers.[26] Her focus (with only one unnamed male wood-turner present) celebrates women's creativity rather than work by the Valley's better known resident artists, Ashley Jackson and Trevor Stubley.[27] A more personal relationship emerged too: outings with a married friend Vera Waddington combined their respective interests. Vera painted while Lockwood took photographs that enabled Vera to finish her paintings. Meticulous in her hobby, Lockwood's own recognition of her films' value led her to contact the Imperial War Museum.[28] That step led to their subsequent regional preservation. Produced in, about and for people she knew, her footage was underpinned by mid-century values of public service and conservatism. The Holme Valley was geographically remote from newsworthy national and international events but wider influences impacted locally. It also generated its own news. Covering these visual stories helped Lockwood and others make sense of their lives and identities.

Adjusting to Modernity

Lockwood's cine practice may be compared with that of another Yorkshire teacher/filmmaker who lived and worked virtually all her life less than ten miles away although they may have never met. Lucy Fairbank (1890–1983) was born to a mill-working mother and, from further down the Colne Valley, a local businessman, possibly also in textiles. Her unmarried parents lived together until her mother's death when Lucy was nineteen. Although retaining her mother's surname, Fairbank was acknowledged by her father and his financial support enabled her travels and filmmaking. She became a pupil teacher where she had attended school and co-ran the infant department at Linthwaite Council School prior to her retirement in 1952. Private archives, entrusted to Ian Baxter, a former pupil, friend and filmmaker, attest to Fairbank's extensive output and local screenings that continued until she was in her seventies. Talking and watching her films with Ian, and unlimited access to her films and papers, form the basis for exploring the localised outreach of another pioneering teacher filmmaker.[29]

Fairbank's life challenges clichéd notions of Britain's unchanging traditional northern working communities. Unlike her mother and grandmother, she completed her school education, and later, as a much travelled village teacher and a stalwart of the Methodist Church, she acquired considerable respect. Her well-shot films of overseas holidays and her intimate portraits of local places and people as a trusted and familiar insider blur conventional class divisions during the interwar and post-war years, although outside cine club circles, her social networks were largely defined by non-conformist chapel and classroom.[30] Recurring imagery of young women socialising together at local events or on outings suggest modernising lifestyles, independence and femininity within the constraints of social, economic and political provincialism (Buckley and Fawcett 2002: 90–1).

Fairbank learnt to film, edit and title from other early members of Huddersfield Screen Players (Huddersfield Film Makers Club) in the early 1930s.[31] Club involvement continued over thirty years as she entered competitions and made wedding films for other members.[32] Regular attendance at evening meetings was limited by not having a car and no surviving evidence points to her taking part in group productions. Fairbank filmed alone, although occasionally she filmed club outings, attended club dinners and featured in other members' family films. She used an expensive 16mm Siemens D camera with interchangeable lens and a light meter. She became proficient at rapid changes in response to the constantly shifting Pennine light and by the mid-1930s she used colour film in bright sunshine. She experimented with slow motion as seen in playground sequences and simple trick photography among the ruins at Fountains Abbey also shot during the 1930s.[33]

Calligraphy, artwork and other classroom skills informed her cine practice. She annotated hand drawn route maps on travel films and her captions combined purchased frame motifs and fonts, cut out lettering, and drawings in ink, chalk or watercolour. Inserted handwritten intertitles and place names filmed from her classroom blackboard or a slate propped up in the garden added opinion, humour and a sense of narrative. She included chanced-upon written text too: the names of ships and buildings, Sunday school and brass banners in local processions and perhaps most strikingly, the sense of urgency in headlines on newspaper stands filmed while travelling home from Paris in August 1939 – 'Germans told to leave Britain' (*Daily Sketch*) and 'Roosevelt again appeals to Hitler' (*Daily Mail*).[34]

Fairbank's surviving cine production fell into five categories – weddings, children, travel, local and regional. After she died, some films were discarded as unimportant, notably films of friends and holidays in emerging tourist destinations. Discussion here draws upon material that exemplifies how her stories of gender, class and locality fit into larger narratives of national change even though identities are no longer known for some of the people she filmed, including three laughing young women in Paris and others visiting the pleasure gardens at Alton Towers.[35]

Fairbank's teaching career structured much of her cine activities for years. She filmed during summer holidays abroad usually with another teacher companion and occasionally had an overseas Easter holiday too. She made numerous shorter films about her dogs, garden, local outings and seeing friends. Filmmaking offered a creative alternative to school's repetitive 'daily round' (a recurring caption) and was an integral part of her teacher identity. Children became accustomed to being on camera although some regularly waved and smiled as she filmed. After her holidays, she often finished films by recording school activities in the playground.[36] She documented open air lessons including the slim bob-headed 'top girls' involved in skipping and dancing routines wearing printed cotton frocks. Well-handled atmospheric contrasts occur in interior sequences. In dark crowded classrooms she caught shafts of sunlight entering through high Victorian lancet windows to light infant faces and hands as they worked on varied activities or had an afternoon rest.[37] She brought her empty film reels to school for creative play. Focused and well-composed, Lockwood's imagery conveys a rich sense of period. Camera use outside lessons was more contemplative. It demarcated the limitations of Fairbank's ordered term-time world: school railings, separate doorways for older girls and boys and the frieze-filled walls of her empty classroom that contrast with the increasing political uncertainties beyond (Figure 6.1).[38]

Figure 6.1 Still frame from *Films from Miss Fairbank* (*c.*1936).

A school visit to Glasgow's Empire Exhibition (1938) disclosed Fairbank's filmic response to modernity.[39] Images of mills and chimneys gave way to the glass, steel and prefabrication of futuristic pavilions, towers and spectacular landscaping that promoted late imperial ambition. Her captions condemned this bold, bright vision as 'severely modern' and she preferred the reconstructed Highland *clachan* (traditional blackhouses) as 'about the only thing in the Exhibition that does not point to the future'. Lingering shots of the modest stone dwellings in their lakeside setting seem closer to the material conditions of Pennine life. Travel sequences provided visual continuity: shots recorded the train's arrival and pupils boarding. Profiled against the landscapes beyond the carriage windows, children's faces revealed changing expressions and responses to the novelty of waiter-served meals. The film long remained popular among audiences where pre-war childhood experiences sustained shared memories and continuities.[40]

Much preparation often went into Fairbank's film projects. Her earliest travelogue of visiting Oberammergau's Passion play tercentenary anniversary with her teaching colleague, Clarice Mountain, was no exception.[41] After visiting in 1930, she decided to return with a camera. Her 'scenario . . . to make 500 feet of travel film' listed shots, views and locations to evoke the journey: luggage labels and carried bags, boarding/alighting from trains, meeting friends, details of performers and performance context, en route sequences 'if there is an observation car at the back of the train' and 'going through swing door of hotel at night' during their return via London. Unplanned opportunities, including the brief appearance of Adolf Hitler being greeted by saluting crowds, attest to Fairbank's flexibility, eye for visual details and story-telling.

A surviving script offers, in Chalfren's words, a parallel verbal account (1987: 129). It displays an unpretentious, conversational and gently self-assured everyday tone, evincing the modernising conservatism of the interwar years. National stereotypes recur: the 'quaintly dressed' Dutch were 'straight-forward' with 'cleanliness that appeals' although dress codes were complex and, to some audiences, she revealed that 'on the Isle of Marken . . . a bare headed woman would lose her respectability'. Inhabitants of Oberammergau, including older men in traditional lederhosen who posed for the young foreign filmmaker, were 'hardy and independent folk; poor and unpretentious' and, viewers were reassured, 'yet in spite of their poverty – extremely happy'. Anecdotes punctuated her crafted scripts: 'Could we have been filmed in our plight, Laurel and Hardy would have had rival film stars', she quipped recalling a rough North Sea crossing. The political consequences of Chancellor Hindenberg's death were understated as film and script acknowledge the 'solemn and doleful' atmosphere of bells tolling as they reached Cologne. In Munich, level-headedness prevailed: 'after all, it would not be too dangerous to be seen carrying a camera'. Arriving in the aftermath of the Austrian Chancellor Dollfus' recent murder and 'his picture draped around with crepe . . . displayed in every window', she noted 'more evidence of poverty than had been seen before in our wanderings' (in 1930). Observations continued: 'trade seemed bad', women swept the streets and 'the stores were very quiet'.[42]

Such eye-witness accounts enhanced Fairbank's authority as she linked audiences directly to wider places and people in the news. She made films until 1941 (possibly when she could no longer access film) and she recorded the early post-war weddings of friends and former teaching colleagues, including (despite being 'mortified') her close friend Clarice. Film shows resumed in the late 1940s and featured her pre-war overseas travel in and beyond Europe.[43] Foreign holidays restarted in 1951 to diverse destinations as shown by her notebooks over the next decade. Among numerous titled films, she produced *Camera Looks Down on Colne Valley* (1956–9), a well-made colour film about where she lived. A local historian offered to write a script but surviving notes suggest that she created a written record following her own filming (Figure 6.2).[44]

Figure 6.2 Still frame from *The Camera Looks Down on Colne Valley* (1956–9). © Lucy Fairbank Legacy archive/Ian Baxter.

Fairbank's local films enabled audiences to revisit familiar places, their children's activities and their younger selves. Shared viewing enabled companionable reminiscence. Sometimes she retained poorer quality sections or when frequent film changes occurred for personal reasons. Imagery shows how gender, age and status affected how people responded differently to being on camera: sometimes with mimed exaggeration and addressing the lens directly; elsewhere, with restraint and courtesy, but rarely indifference. Pre-war frivolities involving smartly dressed women as they smoke and play back garden games have an informal intimacy that recurs in later scenes of friends together.[45] Her focus was selective, often reflecting how and where she felt happier filming: hikes with women on breezy summer days, children playing, mothers pushing chunky prams along country lanes, church walks, feeding farm animals and householders who interrupted domestic duties as they pose laughing and mouth silent comments at the camera. There is an elegiac feel to such sequences, despite the abandoned cottages, rundown farmyards and new communication masts: they were moments to remember. Companionship weaves through these films but Fairbank's retirement did not obscure her sense of change and industrial decline. She recorded the canal's abandonment, infilling and replanting with cherry trees and flower beds, most notably in the Valley bottom settlements linked by Huddersfield Narrow Canal. Her recurring shots of dark shiny pipes among the churned up mud resemble wartime gun emplacements and seem poised to violate the soil of her Valley. Recording for posterity had been unintentional in 1934. Post-war she recognised the camera as a tool of witness.[46]

As homes gained televisions, Fairbank continued with her film shows. Rarely travelling beyond the Valley, she went by taxi or an organiser's car to village halls, churches and chapels. Over ten years, she gave 118 evening film shows mainly during darker winter months when projection was easier. Typically, she stood in the middle of the hall by her projector as she talked to people who rarely travelled very far from home.[47] Ticket sales raised funds for her own church and other groups within the Valley,[48] reflecting Methodism's diverse affiliations, her voluntary interests and perhaps her own sense of acceptance. Her film selection varied for different occasions but apart from using bought footage within a Coronation film (1937), she only showed her own films.

For those growing up in the 1950s, Fairbanks film shows were 'something different' and 'novel alternatives to playing out or an evening at home'.[49] Her notes reveal the character of these occasions: 'Badly organised and supported. Not worth going back. Raised two guineas.'[50] The next two entries admitted problems too: 'Not very enjoyable. Screen had not been fetched.' After it was collected by car and 'brought in through the window', she noted she 'got neuralgia' and that for next time she would 'fix up with a different group'.[51] The following month, wintry conditions caused latecomers and kept people away. Advance ticket sales dropped and she charged less but 'gratifyingly' raised £9.00 towards church funds.[52] Tensions occurred: 'A very large audience but shabby opening. No introduction . . . No national anthem. Next time the minister will be given his place.'[53]

Technical problems persisted as Victorian venues, pre-war equipment and Fairbank grew older: 'Loose wire . . . caused fuse in plug. Total disaster. After twenty minutes got going.'[54] Yet, when everything went to plan, there was a pleasurable sense of achievement: 'Very good evening. The little school was filled. The people were . . . happy. Children behaved in a splendid manner.' Film shows ceased sometime after making her last film as the projector, screen and transformer became too cumbersome for her to move around.[55] Her final entry suggested it had been worthwhile: 'Good crowd. Satisfactory receipts.'[56] It was a fitting epitaph for a filmmaker whose films enabled her to share her curiosity and responses to the changing world around her.

Tradition and Transgression

Opportunities for relatively well-paid employment for educated women, including teaching, grew in the expanding post-war state sector: in 1955 the Ministry of Education appealed to married teachers to return to the profession (Sinfield 1997: 205; Todd 2005: 103). More cine using women teachers recorded on-site activities, visits and residential journeys in new secondary modern schools. They echoed their male counterparts who had filmed in grammar schools and occasionally in technical schools between the wars although they tended to focus on smaller events rather than speech days and prize-giving and other whole school occasions. Their imagery negotiated their own evolving identities and reflected the impact of current debates on employment and domesticity upon changing expectations for girls and young women. While some senior unmarried teachers, including Dean Norris, recorded the early years of a comprehensive school opening in West Yorkshire and its emulation of grammar school traditions, other teachers strove to capture innovation and change.[57] Some newly qualified secondary school women teachers were more mobile than their pre-war junior and infant school predecessors as they sought their first teaching post. As a result, their films tended to focus less on community events and more on school life including their own involvement in changing educational provision for Britain's teenagers.

School fashion shows, recorded at Hope Park School, Prestwich, for example, recognised pupils' non-academic achievement and celebrated current youth ideals of being attractive and stylish. Camera work of modelling sessions and catwalk routines in the school hall validate fresh approaches to the teaching of domestic science and needlework. Girls and garments recorded on 16mm signal the school's acceptance of closer-fitting outfits, changing hem lengths and self-confident adolescent body language unimaginable ten years earlier.[58] Mrs Buxton's filmed close-ups of girls' bodies as they perform sequential rolls, jumps, stretches and apparatus work were also far removed from callisthenic routines filmed in previous decades.[59] From their occurrence amongst family films, these controlled movements of young bodies in leotards suggest professional enjoyment and pride in pupils' prowess. Despite the strong visual effects caught in the patchy sunlight and shadows of a school hall, they seem to have been more of a personal record of pupils and practical work, than for public viewing, as do her films of swimming in the school's newly built pool.[60]

Teachers also filmed pupils' travel experiences to European and Mediterranean destinations within a fast-changing holiday industry in the 1950s and 1960s.[61] As overseas travel was still a novelty for many youngsters, educational holidays combined sightseeing and leisure. A secondary school visit to Elba involving two women teachers recorded young fishermen as they joined adolescent girls relaxing on a beach.[62] Added titles observed that 'Our sea nymphs attracted many admirers – naturally' and successive sequences and cut-aways show how they sat and danced with the girls whose responses to their presence and being on camera varied. 'So our holiday ends with tearful girls whispering *arrivederci* hoping to return some time' the film coyly concludes as if redirecting attention from the numerous waiters, boatmen, drivers and other young men who also feature within these holiday film memories. Made possibly for sharing with an adolescent audience rather parents, and even though the filmmaker's identity – as a man or a woman – remains unknown, the film highlights the liberalism and sexual mores of another era. This film is a reminder that although retrospectively filmmakers and their work may seem to fit with a given moment in time, it would be misleading to ignore the varied settings in which teachers taught and filmed, as seen in the next section.

Out with the Girls

The surviving films of Ellaline Jennings (1909–2013) reveal the visual practice of an unmarried art teacher who worked in the heavily industrialised area of St Helens, Lancashire.[63] Between *c.*1947 and 1964, she recorded how two local authority secondary schools merged following wartime educational reform and captured that story of change for parents and children, as an all-girls school became co-educational. Although she filmed mixed sports days, visits and the school's expansion, her earlier footage of school journeys, undertaken with the help of another single colleague, Doris Crompton, is of greater visual quality and interest for the apparent pleasure derived from working with film within a single-sex setting.

Jennings, born into a family with wide-ranging regional artistic and literary connections, first filmed with a borrowed 8mm camera, won by Crompton's uncle as a result of a competition run by the *Liverpool Daily Post*. The prize indicated the current popularity of cine activity and Crompton's father, a local camera club member, helped the two young teachers to produce a film for parents. Jennings purchased 16mm equipment in 1948 with funds raised by pupils collecting jars for the local jam factory and advice from members at St Helens Visual Arts Society. The girls' willing involvement in their teachers' filmmaking is evident in numerous close-up and medium shots around the school and on week-long holidays in the Lake District. A film made to celebrate the school's tenth anniversary detailed daily routines and lessons. Prefects ringing a bell for assembly and the controlled procession of lines of girls into the school hall echo tropes of restraint and order found in other amateur school films. Little details caught Jennings' attention: girls walking or cycling to school, a pupil with glasses supplied by the new National Health Service or a prefect's badge. She filmed a BBC record on a turntable during a singing lesson, disciplined physical education routines and dance movements. Creativity within drama and art lessons, along with scenes of the girls engaged in domestic science (baking, sewing and ironing) disclose Jennings' documentary aesthetic but also a secondary school self-confident about its differentiated curricular provision.

Successive residential visits to the Lake District were filmed in black and white and later in colour.[64] Journeys framed each visual narrative; they introduced the teachers and pupils and enabled subsequent viewers to be armchair travellers. The 1951 film used subtitles, cut-aways to the classroom calendar and in-camera editing to show an initial meeting, collecting weekly contributions and how pupils painted their own map extracts. Jennings filmed over-shoulder views and captured girls' faces in profile as they worked alone or together. Their varied school clothes reflect the lingering influence of rationing. Colour sections revealed the brilliance of spring sunshine, flowers and lingering snow on the fells. Girls walked along holding hands and encircling their arms around each other's waists.

Figure 6.3 Still frame from Ellaline Jennings, *Grange Park Girls in Langdale* (1948). © North West Film Archive at Manchester Metropolitan University.

A relaxed and uninhibited atmosphere, intensified by cut-aways to sky, flowers and landscape views permeates these informal shots of pupils and teachers (Figure 6.3).

Jennings captured the girls' physical freedom of being alone, in pairs or small groups in the countryside. Sequences disclose facial expressions registering delight and contemplative pleasure as girls and teachers clambered among rocks, paddled in streams, picked flowers and fed lambs. They hiked with improvised walking sticks and wartime canvas kit bags or rucksacks and sometimes just stood or sat closely. Local festivals, church interiors and visits to the homes of artists and writers enriched the itinerary and offered scope for varied close-ups and composition. Filming captured unexpected encounters with other hikers and a group of landscape painters but much was planned and reliant upon prior knowledge of earlier visits. Signs and way-markers were supplemented by edited-in place names on black and white film; some indicate locations but others convey narrative as they give distance and the route ahead, followed by a panoramic view or image of walkers setting off. Shots from different vantages again suggest in-camera editing and

Figure 6.4 Still frame from Ellaline Jennings, *Lakeland Holiday* (1952).
© North West Film Archive at Manchester Metropolitan University.

reveal that Jennings often went ahead to film as the group approached. Views of colleagues, accommodation, listening to the radio, playing tennis and enjoying the gardens completed the week's record. Packing and stowing bags, boarding the coach and waving goodbye to the centre's staff led into the journey home along country roads. Shot for screening at school, Jennings gradually moved from filming in black and white to only using colour film stock as materials became more available and affordable. The films offer well-made portraits of adolescent and pre-adolescent girls in beautiful surroundings of wide open skies, plunging hillsides and sweeping views (Figure 6.4). They reveal the emotional intensity, uninhibited physicality and conviviality of a short-lived group experience. There was vicarious enjoyment too for the parents: a chance to see children's achievements away from home and proof of money well spent. For Jennings, her films may have been personal endorsements of how meticulous planning and leadership brought the satisfaction of a job well done. Perhaps that fulfilment lessened over time as although the educational holidays continued through the 1960s, later films of the boys' visits were very short.

Had Life Been Different

For Joyce Skinner (b.1920) teaching seemed a viable career option but film remained her passion.[65] Following her interrupted wartime secondary school teacher training, she specialised in art and physical education and rose to deputy-head level.[66] As a single person, she could be flexible and responsive to opportunities in and away from school. She co-founded the South Birmingham Cine Society in the early 1950s, where she and other women made two films together while male members formed a sub-group of 'keen types' briefly to work separately.[67] Skinner became club chair and donated a trophy that she won on numerous occasions. She laughed at the idea of being a feminist and seemed undaunted by working alongside professional men, either in school or as a filmmaker. At the club, 'the men just automatically accepted me' and her competition successes drew respect. Skinner's commissions sometimes brought in modest payment and barred her from later *Amateur Cine World* (ACW) competitions (Figure 6.5). Her cine interests began with a borrowed camera and led to films about school, including training on an improvised ski slope in the hall, visits

Figure 6.5 Photograph of Joyce Skinner filming *Power in Trust* (1966). © CEGB.

abroad and educational cruises.[68] After retirement she spent a further twenty-six years using evolving formats.

Early on, Skinner made an instructional film for the All England Women's Hockey Association that involved her filming at Wembley alongside BBC camera crew.[69] Chance encounters led to projects that reflected the dynamism and creativity fuelling the South Midlands post-war economy. She made commissioned films about electricity, accident prevention and safety, elderly care and disability, young people and career options.[70] Her later documentaries covered crafts and traditions, wildlife and travel. A film made on holiday in Tunisia coincided with the country's opening to package tourism in the early 1970s and briefly became official promotional material (Russell 2004). Adopting Super VHS and later digital technologies, she continued to film local and regional life, including her own Warwickshire village during floods, anniversaries and from the air. Invention and an appreciation of nature persisted: recording bird box activities via a small closed circuit camera lens echoed wildlife interests captured on film sixty years earlier. 'If I had known how things were going to progress . . . and there had been the openings, I think I would have enjoyed a job as a filmmaker', Skinner commented.[71] As an amateur, film became a parallel career.

Conclusion

Teachers have represented a heterogeneous sub-group among women filmmakers for almost a century. Their lives and interests reflect new social and personal opportunities offered by work, travel, spending power and the changing nature and expectations of domestic life. For some, their visual practice embodied the patriotism of private lives, finding contentment in their immediate surroundings; for many, film expressed their sense of citizenship that, like their teaching, revealed commitment to public service. Financially secure as professionals, although lower paid than their male colleagues and restricted by gendered recruitment for decades into less senior positions, specific subject areas and often teaching younger children, their film interests brought personal satisfaction and wider pleasure. While professional constraints limited individual ambitions, their filmmaking offered autonomy, challenge and recognition outside school. It brought private interests into the public realm. School life offered a source of visual interest that encouraged willing involvement and later audiences. Other teachers recognised the cine camera's mimetic role in charting progress, as seen particularly in films of young children and some older pupils' involvement in sport and practical subjects.

Evidence of seeking guidance and club involvement varied: single teachers had greater flexibility to take part in club activities but, well into the post-war years, some clubs were more accommodating to married couples than women participating on their own. Film projects and clubs, often started by male teachers, had been a feature of some secondary schools since before the 1930s and particularly during the 1950s although some educational boards encouraged school film clubs too, as in London and Liverpool.[72] School film clubs, run by women teachers, emerged during the 1970s and 1980s, as seen in other initiatives in urban secondary schools.[73] While some rural schools required teachers with access to a car to bring in their own equipment, better equipped settings enabled filmmakers to tackle ambitious projects on- and off-site.

Women teacher filmmakers were not confined to mainland Britain or mainstream education. Although not discussed here, Jenny Isabel (née Brown) Gilbertson (1902–90) had a remarkable documentary and educational filmmaking career alongside teaching for decades (Wade 2004). Another teacher filmed pupils with physical and other learning needs at a time when children with 'special educational needs' were separated from their peers.[74] This also often resulted in traveller children and children from non-white backgrounds being disproportionately represented in special education and, although subsequently criticised as being flawed educational thinking, it opened new career opportunities for women teachers. Films from the 1970s reveal that children with Down's syndrome as well as pupils with cerebral palsy and other physical disabilities travelled to new specialist settings for separate education. Camera using teachers recorded supported learning for individual pupils of different ages and ethnicities. They filmed as younger children engaged in water and sand play or worked with apparatus and inflatables in therapy settings. Lessons, school meals and other daily routines were filmed too. Maureen Holden also recorded winter walks, a summer concert, seasonal celebrations including Bonfire Night and Father Christmas distributing presents as well as longer countryside visits in North West England.[75] Such imagery challenges what Landzelius (2004: 279–97) calls the landscapes of ableism still found in many histories of childhood and adolescence and also identifies racialised aspects of past educational policy in England and Wales.

Relationships, routines and performances weave through these teacher/filmmaker visions of past school life. For teachers accustomed to the division of time into timetabled slots, terms and school years, punctuated by holidays, producing film allowed their own control over time. Perhaps this creative repurposing of time was an antidote to temporal demarcations in their professional roles. Live action film may not have led to the experimentation found in animation and fictional school film club productions but it brought satisfaction and external appreciation. From toddlers to teenagers, teachers' school documentaries reflect the power of dominant ideologies in shaping continuities and enabling change. They reveal how the dynamics of social relations and authority between staff and pupils and each other were sometimes unexpectedly informal, as seen in Jennings' films. Their films coincide with decades when education's role in transmitting values, beliefs and codes of conduct was also negotiating changing attitudes towards women, their roles in paid and unpaid work in and beyond the home and concern about preparing girls for adulthood (Spencer 2005: 66–9). Wartime had redefined women teachers' work significantly twice within thirty years and their school films increasingly seem to be as much about the importance of pupils taking part as success, whether in informal unedited sequences or carefully crafted productions.[76]

Many teacher/filmmakers did not only make school documentaries. Other everyday worlds featured too, as did those activities that disrupted habitual routines of everyday life and the dislocations brought by war, disaster, adverse weather and other change. Travel alone or with teacher companions was also a distinctive part of these women's lives and film output. It reflected their income, interests and the confidence to venture further afield, as seen in Lucy Fairbank's travels before and after the Second World War and Joyce Skinner's later holidays and school cruises. Despite outward self-assurance many teachers were essentially private people happier behind rather than in front of the camera. They feature in their own films rarely, if at all, even when they had a close colleague or travelling companion. Yet their films and lives disclose that, even in the smallest setting, their localised worlds of mid-century Britain were not immune from broader concerns, and infinitely more complex, networked and with a sense of agency than suggested by their eponymous fictive classroom equivalent, Miss Read.

Inevitably the pace of school life affected these filmmakers' endeavours. Joyce Skinner's output of over fifty films in sixty years, nearly half being made for professional use, seems unimaginable within contemporary teaching and reinforces the cross-over between amateur and professional activity. Her work highlights an understated third strand in amateur activity too – the amateur production used in professional contexts. Ellaline Jennings' filming over many months of the build-up to her girls' residential visits now seems an impractical time commitment too but no clues survive about other films she may have made outside school.

Kathleen Lockwood achieved an almost unbroken record of filming of which only a relatively small and early part featured her pupils. Retirement brought fresh opportunities for making and showing films, ambitious new projects, as in the case of Lucy Fairbank and alternative outlets for creativity as still seen in Jill Lampert's embrace of digital filming after leaving teaching.[77] Nonetheless, this exploration of personal and professional subjectivities and circumstances invites further lines of enquiry: to uncover the fuller involvement of teachers in both professional and non-professional film activity and to delve into within other professions where women also became committed filmmakers.

Notes

1. Concerns over the need to regulate taking and sharing images of children has grown as internet use and misuse has grown. Legislative measures introduced between the late 1970s and 2004 are invoked by Britain's schools and many child-related organisations to justify current policies that limit photography or filming of children.
2. At individual public archival level contemporary decisions also reflect changing attitudes towards socially acceptable forms of showing children in relation to cataloguing, conservation and making archived footage available.
3. No systematic study of films made by school age pupils has yet been attempted. In addition to films listed in Britain's regional archives, chance references suggest there was a proliferation of filmmaking particularly in secondary schools from the mid-1950s to the late 1960s, as seen in the *BFI Distribution Catalogue* 'Amateur Cine World' (1969) in which thirty-one secondary school productions (mainly fiction) were listed.
4. George Higginson (*1929) *School* (4:35min, b/w, silent), NWFA no. 2867; (1935) *Dancing Display at Beech House* (21:09min, b/w, silent), NWFA no. 2861.
5. Eileen and Ray Norris (*1959) *The Harvest* (3:49min, b/w, sound), NWFA no. 662; (1959) *Farewell Picnic, Party for Mrs. Clarke, July 1959* (5:15min, b/w, sound), NWFA no. 666; (*1959) *Open Days at Linaker Street Infants School, Southport* (16:16min, b/w, sound), NWFA no. 667.
6. For almost a year Norris corresponded in doggerel verse that reflected her responses to watching the films again: 'Oh days gone by, oh happy days / Of children and their childish ways / Of people who are no longer here / Memories that are -oh- so dear.' See Eileen and Ray Norris Collection, Acquisition files, NWFA no. RR104.
7. See Mary Corner Collection, Acquisition Files, NWFA, no. 1577 covering over thirty-five films made over twenty years on 16mm, 9.5 and Super 8mm, *c*.1965–84. Films include: (*1965/66) *Nursery School Activities* (16mm, 15:48min, colour, silent), NWFA no. 5573; (*1965/66) *Play is Education*

(16mm, 10:05min, colour, silent), NWFA no. 5581; (*1965/67/68) *Andrea's Art (and other scenes)* (16mm, 24:03min, colour, some sound), NWFA no. 5572 (RR1577/3); (1968–71) *The Nursery School, Howard Street* (16mm, 15:45min, colour, silent), NWFA no. 5572.

8. Mary Corner and Jean Hartley (*1966/68) *A Day in a Nursery School Kitchen* (16mm, 16:21min, colour, some sound), NWFA no. 5574.
9. DFA (Northern Ireland), Grace Foster (1970s) *Super 8 Stories: The Foster Family*, available at <http://digitalfilmarchive.net/media/super-8-stories-the-foster-family-534> (last accessed 17 April 2018); (1970s) *Super 8 Stories Extra Footage: Mersey Street Primary School*, available at <http://digitalfilmarchive.net/media/super-8-stories-extra-footage-mersey-578 Foster Family> (last accessed 17 April 2018).
10. See also discussion on using still photographs in eliciting memories in Thomson and Freund (2011).
11. Details are drawn from interviews, archival sources and private papers throughout this section including the Yorkshire Film Archive (YFA) and Holmfirth Camera Club Archives.
12. Angela Heywood in conversation with the author, March 2014.
13. Details of YFA films are available at <http://www.yorkshirefilmarchive.com> (last accessed 17 April 2018).
14. Heywood's memories are corroborated by entries in the Holmfirth Camera Club minute books, 1940–90, owned by the club and accessed via their officers (summer, 2016).
15. See for example, Kathleen Lockwood (1975–9) *Changing Face of the Holme Valley* (21:40min, colour, silent), YFA Id. 807; (1940–50) *Holme Valley in the 40s and 50s* (15:00min, colour, silent), YFA Id. 796.
16. See Chapter 2.
17. Angela Heywood in conversation with the author, March 2014.
18. Holmfirth Camera Club Minute Books 1940–90, pp. 1–7.
19. Anon., 'Kathleen Lockwood. Obituary,' *Holme Valley Express*, 27 June 1997.
20. Angela Heywood in conversation with the author at her home in Honley, near Holmfirth, West Yorkshire, March 2014.
21. Kathleen Lockwood (1971) *Water, Water, Everywhere* (Super 8mm, 13:20min, colour, silent), YFA Id. 788; (1975–9) *Changing Face of the Holme Valley* (Super 8mm, 21:40min, colour, silent), YFA Id. 807; (1984–8) Holmfirth 1984–1988 (Super 8mm, 26:40min, colour, silent), YFA Id. 792
22. Kathleen Lockwood (1939)*When We Were Young* (Standard 8mm, 10:26min, b/w, silent), YFA Id. 812; (c.1968) *Living World in My Garden* (Super 8mm, 36:40min, colour, sound), YFA Id. 798; (1970s) *Nature Around Us* (Super 8mm, 26:40min, colour, silent), YFA Id. 795.
23. Kathleen Lockwood (1970s) *Disability, Satisfaction and the Garden* (Super 8mm, 31:00min, colour, silent), YFA Id. 799.
24. Kathleen Lockwood (1940–50) *Holme Valley in the 40s and 50s* (Standard 8mm, 15:00min, b/w, silent), YFA Id. 796.

25. Sarah Easen, 'Mary Field (1896–1968)', British Film Institute, Screenonline, available at <http://www.screenonline.org.uk/people/id/581940/> (last accessed 17 April 2018). Lockwood's film, *When We Were Young* (1939), post-dated Mary Field's involvement with the pioneering natural history series *Secrets of Nature* produced by British Instructional (later Gaumont-British Instructional).
26. Kathleen Lockwood (1975) *Arts and Artists in Holmfirth* (Super 8mm, 26:40min, colour, sound), YFA Id. 800; (1980) *Arts and Crafts in the Holme Valley* (26:40min, colour, silent), YFA Id. 805.
27. Kathleen Lockwood (1975) *Ninth Art Exhibition* (Super 8mm, 11:40min, colour, silent), YFA Id. 791.
28. Angela Heywood in conversation with the author, March 2014.
29. Ian Baxter in conversation with the author at his home in Linthwaite, West Yorkshire, where he maintains the Lucy Fairbank Legacy archive, and has screened and discussed her films during visits between 2012 and 2018.
30. See for example her uninhibited filming in colour and black and white of guests, cars and entertainment among local well-to-do and the seasonal charity offered for local children (not her pupils) by an influential entrepreneur and employer, in Lucy Fairbank (1938) *Golcar Baptist Garden Parties* (16mm, *c.*7:00mins, b/w and colour, silent); (*c.*1951–2?) *W. E. Crowther's Christmas Party* (16mm, *c.*5:30mins, colour, silent), Lucy Fairbank Legacy archive.
31. No minute books survive from the pre-war years although club historians and officers attest to this early involvement. Trevor Spencer in conversation with author at the University of Huddersfield, 21 June 2014.
32. Ian Baxter's parents had their own wedding filmed in colour by Lucy Fairbank in the late 1930s and her own friendship with the family led to him and his siblings featuring on some of her few wartime films, although she had stopped filming at school by the time she became his teacher. Fairbank continued to film weddings into the 1950s.
33. Lucy Fairbank (1934) *Linthwaite School Playground* (16mm, 10:00min, b/w, silent), YFA Id. 3408; (1938) *Beautiful Yorkshire, 1935–1938* (16mm, 12:00min, b/w, silent), YFA Id. 3411.
34. Lucy Fairbank (1939) *Holiday in France August 1939* (16mm, *c.*11:00mins, b/w, silent), Lucy Fairbank Legacy archive.
35. Lucy Fairbank (1935) *Paris at Easter* (16mm, *c.*5:30mins, b/w, silent); (1938) *German Circle Visit to Alton Towers* (16mm, *c.*5:30mins, b/w, silent), Lucy Fairbank Legacy archive.
36. For instance, sequences for *Linthwaite Council School 2* (1936) (16mm, 16:00min, b/w, silent), YFA Id. 3409 used reels bought to record sailing on RMS *Queen Mary*'s third Atlantic voyage and returning via the RMS *Aquitania* in (1936) *Holiday Memories* (16mm, 16:15min, colour and b/w, silent), YFA. Id. 5198.
37. Lucy Fairbank (1934) *When the Heart is Young, Linthwaite Council School* (16mm, 11:00mins, colour and b/w, silent), Lucy Fairbank Legacy archive.

Catalogued also as *Linthwaite School 1* (16mm, 10:00min, b/w, silent), YFA Id. 3408.

38. Lucy Fairbank (1938) *Linthwaite* (16mm, 16:00min, colour and b/w, silent), YFA Id. 3410.
39. Lucy Fairbank (1938) *British Empire Exhibition in Glasgow* (16mm, 10:19min, b/w, silent), YFA 126.
40. Fairbank's record of screenings at different venues through to the early 1960s included date, film programme, audience numbers and responses, as well as technical details and her overall responses to the occasion. Source: Lucy Fairbank Legacy archive.
41. 'Scenario of our holiday 1934' and other planning notes are derived from private papers and notes held by Ian Baxter as part of the Lucy Fairbank Legacy archive, Linthwaite, West Yorkshire.
42. Lucy Fairbank (1934) *Through Holland and Germany to the Passion Play at Oberammergau* (16mm, *c.*43:30mins, b/w, silent). (Film and handwritten script of same title.) Also available as a three-part journey catalogued as *Huddersfield to Nuremburg* (16mm, 16min, b/w, silent), *Munich to Innsbruck* (16mm, 17:30min, b/w, silent) and *Lucerne to London* (16mm, 10:00min, b/w, silent), YFA nos. 3405–7.
43. Lucy Fairbank (1939) *Holiday in France August 1939* (16mm, *c.*9:00mins, b/w, silent); (1935) *Paris and Norway* (16mm, *c.*11:00 mins, b/w, silent); (1936) *Holiday Memories* (16mm, 16:05min, b/w, silent), YFA Id. 5198 and (1937) *Switzerland* (16mm, *c.*11:00 mins, b/w, silent), Lucy Fairbank Legacy archive.
44. Tom Pearson according to Ian Baxter. No further details known.
45. Lucy Fairbank (1935) *Wellhouse, The Hub of the Universe* (16mm, *c.*11:00 mins, b/w, silent); (1938) *Golcar Baptist Garden Parties* (16mm, *c.*7:00mins, b/w and colour, silent), Lucy Fairbank Legacy archive; see also Norris Nicholson (2012a: 126–9).
46. Lucy Fairbank (1956–8) *The Camera Looks Down on Colne Valley* (16mm, 65:00min, colour, silent), YFA 3413.
47. Ian Baxter in conversation with author at his home in Linthwaite, 11 March 2016.
48. 'Tickets were 1/3d (c. 7pence) and 6p (3pence) for adults and children and she later claimed with pride to have raised over £1000 for different organisations.' Cited by Ian Baxter in a letter to R. G. Fairbank, 4 December 1996.
49. Cyril Pearce in conversation with author, recalling attending Lucy Fairbank's film shows as a child.
50. Lucy Fairbank, *Notes*, 30 October 1955, St John Ambulance, Slaithwaite (£2.10 equivalent).
51. Lucy Fairbank, *Notes*, 22 January 1955, Linthwaite Church.
52. Lucy Fairbank, *Notes*, 26 February 1955, Golcar.
53. Lucy Fairbank, *Notes*, 4 March 1958, Linthwaite Church. Sound recording of the national anthem still occurred at some cinemas in the late 1960s, and

its inclusion at the start of orchestral concerts at some civic and public venues continued into the 1980s, so this was possibly less of an oversight than an assertion of socialism in a Valley proud of its radical leanings.

54. Lucy Fairbank, *Notes*, October 1958, Deanhead Church.
55. Letter from Ian Baxter to R. G. Fairbank, 4 December 1996.
56. Lucy Fairbank, *Notes*, 16 November 1963, Deanhead Church.
57. Ian Baxter in conversation with author at his home, Linthwaite, 2016.
58. Unknown (Hope Park Girl's School in Prestwich) (*c.*1964–7) *Hope Park Mannequin Parade* (16mm, 12:25min, colour, silent), NWFA no. 4452.
59. Mrs D Buxton (Sutton County Secondary School for Girls, Ellesmere Port) (1966) [*School Gym Club I*] (Standard 8mm, 4:43min, colour, silent), NWFA no. 2702; (1966) [*School Gym Club II*] (Standard 8mm, 4:40min, colour, silent), NWFA no. 2703.
60. Mrs D Buxton, 1959, [*Synchronised Swimming*] (Standard 8mm, 8:10min, colour, silent), NWFA no. 2704.
61. Many male teachers produced school journey films in the later 1930s and early post-war decades. See, for example, George Wain (a Ten Best winner and prolific writer on amateur practice) (1957) *Holiday in Spain* (16mm, 15:06min, colour, silent), NWFA no. 4406.
62. Unknown (Hope Park Girl's School in Prestwich) (*c.*1964–7) *Hope Park Mannequin Parade* (16mm, 12:25min, colour, silent), NWFA no. 4452.
63. See Ellaline Jenning/Grange Park Collection, Acquisition files, NFWA 1367.
64. Films by Ellaline Jennings of different visits to the Lake District with very similar titles may be identified via their catalogue entry under Grange Park or Grange Park Girls' School, NWFA nos. 1514–25; see also 'Death of a grand lady', *St Helens Reporter*, 12 April 2013, available at <https://www.sthelens reporter.co.uk/news/death-of-a-grand-lady-1-5581454> (last accessed 19 January 2018).
65. Joyce Skinner interviewed for the BECTU/BFI sponsored The British Entertainment History Project at her home in Welford by Angela Martin (2014) (60:56min, colour, sound). Copyright: The British Entertainment History Project, available at <http://www.historyproject.org.uk> (last accessed 17 April 2018; now also available via the Media Archive for Central England (MACE)).
66. Barrie Russell, 'Perspective: The Anne Robinson of Woodrush School', 2004, available at <https://www.thefreelibrary.com/Perspective%3a+The+Anne+Robinson+of+Woodrush+School%3b+Freelance+writer. . .-a0118661901> (last accessed 19 January 2018).
67. Joyce Skinner (1962) *A Switch in Time* (16mm, 10:16min, b/w, sound); (*c.*1963) *By Arrangement* (16mm, 15:03min, colour, sound; now also available via MACE).
68. Joyce Skinner (1959) *Any Day* (16mm, 24:05min, b/w, sound); (1961) *Holiday Playtime* (16mm, 13:06min, colour, sound). This skiing instruction film

won a four star award in the *Amateur Cine World's* Ten Best (now also available via MACE).

69. Joyce Skinner (1968) *Improve Your Hockey* (16mm, *c*.22:00mins, colour, sound) was sold in the USA, Canada, France and Australia. Skinner also made another instructional hockey film (1968) *Wembley Way* (16mm, length unknown, colour, sound). Both films were made for the All England Women's Hockey Association, the UK's governing body for women's hockey 1895–1997, thereafter superseded by the English Hockey Association. Online catalogue details do not list either film as forming part of archived materials for the All England Women's Hockey Association Collection (GB 1128 Hockey) now held in the University of Bath Archives and Research Collections, https://archiveshub.jisc.ac.uk/search/archives/98b4ddce-9c0a-3c34-9461-66c5845e5b1f (last accessed 23 May 2018).
70. Other films by Joyce Skinner include: (1964) *Enjoy Them Safely* (Version 2, 16mm, 7:10min, colour, sound). The film won the Glasgow Cup at the Scottish Amateur Film Festival (SAFF) that year and a copy was sent to the British Fireworks Manufacturers' Association. It was then professionally edited and a commentary was added by Kenneth Horne, then well-known on radio for the programme, *Around the Horne*, and distributed as accident prevention material; (1966) *The Choice is Yours* (16mm, 24:56min, b/w, sound) (SAFF Glasgow Cup, 1966) a film sponsored by local industry on careers' guidance and made for Youth Employment in Redditch that featured commentary by the BBC Midlands newsreader Leslie Dunn and led to Skinner being interviewed on BBC Midlands television with Tom Coyne; (1967) *Power in Trust* (16mm, 15:00mins, colour, sound) (produced for Central Electricity Generating Board); (1970) *Tunisia Yesterday and Today* (16mm, 22:53min, colour, sound), (SAFF, merit award, 1970); (1974) *Pastures New* (16mm, 26:41min, colour, sound) (produced for Management Committee of the Warwickshire Cheshire Home); and various titles for the Royal Society for the Prevention of Accidents (RoSPA). Forty-five of Skinner's films may be viewed by arrangement at MACE, available at <http://www.macearchive.org/> (last accessed 17 April 2018).
71. Joyce Skinner was interviewed for the BECTU/BFI sponsored The British Entertainment History Project at her home in Welford by Angela Martin (2014) (60:56min, colour, sound). Copyright: The British Entertainment History Project, available at <http://www.historyproject.org.uk> (last accessed 17 April 2018; now also available via MACE).
72. One talk in Liverpool on the established classroom use of film to make 'certain lessons more agreeable to the children' reported that 'a teacher member of the Association has been granted three periods a week in her curriculum for 'instruction in practical filmmaking', Liverpool Amateur Photographic Association Cine Group, *Amateur Cine World*, September 1955.
73. See for example discussion of Sheila Graber, Valrie Ellis and Mollie Butler in Chapter 8.

74. Maureen Holden (1973–4) [*Belmont Special School – Activities 1973–74*] (Super 8mm, 28:04min, colour, silent), NWFA no. 1370; (1976) [*Belmont Special School – Classroom Scenes and Mayoral Visit 1976*] (Super 8mm, 12:35min, colour, silent), NWFA no. 1367.
75. Maureen Holden (1974) [*Belmont Special School – Days Out and Seasonal Celebrations*] (Super 8mm, 31:12min, colour, silent), NWFA no. 1371; (1974–5) [*Belmont Special School – Various Visits 1974–75*] (Super 8mm, 9:38min, colour, silent), NWFA no. 1373; (1977) [*Belmont Special School – Activities 1977*] (Super 8mm, 16:26min, colour, silent), NWFA no. 1374; (1978) [*Belmont Special School – Activities 1978*] (Super 8mm, 27:27min, colour, silent), NWFA no. 1375.
76. Thirty-one productions made by the Sir John Deane's College Film Unit over twelve years ranged from semi-documentary to surrealistic drama. They include (1959–61) *The Mistress is Not for Leaving* (16mm, 10:23min, b/w, silent), NWFA no. 3885; (1962) *A Matter of Conscience* (16mm, 9:41min, b/w, silent), NWFA no. 3884; (*1963–4) *Throstle and Other Short Stories* (16mm, 22:26min, b/w, silent), NWFA no. 3888; (1964) *The Time Desk* (16mm, 13:46min, b/w, silent), NWFA no. 3886; (*1969–70) *Listen to Me When I'm Talking to You* (16mm, 26:10min, colour, silent), NWFA no. 3889.
77. For discussion of films by Jill Lampert see Chapter 8.

CHAPTER 7

British Women's Media Narratives of Gender and Collective Memory

Two images, four captions and an infinity of possible storylines. The first is a studio portrait showing a woman wearing a beautifully brocaded *fin de siècle* dress and a young boy in a sailor suit, possibly her son. Ill at ease and with an air of anxious vigilance, the woman sits on a simple white chair, her left hand gripping the armrest. The boy stands by her side, his right hand tucked into his trousers' pocket and his left hand resting on the other armrest, almost touching the woman's right hand. Neither are smiling. The image has two captions: 'I was happy to have one mistress only, and she raised our child', and 'Their passion fizzled out' respectively.[1] The second image is a snapshot of four African men recorded in the early 1970s, somewhere on a rural dirt road. One of the men is walking towards the camera, sporting a fashionable hat; another is staring at the camera while posing in front of a utility pole; the third is standing behind them, stopped in mid-action, hands on hips; the fourth man is busy in the background and possibly unaware of the photographer's presence. The two captions for this image read: 'But she dreamed of far-away places' and 'He left for the furthermost away place'.[2] These two photographs belong to a set of thirty-six family photographs reproduced as postcards and used by Valérie Mréjen when designing *Images en quête d'histoires* (2017) – a media project in which the participants arranged these images to create separate collective histories and personalised narratives. Mréjen's project resembles a Lego-images game which, owing to its multiple narrative options, brings into dialogue media ethics protocols in place when using private or public archival photographs and Umberto Eco's claim that '[t]he attempt to look for a final . . . meaning leads to the acceptance of a never-ending drift or sliding of meaning' (Eco 1992: 32). Media scholars regularly apply this Lego-style visual narratorial exercise when analysing still or moving amateur images – a by-product methodology prompted by the need to negotiate constructions of collective master narratives in relation to individual visual identity formations. Importantly, issues of gender, race and private memory raised by amateur films, and amateur media in general, whether analogue or digital, amplify the 'never-ending drift of meaning' within ongoing contextualised assumptions about what might have been the photographer's/filmmaker's deliberate or involuntary choice of topics. Most (every?) scenes selected from amateur films/media are by default similar to the images used by Valérie Mréjen in her media project: they invite a multitude of interpretations while simultaneously guiding the viewer, the critic or the theorist towards a particular example of cultural memory (Hirsch and Smith 2002).

Such images offer fluid historical records that combine personal stories, collective traditions and technological developments – records of exceptional importance if produced by marginal groups such as, for instance, women amateur filmmakers. In this case, questions of identity representation risk being ideologically taxed should feminist discourses about the politics of the female body or of women-specific cultural ghettoes be given precedence; this is particularly relevant if the overall theoretical goal is to '[retrieve] many women from oblivion as historical actors' (Chedgzoy 2007: 216). Instead, a more flexible methodology concerned with the thematic, aesthetic and moral choices made by women amateur filmmakers, and with their narratorial agency evident across records of mundane or extraordinary events, could present insightful perspectives on the politics of recurrent, possibly gender-specific, visual autobiographical practices. Rather than being seen as 'historical actors', women producing visual testimonies of their times, gender and contextualised cultural settings, are de facto creators of specific discourses of historical consciousness, one that inevitably echoes precise combinations of factual details and their implicit structures of meaning. Like most story-tellers, amateur or professional, lay or academic, women amateur filmmakers take on two roles: the one (also) shared by most historians who often abide by recurrent master narratives when configuring their material of study in conformity to a '"framework" of preconceived ideas', or with a 'preconceived selective point of view', and the one in which they negotiate nuanced visual autobiographies against fixed cultural standards (White 1978: 106).

It is possible to argue that, while being inevitably dependent on their response to existing mythologies of the female self, women have been attributed a non-universal human kind of selfhood, which they need to confront if willing to acquire the right to an 'I' of personal experience (Smith 1993: 11). Moreover, it is often through visual records and artworks that female identity becomes manifest as an ongoing personal narrative which is constantly constructed and challenged across the (female) author's social interactions and developments. Lastly, whenever women artists (including women amateur filmmakers) move away from being a 'subject of research' (Bock 1991) to become their own self-reflexive object of analysis, the individual (female) identity formation process is in dialogue with in-group narratives of selfhood while simultaneously primed by their emotional and social responses (Hammack 2008). There are usually two resulting narrative strands: either a triumphalist gendered-body-immolation visual artwork/act presented in response to the male subjectivity-driven master narratives, or a more nuanced, sometimes even accidental, dialogue with their given social and cultural orders. While the former narrative strand is persuasively meant as a rejection of mainstream constructions of female selfhood, the latter visual narrative framework does not necessarily abandon the right to appeal man-made master narratives of gendered identities. Instead, it allows women's authorial agency to translate rather than enforce social and gendered tensions which, in turn, permit their personal narratives of identity to change traditional gender taboos.

The politics of self-representation among women amateur filmmakers discussed in this book does not seem to include, to the best of the authors' knowledge, examples of equally assertive, combative and uniquely creative visual narratives as those found in works by, for instance, Leonora Carrington, Paloma Varga Weisz, Grace Lau, Frida Kahlo, Dorothea Tanning, Louise Bourgeois, Leonor Fini, Georgia O'Keeffe, Jo Spence, Claude Cahun or Tracey Emin – a hurriedly abridged list of the many exceptional female visual artists who imposed, and continue to propose, revolutionary critical and self-critical perspectives on constructions of female selfhood, and of the female body as objects and subjects of reversible gazes within popular culture. The British amateur filmmakers discussed in this volume have not employed any of the features specific to feminist guerrilla visual narratives produced against male-dominated master narratives, and which would have perhaps allowed for images of female bodies subjected to visual self-immolations – including the explicit 'terror' of metabolic intimacy, of eviscerated vaginas and amputated breasts,[3] to avoid the risk of scopophilia in male audiences. Despite not making the female body their visual Procrustean bed for social and cultural debate, amateur filmmakers such as, for instance, Lucy Fairbank, Eleanor Dalyell, Nat and Nettie McGavin, Audrey Lewis, Lady Mary Douglas-Hamilton, Enid Semple Briggs, Wilma Gladstone or Marjorie Alexander, offer different, albeit often equally intriguing, critical pathways to understanding issues of female visual taxidermy and emotional geographies, and of intrinsic voyeurism with its ensuing self-referential narcissism.

Like any other artistic expression, their amateur filmmaking practice implicitly demanded public recognition of their technical skills, choice of themes and life stories, and of their privileged access to special contexts and social networks. Their visual narratives of individual identity and gendered collective memories are mostly anchored in the ways in which their immediate world 'responded' to their recording of it, by self-revealing instances of specific histories and, consequently, by shaping 'certain kinds of [gendered] imagery' (Chadwick 1996: 8). This type of imagery can be found across most types of written and/or oral story-telling used to define women's identities in a given context while, at the same time, their roles within domestic settings continue to be perceived as the family's 'historians' and as 'the guardians of [the family's / collective] memory' (Spence and Holland 1991: 9). For instance, by way of documenting, celebrating and re-memorialising British memsahibs' life in India in the early and mid-twentieth century, Mary Thatcher – the first archivist of the Centre of South Asian Studies (Cambridge) – had compiled and distributed in the late 1970s and early 1980s the 'Questionnaire on Life in India during the British Raj for wives of I.C.S. and other administrators'. In response, she received numerous and detailed accounts from obliging former memsahibs, all diligently answering questions such as 'What sort of houses did you live in?', 'Can you describe a typical day?', 'Did you go on tour with your husband?', 'What social life did you have in India?', 'Did you do any welfare work?'. The visual equivalent to such questions are also found in many films made by British women amateur filmmakers such as Lady Kendall, Lady Dalyell or Barbara Donaldson, to name just some of those discussed in this volume. However, neither the interviewees nor the colonial amateur filmmakers could fix 'into images' answers to some of Mary Thatcher's more intimate, more conceptual questions such as 'If someone says "India" to you suddenly, what is the image or memory that springs to your mind'.[4] From this perspective, it could be argued that negotiating private memories of collective history is predominantly an exercise in deciphering emotional, visual and cultural priming – an exercise that also gauges British imperial past within renewed degrees of historicity, and in which events are remembered within shifting timeframes (Geppert and Muller 2015).

Aiming to assess whether gender constructions are the prerogative ('in the eye') of the beholder, this chapter is primarily concerned with the relationship between male-dominated (popular) master narratives of exploration and the personal visual narratives of female (collective) identity evident in several examples of amateur films made by British women amateur filmmakers in the second half of the twentieth century. For this purpose only two case studies have been selected – the amateur footage recorded by Eileen Healey of the international all-women mountaineering Cho Oyu expedition in 1959, and several exceptional sequences filmed by Rosie Newman during her first trip to India in early 1930s.

'Woodsmoke, Whisky and Wild-looking Women'[5]

Some men negotiated the discomfort of being filmed by means of masquerading, of hiding behind self-deprecating humour and self-inflicting clowning gestures. One such example is offered by the man who accompanied Maharaja Vijaysinhji of Rajpipla, Ella Atherton and a stylish young woman during their visit of the New York World's Fair in 1939. In a series of short scenes, the group is seen eating ice cream from small conical cups, each of them smiling and giggling in response to the awkwardness of having to pose for the camera while licking the quickly melting ice cream. Either Ella or the other woman in their group – both carried a Kodak Six-20 Brownie Junior film camera[6] – recorded a close-up shot of the man. Perhaps primed by the others' slight embarrassment and tendency to make fun of the situation, he starts laughing while covering his face in dripping white ice cream, albeit careful to hold the cone with sufficient dexterity to avoid damaging his elegant pinstripe suit. This is an example of the many occasions in which men chose humour as a defence mechanism when subjected to a woman's cine scrutiny, or when fighting the inherent awkwardness of being powerless in terms of securing a flawless visual identity. The other options would be either the studio-pose look or an abrasive refusal, as in the case of the Nepalese Lamas who declined straightforwardly to be filmed or photographed by Eileen Healey and Micheline Rambaud when, in the autumn of 1959, their paths crossed near the Tengboche Monastery on the ancient trade route between Tibet and Nepal. Eileen and Micheline were part of the first international all-women mountaineering expedition climbing towards the Cho Oyu summit. Disregarding their request, Micheline filmed the Lamas anyway, whether because she didn't know or because she chose to ignore their spiritual beliefs and political anxieties – that the camera might steal their souls, or that their published photographs could reveal their location; the latter posed an serious risk to many Tibetan monks who at that time followed in the footsteps of the 14th Dalai Lama by seeking refuge in northern India. This was an exodus that started in March 1959, only a few months before the expedition begun. In turn, Eileen opted for a more considerate approach, which she later explained in her diary to have been based on technical reasons only: 'I did not bother, the light was bad and I had so little film.'[7]

The first case study discussed in this chapter explores how two women produced significantly different visual histories and, consequently, conflicting re-memory processes about gender roles during postcolonial territorial explorations. While Micheline Rambaud's film of their tragic ascent, *Voyage sans retour*, won the l'Union Internationale des Associations d'Alpinisme Award at the Trento Film Festival of mountaineering and exploration in 1960, Eileen Healey's amateur film of the same expedition failed to secure full sponsorship or to be acknowledged by British TV producers as a valuable historical record, on account of not showing the tragic events that marked their ascent.[8] Shortly after the expedition, Eileen's film was shown occasionally to members of various climbing clubs and then, years later, in a digitally restored version, at the Kendal Mountain Festival in 2009. Importantly, while both women were amateur filmmakers, the French camerawoman opted for the aesthetic guidelines and narrative style common to poetic documentaries such as, for instance, *Rain* (dir. Joris Ivens, 1929), *Night Mail* (dir. Basil Wright, Harry Watt, 1936) or *Man of Aran* (dir. Robert Flaherty, 1938), to name just a few, while the British amateur filmmaker preferred a chronological and candid description of the events – her simple, unswerving filming technique producing in the end a reliable visual record of the expedition.

On 21 August 1959, the international all-women expedition led by Claude Kogan started the ascent on the China–Nepal border toward Tibet's Cho Oyu summit, the world's sixth highest mountain (26,906ft /8,200m) and a training ground for those aiming to climb Mount Everest.[9] Theirs, the fourth expedition after Edmund Hillary who did the first reconnaissance of the north-west face in 1952,[10] was also one of the early expeditions with the highest rate of casualties involving experienced alpinists: four deaths – Claude Kogan, Claudine van der Straten-Ponthoz, Sherpa Ang Norbu and Sherpa Chewang. Moreover, unlike most previous women expeditions, the 1959 Cho Oyu ascent was almost entirely funded by the twelve members of the team and by in-kind sponsorship from food and clothing private companies, alongside some financial backing offered by the *Daily Express* and *Paris Match.*[11] The expedition had also been met with resentment, mild sarcasm[12] and harsh suspicion regarding its members' expertise and skills as suitable alpinists – 'in those days, it wasn't easy to finance an all-women exhibition since, for some people, and even for mountaineers, we were *just* women'.[13] Eileen Healey, a bacteriologist from Brighton,[14] had to secure funds to cover her participation in the expedition as well as the costs of her film equipment. She contacted the Eastman Kodak Company for sponsorship but, before an evaluation of her fund-raising proposal was worth pursuing, she had to prove that the expedition was accredited by the Royal Geographic Society or the Mount Everest Association.[15] Seeking advice and help regarding a possible broadcast, she later approached among others John Grierson – the founder and leading figure of the British Documentary Movement in the 1930s, who was working for Scottish Television in the early 1960s.[16]

On the other hand, Micheline Rambaud had less to worry about financing her filming equipment and film stock since Claude Kogan commissioned her to film the expedition, and there was also help available from her family's business – her father ran a photographic studio in Grenoble. Irrespective of their social and professional background differences, both Eileen and Micheline were passionate mountain climbers and shared an important lineage of visual literacy promoted by women photographic or filming at high altitudes – a cultural tradition led among others by Elizabeth (Lizzie) Le Blond who has been an outstanding alpinist, the founder of the Ladies' Alpine Club (London) in 1907 – the first mountaineering club for women[17] – and a prolific amateur filmmaker and photographer active in the late 1890s and early 1900s.

In spite of their common interests and networks, Eileen and Micheline's films about Kogan's expedition in 1959, which they recorded almost simultaneously while both using colour footage, diverge on two critical levels: the style of filming, and the message proposed by the final edited versions of their respective footage. The storyline rather than the visual schism is initially perplexing since both cine women witnessed the same events, except on the few occasions when Eileen would climb ahead to help set up the next camp. They even shared some of the colour footage, a fact recorded by Eileen in her diary entry on Saturday, 10 October (1959), when she mentions having filmed that day 'for both Micheline & myself".[18] It could be argued that their films differ in their authorial and storyline agendas simply because the filmmakers' personal memories of the expedition underwent (cathartic) narrative shifts. Consequently, the editing of their own footage might have been determined by how each of them related to the memory of the events rather than to the factual information revealed by the images themselves – an instance best described by Hans Belting when noting that the poetics and philosophy of photography, and implicitly of visual culture in general, are determined by how the 'gaze of two beholders looking at the same picture diverge where the memory separates them' (Belting 2014: 148).

Together with their mountaineering companions attempting to reach the Cho Oyu summit in the autumn of 1959, Eileen and Micheline were also authentic 'wom[e]n with a pluck' – a term coined by the *Daily Express* in 1924 when publishing extensive coverage of the feats and ordeals experienced by Stella Court Treatt who accompanied her husband in a sixteen-month expedition from Cape Town to Cairo by car (Zalmonovich 2009). Women like them would forgo the comforts and routine of their respective modern societies in exchange for being able to challenge preconceptions about their physical stamina and exploratory resilience. Often, they recorded in writing or with still or moving images some of the sacrifices they had to make and the subtle drifts in their self-awareness.[19] For instance, Stella Court Treatt noted during the 1924 expedition that

> I am trying to forget that I am a woman; it isn't always easy, but I am sure it is the only way to get through . . . To-day I present a quaint picture of a boy with my long mane shorn off . . . I dream of my missing hair as a fox does of its lost tail. (Zalmanovich 2009: 207).[20]

Scenes of women washing their hair or having it cut – a minor but critical rite of passage in preparation for their journey and its challenges – also appear in Eileen and Micheline's films. Eileen filmed one of Tenzing Norgay's daughters, Pem Pem, who participated in Claude Kogan's expedition, washing her long hair in the river, and followed it with images of Claude cutting Claudine van der Straten-Ponthoz's hair. Filmed also by Micheline, the latter scene became iconic and highly emotionally charged shortly before the expedition was aborted. While both Eileen and Micheline used colour footage and paid great attention to details, the crucial differentiating feature of their filming style, and which transformed this moment in two different vectors of collective memory, was their choice of framing. Eileen used shoulder-level straight forward angles and filmed at length such that Claude and Claudine's interaction during the haircut scene was recorded in detail, intimately but not intrusively (Figure 7.1).[21]

Micheline opted for a different approach such as sharp low or high angles, a focus on the pair of scissors seen as if plummeting from the sky, close-up shots of Claude sticking out her tongue to concentrate better on her task, detail shots of Claudine's ruffled hair and of her raised eyebrows. In short, Eileen documented the scene while Micheline romanticised it.[22]

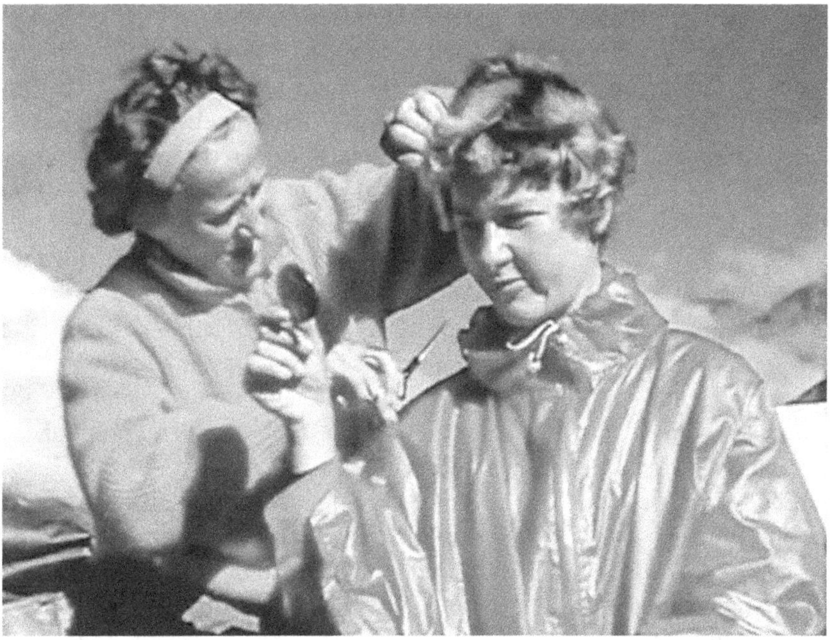

Figure 7.1 Still frame from Eileen Healey, *Cho Oyu Expedition* (1959). © Alpine Club Library.

This is also evident in their written and oral testimonies. For instance, Eileen was more interested in, and valued the opportunity to secure, correct images of the expedition – 'I started [by walking] in front to photograph the Sherpas, and then stopped behind [the party] to photograph them; it was a perfect day and we wanted to photograph the mountain from any view point',[23] or 'I realised that [Claude Kogan] was valuing me more as a photographer than a mountaineer' (Healey 1960: 15). Micheline claimed later that she refused to make a 'big arms and hairy calves' film, one typical of mountaineering visual records of men-only expeditions,[24] and that, instead, she preferred to document the behaviour of European women when at high altitudes. It is one of Micheline's remarks that pivots the core difference between her and Eileen's approach to filming the expedition – 'I wanted to make *a feminine* film about the women taking part in the expedition', one that would reflect faithfully 'in time and space [our] exhaustion at every step of the way, . . . our joy of discovery, [and our] desire to reach our mountain' (emphasis added).[25] In her film, Micheline included detailed scenes of the crew members giving each other toe massages, of Sherpanis stuffing hay in their boots before setting off with their heavy loads fixed with a tumpline (strap placed across the top of the forehead),[26] of Sherpas cooking and eating, long panoramic views of the mountains, and close-up shots of flowers and of peoples' faces.[27] Her framing and editing was respectful of the core aesthetics of poetic documentaries, and was buttressed by a voice over commentary rich to the brim with poetic licence. She entitled her film *Voyage sans retour* ['A One-way Journey' or 'Journey without Return'] but it seems reasonable to suggest that, given her choice of filming style, one reminiscent of Basil Wright's, perhaps *Song of Cho Oyu* would have better suited her overall interpretation of the expedition. However, what discounts Micheline Rambaud's discourse as a valid historical record is not her visual narrative style nor her tendency to romanticise the story in the traditional vein of feminine sensibility – the stigma of women's stereotypified identities, always vehemently repudiated by feminist scholars – but her censoring of two key events. First, Sherpa Wangdi's return after an unsuccessful and tragic reconnaissance trip to Camp 4 during which his companion, Sherpa Chewang, died in an avalanche, and in which he failed to reach the three missing alpinists – Claude Kogan, Claudine van der Straten-Ponthoz and Sherpa Ang Norbu. Having miraculously survived the avalanche, Wangdi managed to return to Base Camp exhausted, starving and with third degree frostbites. Eileen introduced her sequence of Wangdi's return with images of Claude and Claudine walking up a knee-deep snowy slope – 'Last sights we have of them. These two and their faithful Sherpa never returned.'[28] Then she edited in scenes of Wangdi's hands heavily bandaged, and of him cocooned in a thick windbreaker jacket, wearing sunglasses and with his face treated for frostbite. Another of Eileen's scenes shows him walking slowly towards the camera on a mountain path and holding in his bandaged hands ski poles in lieu of crutches (Figure 7.2).

She also included scenes of the heavily stacked glacial stone memorial built by the Sherpas in memory of Ang Norbu and Chewang. In turn, Micheline chose a different narrative. In her voice-over commentary, she introduced the scenes of Wangdi covered in frostbite with a generic statement: '*A* Sherpa who made a miraculous escape after having been caught in an avalanche requires immediate help for his frozen hands/frostbite' (emphasis added).[29] She then used several close-up and medium shots which show in great detail blood-stained bandages being unbearably slowly peeled off Wangdi's fingers, his frostbite-swollen hands, his tumefied face, as well as images of Dorothea Gravina serving him a shot of Martel cognac, and a short scene of him entering a tent where he was going to receive an injection. A playfully condescending voice-over commentary confirms that 'that' Sherpa preferred the cognac rather than the

Figure 7.2 Still frame from Eileen Healey, *Cho Oyu Expedition* (1959). © Alpine Club Library.

injection. She illustrated the commentary with an image of one of the European alpinists holding a fully filled syringe, needle glistening in the sun, and following Wangi into the tent. Micheline then continued her visual story-telling with slow panoramic views of the Cho Oyu, and poetic remarks about how the women mountaineers kept prospecting it with their gazes while planning their ascent. There is no mention in her film of Claude, Claudine, Ang Norbu and Chewang missing or possibly being dead – a certain fact by the time she zoomed in with clinical curiosity onto Wangdi's painfully deformed fingers. The following sequences, and until the end of *Voyage sans retour*, are packed with romanticised allusions, both visual and verbal. She refers to the treacherous terrain – the slightest absentmindedness could have catastrophic consequences;[30] the hardship constantly faced by the climbers while careful to never fail in their enthusiasm for the expedition; the supreme role of the *réchaud à gaz* (camp stove) in securing the survival of the alpinists; and, finally, to the way in which the 'primitive people of the sky have gathered in front of God' and together with the European women climbers, the Sherpas and implicitly the viewers, 'wait for the souls who love the summit'.[31]

Throughout her film, Micheline has skilfully avoided mentioning the tragedy that led the surviving team to abort the expedition. She nevertheless succeeded in making a poetic documentary about events that mirrored what most people learnt from newspapers or later from reading Stephen Harper's book, *Lady Killer Peak. A Lone Man's Story of Twelve Women on a Killer Mountain* – the British journalist banned by Claude Kogan from joining her team, and who claimed with inveterate arrogance to have had access to, and a perfect understanding of, what the all-women expedition experienced during the ascent.[32]

Eileen Healey told a different story from those promoted by Rambaud or Harper – she diligently documented each stage of the expedition, and established herself as an astute judge of visually significant and revealing details. At the time of the Cho Oyu expedition, she already had extensive experience as an amateur photographer,[33] colour film always being her favourite stock, but little to no practice with a film camera. To film the expedition, she borrowed her husband's 16mm Cine-Kodak Royal Magazine Camera. Her filming skills could hardly match Micheline's proficiency in framing, and later editing; however, she succeeded where the more skilled French amateur filmmaker failed – she filmed with the dexterity and responsiveness of an 'insider'; she recorded from *within* most of the events that shaped their tragic ascent. Her film camera was not a tourist's tool, an explorer attentive only to scenic or visually marketable details and events. Eileen avoided sharp or surprising angles, dream-like panoramic views of the mountain, or striking details of harm and pain – proving her ethnographic flair, she included in her film a scene showing a porter killing a goat by traditional means, while avoiding the predictable shock effect of showing Wangdi's frostbite-mutilated fingers. Restored and revised in the early 2000s, the final edit of her film includes a map showing Kogan's planned route (in red) for the ascent as a counter option to the one (in blue) used by Herbert Tichy, Sepp Jochler and Pasang Dawa Lama in 1954, matter-of-fact intertitles (Figure 7.3), and her own voice-over commentary that is equally straightforward and highly informative regarding names, dates and locations.

Since it depicts in chronological order each stage of their expedition, Eileen's film reveals credible and crucial information while successfully avoiding emotional or sentimental undertones even when showing beautiful flowers, women villagers and their crafts, young children, porters, Sherpas, Sherpanis or the splendid landscape. Her film, more so than Micheline's poetic documentary, guides the viewer through the visual discourse without employing a tourist gaze or priming the audience to adopt a melancholic, sorrowful perspective. Consequently, Eileen's amateur film offers a

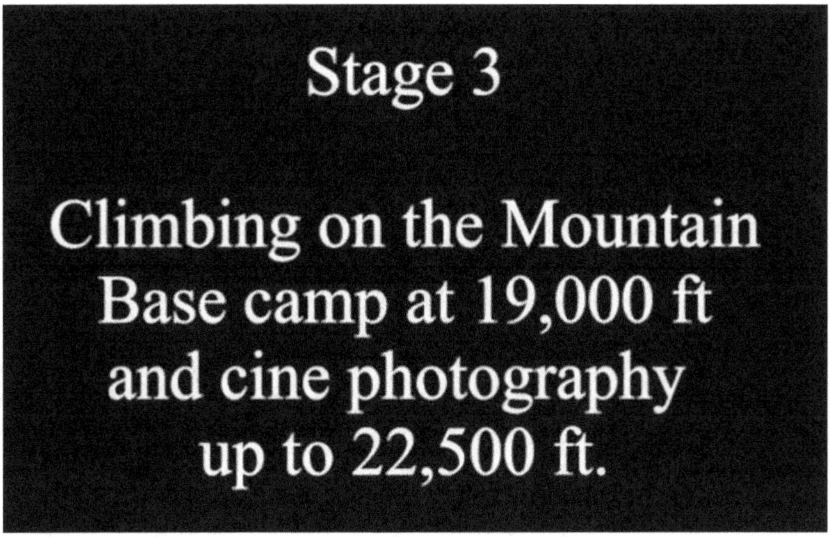

Figure 7.3 Still frame from Eileen Healey, *Cho Oyu Expedition* (1959). © Alpine Club Library.

realistic, unsentimental, coherent and accurate visual documentation about the expedition,[34] a cine narrative that matches her own and the other climbers' diaries of the ascent. As such, it is to date the only visual record of the expedition that mountaineers as well as historians can use in their research of the first international all-women ascent towards the Cho Oyu summit in 1959. Notably, Eileen concluded her film with a short sequence showing Sherpanis and porters leaving the camp for Namche Bazaar, Dorothea checking their heavy loads, and a general view of the snowy summit. These images she underlined with the voice-over commentary: 'It is a glorious day and each man of the party would have their own particular memories of the time they spent on the mountain, with its joys and its disappointments. An appropriate moment to finish the filming.'[35]

While Micheline Rambaud's film presents in a flamboyantly poetic style some of the events that defined their expedition, and not always in chronological order or in the spirit of full disclosure, Eileen Healey's amateur film offers a credible and valid example, in style and storyline, of a historical account of their ascent as well as of a feminist visual narrative. In spite of her original goal to secure a distribution contract and so to reach an ethno-entertainment orientated audience, Eileen's film proved over time to be an authentic feminist visual account. This is precisely because her amateur film scenes documenting Kogan's all-women expedition and their experiences in the autumn of 1959 resulted in an exceptional account *about* women, and therefore become an inspiration *for* women.

The core theoretical issues prompted by the comparison of these two sets of amateur footage (one later edited into a poetic documentary) concerns the filmmakers' approach to chronology and references to death and failure. Their different methods in dealing with the chronology of collective trauma had implicitly produced two different memory accounts, both narrated from individual albeit gender-cohesive perspectives: a feminine (sentimental, romanticised) documentary and a feminist amateur film-chronicle of the women's expedition. Their distinctively divergent narratives also raise issues of how individual constructions of identity within a group relate to master narratives informing significant events. Given that in most societies, any threat to, or loss of, a group's collective memory leads directly to a stronger connection with that group's traditional core values and iconographies – usually male-designed and dominated master narratives – it seems reasonable to argue that each of these two films has responded to similar cultural and individual tensions. For instance, Micheline's film appears to have responded to and conformed with mid-twentieth-century popular expectations of women being humoured when aiming to undertake exceptional (male-domain specific) tasks, and being similarly pardoned in case of failure, as long as their recounting of their experiences verged on the tropes of self-indulging feminine sentimentality. Her film then reconnected with, and subscribed to, the master narrative of successful alpinist feats, which were traditionally the privilege of men with *gros bras* and *mollets poilus* (big arms and hairy calves). In contrast, Eileen's film provokes the audience into a dialogue about hardship, tenacity, cross-racial empathy, community-driven commitment, camaraderie tested and strengthened by natural disasters, insights into styles of leadership and, ultimately, about women continuing a social and cultural ascent beyond the story of a tragic mountaineering experience. Her colour amateur film of the Cho Oyu ascent offers clear and credible access to information about Claude Kogan's expedition, and simultaneously invites new audiences to write their own plausible story of the events depicted as if undertaking an exercise in postcolonial critique where the ultimate text 'floats in the vacuum of potentially infinite range of possible interpretations' (Eco 1992: 41).

'Historian in Celluloid'[36]

A short scene from a late colonial amateur film shot in Kodacolour shows a group of people on a train platform somewhere in India in the early 1930s.[37] Among them is a Caucasian woman with light-blond hair, head uncovered and dressed in a white sari (possibly a widow?); importantly, she is not wearing a *choli* – the under-blouse. Her brief cine portrait was filmed in a medium long shot and from profile, thus allowing the viewer to notice that her sari has unfastened just enough to reveal most of her right breast. The woman appears unaware of this wardrobe malfunction as well as of the filmmaker's presence. Moreover, the viewer, in most cases, would also be oblivious of the filmmaker's gender but presumably ready to predict it based on the topic addressed in this short scene. There are other similar scenes or short sequences where the travelogue-driven themes and topics, the filming style and the filmmaker's access to particular social events creates a space for interpretation charged with cultural assumptions, one in which attitude heuristics takes centre stage.[38] For instance, by what means could an audience estimate within accurate cultural norms the gender of another amateur filmmaker who recorded, this time in black and white, a short sequence showing a group of Indian women dressed in saris, their heads covered with *pallu* – the loose end of the sari – and slowly approaching a group of seated onlookers; one of the women is then shown performing a simple-movements dance. Similar to the previous colour scene, this sequence is also filmed in a medium long shot and, once again, there is no direct acknowledgment of the filmmaker's presence on the part of the woman being filmed (Figures 7.4 and 7.5).

Rather than being a theoretical quiz, this analytical approach could help to translate social expectations of gendered narratives and identity

Figure 7.4 Still frame from Wilson-Pemberton Collection, Film 20 (1932). © CSAS, University of Cambridge.

Figure 7.5 Still frame from Wilson-Pemberton Collection, Film 20 (1932). © CSAS, University of Cambridge.

representation, and consequently dismantle stereotypical representations of gender and gender-affiliated media (self-)representations. It could also help to identify, and possibly amend, ongoing tensions between cultural assumptions and cognitive biases. Since the return-of-the-gaze cannot be applied in the study of these two scenes – a theoretical framework tested in Chapter 5 – to estimate the social and gender dialogue between the filmmaker and his or her subject, another critical perspective is then required when dealing with the baseline cultural assumptions employed by an audience when predicting the gender of an amateur filmmaker. For instance, the same could be said about colour footage filmed at night and showing the bombing of London during the Second World War, of aircraft manufacturing, of wounded soldiers on hospital beds, or of Canadian troops on exercise in Hampshire in the summer of 1941 (Fish 1997: 32).[39] During an informal focus group organised with the help of several undergraduate students taking a course in visual anthropology and new media,[40] as well as in conversations with scholars working in the field of imperial history and physical sciences, questions of predictable gender-specific authorship were consistently answered by providing a stable binary criteria: men would most probably film topics relating to social or economic infrastructures, technology, warfare, urban networks, the world *in action* and topics with a high incidence of sexual innuendo. On the other hand, women would be expected to record the more intimate features of a society such as kinship networks and their celebrations or mundane interactions, landscape, children or pets at play, people emotionally scarred by ongoing wars rather than bomb-shattered bodies or buildings – in sum, detailed rather than general views of core social relationships, and most probably, as a rule of thumb, few if any scenes of sexual content. Such baseline cultural assumptions, while translating deep-seated and highly active attitude heuristics at work across varied social and cultural networks, remain nevertheless often inapplicable to studying amateur media. The two colonial amateur film scenes described above challenge this set of assumptions.

Based on a *prima facie* interpretation of these images, it could be assumed that the filmmaker recording the fair-skinned woman who involuntary revealed her right breast must (could) have been a man, given the extra few seconds and additional colour footage invested in a cine portrait inferring sexual arousal. Equally, the black and white film scene showing a fully dressed Indian dancer performing for a public audience could be simply representative of a female amateur filmmaker's interest in detailed examples of regional traditions. However, once told the gender of the two colonial amateur filmmakers – Rosie Newman filmed the scene on the train platform in India and footage documenting life in Britain during the Second World War, while Raymond C. Wilson recorded the black and white sequence of Indian dancers – the group of undergraduate students and junior research fellows adapted their interpretation of these scenes by exchanging attitude heuristics with hindsight heuristics while still preserving the gender-specific narrative coding.[41] An apt example of this shift in perception and interpretation was offered by one researcher who concluded: 'I don't think a man could have filmed such topics any better than she did.'[42] Apart from the swift revision of verdicts about gender-specific choice of topics, it is also possible to identify on this occasion the implication that Rosie Newman, as a (British) woman amateur filmmaker, was now seen as someone who overcame the social expectations and cultural assumptions of being, by default of her gender, prone to an unfailing amateurism; as someone implicitly less technically savvy and so predisposed to employing poetic licence and to creating sentimentalised views of social landscapes and events – a traditional (gender-confirmed) romantic and romanticising perspective.

This opinion is echoed, albeit in stronger terms, by the voice-over commentary accompanying 'A World Away', the first episode in the four-part BBC programme *The Thirties in Colour* (executive producer David Okuefuna, 2008)[43] – an episode focusing almost entirely on Rosie

Newman's amateur film collection. For instance, several historians interviewed about the historic merit of Rosie's films concluded that, as a member of the British upper class and, implicitly, a proponent of elitist views about the world at large, she has been understandably incapable of identifying with, and recording, images of historical importance. For instance, she allegedly failed to 'fully appreciate what was happening in front of her lens' when filming a political meeting on Chawpatty Beach in Bombay in 1931,[44] or that she 'didn't really understand what she was seeing' when filming the brothel area in Madras, or that she missed recording even a simple picturesque view of Everest although all she needed to do was 'to pan over to the left' after having filmed Kangchenjunga. Overall, and in spite of having produced numerous colour ethno-travelogues and amateur documentaries – that is, filmed, edited, wrote intertitles and added musical accompaniment to her films, for most of which she has also published complementary books[45] – Rosie Newman was henceforth discredited as a reliable visual chronicler of the places and events she recorded. In the case of the voice-over commentary for the BBC documentary, it is less a question of how attitude heuristics predetermines the reception of gender-specific narratives, although this process is still at work. Instead, it could be argued that this commentary reflects a circular example of representative heuristics in that Rosie's social status – the epitome of British upper class – authorises the assumption that her cine portraits of the world around her would echo her class-specific limits of social mobility and social awareness, whether the topic was, for instance, interwar England and Scotland or the end of the British Raj.[46] Such alleged limits of awareness and interpretation demote her amateur films from offering relevant historical information to being just some ready-made cine postcards according to her own ('class') view of the world – a thesis proposed by several interviewees when remarking that:

> Rosie was filming the Britain she wanted to see, the Britain she thought her audience would want to see, and giving it a kind of validation . . . and reassuring herself, reassuring her audience that this was really what Britain was all about, a kind of merry England evoked by hay stacks and horses in the fields

or that '[t]his was the Britain she wanted to exist, and that she believed really did exist, so it was partly self-delusion on her part'.[47]

It is precisely such images of events and social interactions allegedly marked by political unawareness, the mundane or the idyllic that, with hindsight, give a chilling and tangible sense of the unpredictable and brutal historic context experienced by most Europeans in the interwar period. Moreover, scenes like the ones filmed by Rosie Newman in England,

Scotland, France and India before the start of the Second World War reveal crucial cultural contexts that translate social hierarchies, whether directly or by proxy. Such images also supplement the large number of amateur films made *during* the war and which also showed almost exclusively scenes identical to a carefree pre-war lifestyle. For instance, this identical narrative and visual rhetoric is found, for example, in the home movies made by SS officers while on leave and enjoying precious time with their families and friends in social settings which, were it not for their uniforms, would deceive most audiences when assessing the respective historic time. Therefore, issues of 'self-delusion' are perhaps less applicable as quick armchair psychoanalyses of amateur filmmakers' motivations for compensatory narratives of their lives and times, and more relevant to understanding how attitude and representative heuristics secure the ongoing stereotypification of visual narratives produced by people belonging to a specific gender and/or class. Although Rosie Newman is praised by most scholars, media producers and by her audiences, then and now, for her courage when filming at night the Blitz in London, or for her tenacity in securing access and the permission to film British and French military sites and operations, which were otherwise unavailable to most civilians, these achievements are recognised as the result of her personality and social and political networks rather than the result of her own interest and awareness of key historical moments. In reading the books she published as supplements to most of her films, it becomes clear that she was well aware of the ways in which her work was often framed in inflexible classist and misogynistic terms. For instance, she notes in her volume, *The France I Knew: The Story of the Film*, that, following the news of her having obtained a special military permit to show some of her films to the British Expeditionary Forces stationed in France, 'a friend remarked, I thought rather rudely, "Your face is your fortune, otherwise they would have given you a good rebuff"' (Newman 1943: 24). Perhaps an even more excessive and injurious judgement of her work as a visual historian of her time was the accusation of 'masquerading under The Woman Voluntary's Service', which she joined at the start of the Second World War.[48]

In light of Newman's contemporary mid-twentieth-century cultural and social ideologies, which she had to negotiate in terms that now define her as a pioneering woman filmmaker – 'amateur' remains a disputable classification in the case of her film collection – and of early twenty-first century studies of her work, it seems reasonable to suggest that, while persistently dismissed as a self-promoting socialite with an expensive hobby, of elitism, and political naivety, Rosie used her film practice as an icebreaker through social classes (represented or alluded to) and across imperial contexts, and, for want of a better expression, made her cine camera her shield and weapon. Hers is not a solitary example of how often the historical merit of certain amateur films, the amateur filmmakers' technical skills, and validity of their political or social interests are judged based on the audience's attitude heuristics – a process immediately at work once the filmmaker's gender has been acknowledged and consequently primed the viewers' interpretations and reception of the respective images.

Without attempting an unwarranted theoretical 'devil's advocate' exercise in amateur film studies, the scenes and sequences used in the 'A World Away' documentary as examples of Rosie Neman's social unawareness of wider ideological, class and economic crises, offer upon closer examination the opposite thesis and recommend her as someone fully aware of such issues while also possessing finely tuned diplomatic skills. For instance, rather than disparagingly reject the historic worth of her scenes of, for instance, the Chawpatty beach in Bombay, the brothel area in Madras or of the 'missing' Everest, it is markedly more applicable to contextualise them by analysing the ways in which Rosie filmed them, her use of intertitles and her notes published in the books describing these ethno-travelogues. By the time Rosie Newman filmed her short scene of the Chawpatty beach in Bombay in 1931, the place had made the news across Indian and British newspapers at least thrice: first in April 1919 when it hosted a large protest against the Imperial Legislative Council's decision to pass legislation (the Rowlatt Act) allowing specific political cases to be tried without juries; second in August 1920, when Lokmanya Bal Gangadhar Tilak, a key leader of the Indian Independence Movement, was cremated on the beach; and in April 1930, when Kamaladevi Chattopadhyay and Sarojini Naidu, noted Indian freedom fighters, lead a 'Salt Satyagraha' in support of Mohandas Karamchand Gandhi's twenty-four-day Dandi March (Dandi Satyagraha) – a nonviolent civil disobedience act against the British salt monopoly.

On that sunny January day when Rosie filmed on the Chawpatty beach, instead of recording the visual 'fodder' of choice for most amateur filmmakers on such occasions – frothy waves, families bathing, children playing and so on – she aimed her camera at the crowds and recorded a precise, somewhat slow-paced panoramic view of their meeting. At the beginning of her sequence, a South Asian man looked straight at this European woman holding her film camera at eye level while accompanied, as was the custom, by a male chaperone belonging to the British official ranks. Judging by Rosie's framing and filming style – one-take sequence – it could be argued that her images indicate acknowledgement rather than unawareness of the importance of the scene 'in front of her eyes' and, implicitly, confirm her alertness to the possible risks to which her filming exposed herself and her companion. Importantly, she did film the 'political meeting' as noted by one of the historians interviewed for the BBC's 'A World Away'. In fact, she 'introduced' the meeting by panning towards it and then stopping the filming shortly after having recorded it. Apart from the historical background defining the Chawpatty beach as a site of anti-British political unrest during the first half of the twentieth century, and Rosie Newman's progressive choice to film demonstrators gathered at the beach, there is a detail in her short sequence that requires further investigation: a flag. The crowds filmed by Rosie that day on the Chawpatty beach had gathered around a red flag; next to it, a man in white clothes stood on a makeshift podium while addressing an audience. Only when viewed the second time and in slow motion does this very short sequence reveal that Rosie has filmed twice (!) this gathering of men and women around the red flag of the Communist Party of India (founded in 1925) (Figure 7.6). It is this crucial detail, and her choice of recording it twice, that confirm Rosie's unquestionable awareness of the social and political context she was witnessing. For a British upper class woman interested in capturing on colour film *glimpses of India* 'to keep alive the memory of [her] wonderful two months tour [of India]', and who 'seized the opportunity of filming rare scenes and incidents selected *almost at random*' (emphasis added), Rosie's short scene of the Chawpatty beach suggests that the implicit haphazardness of her filming was on some

Figure 7.6 Still frame from Rosie Newman, *Glimpses of India* (1935). © IWM, London.

occasions a strategic ideological digression – she displayed a tactful social unawareness, a simulated *incompetence* at explicitly highlighting the obvious social tensions and cultural clashes (Newman undated: 9). Moreover, she would insert such scenes between tourist cine views, like her several beautiful colour shots of Gateway to India filmed on her arrival by sea at Bombay – the type of colonial imagery that duly aligned her amateur filmmaking practice to her British male counterparts such as, for instance, Alexander Gregory Stavridi, Lord George Douglas Hamilton (Selkirk Collection) or Air Commodore Leonard de Ville Chisman (Chisman/Keal Collection).[49]

Issues of not being able 'to really understand what [one is] seeing', to quote the historian decrying Rosie Newman's unawareness of her cine subject when filming the brothel area in Madras, are equally applicable to audiences' ability to identify valid historical information in amateur films, irrespective of whether the audience is the general public or media scholars. Raymond C. Wilson's amateur 16mm black and white film sequence recorded on 21 December 1932, while he and his friend, Mr M. Pemberton, were stationed at the Guest House in Rajgarh (Madhya Pradesh), offers a pertinent example.[50] The sequence consists of two sets of scenes showing a group of Indian women on the terrace of a palace. The first images were recorded from a seated position, indoors, with the silhouette of one of the women dancing at some distance, on the terrace (Figure 7.7). The second

Figure 7.7 Still frame from Wilson-Pemberton Collection, Film 20 (1932). © CSAS, University of Cambridge.

set of images were filmed while standing near the dancer on the terrace and show her simple dance movements. The entire sequence indicates nothing more than a customary visual record of what could have been an itinerant and underprivileged dancing troupe, somewhere in India. The images recorded by Raymond on this occasion seem at a first glance to have *flattened* through their lack of details the more complex context in which this dance performance took place. As is often the case with amateur films, accompanying written documentation can clarify or validate the historic merit of the images recorded. In this case, it is Mr Pemberton's diary that elucidates the pervasive awkwardness of the dance performance – no flamboyant dance gestures, no glittery jewellery and no sign of a music band: the Indian women dancing were prostitutes summoned by the Comptroller to perform in honour of the two British travellers. Further types of services performed by these women were offered, as noted in his diary, at varying prices starting at 4 annas (1/16 of a rupee) and reaching the expensive fee of 1 rupee.[51] The audience, then and now, is offered no indication, whether direct or implied, by Mr Wilson's short sequence about the social context that prompted this dance, and the cultural meaning of it.

Rosie Newman's short sequence of the brothel area, which she filmed while travelling through Madras in 1931 (Figure 7.8), presents the viewer with a richer interpretative framework, alongside a valuable

Figure 7.8 Still frame from Rosie Newman, *Glimpses of India* (1935). © IWM, London.

example of her strategic naivety about certain cultural taboos. For this scene, she also produced an intertitle – 'A quaint street of houses with barred windows'. Words such as 'quaint' and 'barred' create a semantic tension that redirects the reading of her short sequence showing two-story houses with laundry drying on their balconies and, on one occasion, a naked young child, pressing his or her bloated stomach (most probably the effect of protein calorie malnutrition, a common sign of starvation) against the railing while standing next to a woman dressed in a light-coloured sari. It seems reasonable to assume that any tourist happening to walk along such a street would enquire about the meaning of the peculiar urban setting, especially someone who, like Rosie, was in search of 'rare scenes and incidents' across India. Jane Fish, the only scholar to date who did extensive research of Miss Newman's films, remarked in 1997 that 'Rosie was mostly interested [in recording] people and daily life' (Fish 1997: 30) – both topics were covered in her short sequence of the brothel area in Madras.

These images document two key features of Miss Newman's filmmaking practice. First, that she must have often chosen the subject matter for her films, especially if the topic was somewhat unconventional or posed access limitations, whether for social or military reasons. For instance, it could be argued that, in the case of the 'red-light district' in Madras, Rosie decided to film the brothels once aware of their meaning, as otherwise it would have been at least indelicate on the part of her escort, usually appointed by an aide-de-camp, to subject his guest – a female representative of the British upper class – to such an inappropriate context. Second, Rosie used her filming style and her intertitles to reveal a double-meaning footnoted commentary for her images. The intertitle introducing the brothels sequence is deceptive at first – a flat rhetorical question – and so it prompts most viewers, and some scholars too, to pigeonhole her images as accidental recordings of an insignificant albeit somewhat exotic street. The 'exoticism' of it being a satisfactory answer in itself. However, when read in close connection with the images of the young woman standing next to the naked child, her intertitle functions in a richer connotative way: it describes the setting while subtly and yet unquestionably primes her audience to read these images *between the lines*. The semantic tension between 'quaint' and 'barred' is thus translated into an emotional unease and therefore amplifies the viewers' curiosity about what is being shown. Such examples of her amateur filmmaking and, importantly, of her commentary on cultural traditions and discrepancies fit her social portrait – apart from being renown for her negotiation skills, of 'never taking no for an answer'[52] – Rosie

Newman has also been appreciated among her friends for her dry sense of humour and tactful communication skills.

Finally, there remains the issue announced in 'A World Away' of Rosie's laughable faux pas when 'missing' Everest – of her failed tourist gaze at the exact moment when one of the most celebrated subjects of her journey to Darjeeling was, cinematographically speaking, starring her in the face. Indeed, the short colour scene which she filmed of the Kangchenjunga Mountain, followed by a quick panoramic of the snowy peaks on the Assamese horizon line, did not include the crucial image which every amateur filmmaker, photographer or draughtsman traveller in her position would have undoubtingly recorded. This short scene remains controversial for its lack of the 'jewel in the crown' of the Himalayan mountain range. The historian who politely excused Rosie's choice of framing by implying that she must have been misadvised – an indirect way of saying that she wouldn't have been necessarily already aware about were to 'look' for Everest – suggests a shortcut analysis of the images and of her cultural insight and filmmaking skills. A possibly more viable methodology could consider an excerpt from her book, *Glimpses of India: The Story of the Film* (undated), in which Rosie describes her

> first glimpse of the great snow mountains, so often called "The Roof of the World". The giant white peaks of unconquered Mount Everest and beautiful Kangchenjunga, outlined against the clear blue sky, left us a memory that can never fade. . . . That evening we watched one of the gorgeous Himalayan sunsets. . . . The next day we left in a thick fog, which blotted out all views of the mountains.

This written memory cancels at least two possible interpretations of her cine scenes of the mountain range. First, it suggests that she didn't film on the day of her arrival since the colour scene shows large clusters of white clouds instead of a clear blue sky as described in her book. Second, that she might not have filmed on the second day either when, again according to her written description, there was a thick fog. In this case, rather than letting judgement heuristics legislate a critical analysis of her filming skills or cultural acumen,[53] it might be worth embarking on a study of amateur filmmakers', and of visual documentarists in general, memory-building processes in relation to their own acts of recording certain sources of memory, whether in written or visual form.

Overall, Rosie Neman was an avid and agile ambassador between worlds, cultures, classes and disciplines – between Britain and its colonies in the 1930s, between Britain and its Allies in the 1940s, between British aristocracy in England and in Scotland, between military ranks, charities and the wider public, and between commercial, commissioned ethnographic films and newsreels and professionally produced (albeit under the shield of amateur film practice) visual anthropological records.[54] Newman was elected as Fellow of the Royal Geographical Society on 3 February 1936, and received public recognition for her work as an amateur filmmaker and visual historian of (mostly) Britain in the 1930s and 1940s – some film critics praising her *Britain at War* as the 'most interesting and comprehensive documentaries produced during the war'.[55] The unanimous acknowledgement she has received as a proficient, socially aware and philanthropic amateur filmmaker can hardly be credited only to her connections within the upper echelons of the British society of the time, from royalty to military and diplomatic networks. It is then imperative for historians and visual theorists working in British and imperial studies to avoid the attitude heuristics trap – the one directed at gender-subjective narratives, and at the stereotypical gender-specific lack of technical skills and political or social awareness. Rosie Newman's films will continue to present to numerous generations of scholars invaluable research sources owing to her unparalleled access to events, war zones and social networks, which will gradually be deciphered from less politically and class-tinted perspectives.

Conclusion

Several British women amateur filmmakers and their handful of scenes filmed across the world in the second half of the twentieth century challenged in their time, as well as today, common beliefs about their role *as* gender in documenting as well as creating specific discourses of historical consciousness. Persistent acts of social and aesthetic courage, of intellectual curiosity, creativity and perseverance when facing international bureaucratic avalanches or snow blizzards at 22,500ft altitude are found in most of their films, and in all the other women filmmakers' films discussed here or elsewhere. This chapter aimed to highlight the similar cultural and technical crusades on which two British women belonging to distinct social classes embarked in the 1930s and 1950s with the common goal of recording images of worlds away from home–Britain, as well as images of a Britain in which they negotiated issues of popular visual culture and collective memories. While neither Eileen nor Rosie opted (or had access) to record scenes of physical trauma – Eileen's film of the Cho Oyu Expedition in 1959 was judged as 'uneventful'[56] – their colour amateur films prove to be uniquely resourceful visual testimonials of exceptional historical events and people, and of profoundly scarring emotional and psychological traumas. Moreover, their amateur filmmaking practice enable a fertile dialogue between their autobiographical memories and specific, gender-free examples of cultural memory – a dialogue evidenced in their intertitles, voice-over commentary and, in Rosie's case, corresponding books. Films like *Glimpses of India*, *Britain at War* or *Cho Oyu Expedition 1959*, alongside untitled films made by Eleanor Dalyell, Queen Elizabeth II and several Scottish women amateur filmmakers such as Jenny Brown or Nat and Nettie McGavin, challenge fixed interpretative agendas. They also confirm the filmmakers' rich and often revolutionary visual literacies while highlighting innovative perspectives on constructions of female selfhood. Although often obscured by perception biases that miscategorise their films as travelogues, home movies or amateur records of mundanity, most women amateur filmmakers have proved throughout the twentieth century that they were each in their own right a veritable 'one-woman film unit' with an acute flair for re-presenting history.[57] Since representation, whether through optical, virtual or mental images, remains a contested area of finite as well as endless interpretations – 'representation . . . always conveys more than it intends; and it is never totalising' (Phelan 1993: 2) – then Rosie Newman and Eileen Healey, to name just two of the cine women discussed in this book, have ultimately succeeded in inspiring their contemporary as well as future generations of amateur filmmakers. For this role, they sometimes received public recognition even if in oblique ways as, for instance, when Royal Air Force Group Captain A. E. Pratt enquired with the editor of *The Lady* about Rosie Newman's next screening of *Britain at War* in London: 'I make this request as I am myself an enthusiastic user of cine-camera, and I would esteem it a privilege if I could be a member of her audience' (Pratt 18 June 1948). Paying tribute is always a gender-free gesture, something that twentieth-century women filmmakers must have intuitively known every time they tested patriarchal codes of representation with their 'amateur' films.

Notes

1. Original French captions: 'Je me suis contenté d'une seule maitresse qui élève notre enfant', and 'Leur passion a fait long feu', image 32/36, *Images en quête d'histoires*, media project by Valérie Mréjen, Paris: Les presses du réel, 2017). The project resulted in the production of *Quatre enfants*, a two-part film including 'La femme émancipée' and 'Les doubles' short visual essays (<https://www.fraciledefrance.com/images-quete-dhistoires-valerie-mrejen-2/>, last accessed 17 September 2017).
2. Original French captions: 'Mais elle rêvait d'un ailleurs' and 'Il est parti le plus loin possible', image 10/36, ibid.
3. Jesse Kanda's artwork for Bjork's *Utopia* cover album (2017) offers a rich example of how female genitalia can be employed in gendered self-referential

(spiritual?) iconography, within and beyond sumptuously luminous albeit morbid fantasies.

4. Mary Thatcher's 'Memsahibs interviews' files are held by the Centre of South Asian Studies, University of Cambridge.
5. This is the title of Chapter 10 in *Lady Killer Peak* by Stephen Harper who had been appointed by the *Daily Express* to report on Claude Kogan's expedition; she denied him access to the team during the ascent. Nevertheless, Harper announced with the first sentence of his book that 'This is a story of one man, twelve women and a killer mountain . . . told by the man' (Harper 1965:5).
6. The Kodak Six-20 Brownie Junior 620 size film camera was produced between 1939 and 1943.
7. Eileen Healey Diary, entry for Wednesday, 9 September 1959. The Alpine Club Library in London holds Mrs Healey's expedition diary and several of her personal and official letters, as well as newspaper clips about her two Himalayan expeditions, in 1956 and in 1959 respectively. The author would like to thank Nigel Buckley (librarian) and Glyn Hughes (archivist) at the Alpine Club Library for their indefatigable help and valuable advice regarding the Eileen Healey Collection and many other relevant archival sources in relation to all-women alpine expeditions. Grateful thanks also to Tim Healey for granting us the permission to reproduce several still frames from Eileen's amateur film, *Cho Oyu 1959*.
8. See letters addressed to Eileen Healey by John Grierson on 13 February 1960, and from Miss R. Collins, Secretary to Dr [John] Grierson, dated 24 March 1960. Eileen Healey Files, Alpine Club Library, London. See also 'Pinnacle President on the One Show' (<http://pinnacleclub.co.uk/pinnacle-president-on-the-one-show/>, last accessed 12 January 2016).
9. The European alpinists participating in this expedition were Margaret Darvall, Eileen Healey, Colette Le Bret, Dorothea Gravina, Loulou Boulaz, Jeanne Franco, Claudine van der Straten-Ponthoz, Claude Kogan and Micheline Rambaud. The Nepalese alpinists included, among many others, the Sherpas Ang Norbu, Wangdi, Dannu, Gyalzen, Lakpa, Phu Dorji, Da Norbu, Sona Gyeme, Pem Pem, Nima, Nawang Tsering, Chewang, Gompu and Douma. See also Brickell and Garrett (2013).
10. Herbert Tichy's Austrian team completed the first ascent without oxygen in 1954 – the same year Claude and her husband, George Kogan, also attempted to climb the mountain but failed.
11. See 'Details sur L'Organisation et les buts de L'expédition feminine a L'Himalaya 1959. Pourquoi un expédition feminine' by Claude Kogan (1959), in Eileen Healey Files held by the Alpine Club Library, London.
12. See 'Women Scale Himalayas. British team find it slimming' (newspaper clipping; no reference, in Eileen Healey Files, Alpine Club Library). Women alpinists were often quoted in their attempt to echo similar 'marketing' slogans as in the case of Mrs Joyce Dunsheath with whom Eileen Gregory (later Healey) embarked on 'an "away-from-it-all" holiday trip' in the Himalayas

in 1956, and enjoyed a 'holiday from housekeeping!' (*Daily Express Saturday*, 4 August 1956).

13. Original French text: '. . . à cette époque, il n'était pas évident de trouver des financements pour une expédition de femmes, car pour certains, même alpinistes, nous n'étions QUE des femmes . . .' (emphasis in original) in *Rencontres, FFME IMAG*, 7 December 2015, <http://ffme-imag.fr/rencontres_7/micheline-rambaud-raconte-la-premiere-expedition-feminine-en-himalaya> (last accessed 8 January 2017). A similar view concerning most women climbers has been publicly criticised by the curators of the 'British Women Climb' exhibition hosted by the Keswick Museum (29 September 2017 – 16 September 2018 (<http://www.mountain-heritage.org/news/british-women-climb-exhibition-opens-today/>, last accessed 12 December 2017).
14. 'It's not lonely at 20,000ft', *Gazette* (newspaper clipping about Mrs Joyce Dunsheath, Miss Hilda Reid, Miss Frances Delany and Miss Eileen Gregory's (later Healey) Himalayan expedition and prospection of the Kulu Spiti and Lahour areas, North-West Himalaya, in 1956; no reference, in Eileen Healey Files, Alpine Club Library) – Miss Gregory '[b]efore she left England she was a bacteriologist. Now she is looking for a new job.'
15. Kodak Limited official letter addressed to Mrs J. A. D. Healey, titled 'Expédition Feminine 1959 au Nepal' dated 23 July 1959. Eileen has drafted a reply written in pencil on the same letter – 'Thank you for your letter. This appeal is supported by the Everest Foundation who has given us a grant of £500.' Eileen Healey Files, Alpine Club Library.
16. Official letter signed by John Grierson dated 13 February 1960, in which he confirms that 'I shall be glad to see [Eileen's final edit of her amateur film of the Cho Oyu expedition] and give you my word about it.' Eileen Healey Files, Alpine Club Library.
17. Relevant information about Lizzie Le Blond is available at the Martin and Osa Johnson Safari Museum, see <http://www.safarimuseum.com/research/permanent-collection/elizabeth-main-le-blond-collection/> (last accessed 2 August 2017).
18. Eileen Healey Diary of the Cho Oyu expedition, page 52 (manuscript). Alpine Club Library.
19. Micheline Rambaud recalled in an interview for *Le Magazine de la Fédération Française de la montagne et de l'escalade* that at some point during the Cho Oyu expeditions she noted in her diary, 'I wonder why did I choose to die here?' (original French text: 'Je me demande bien pourquoi je suis venue mourir ici?'), in *Rencontres, FFME IMAG*, 7 December 2015.
20. Rosie Newman made wardrobe concessions when filming on-board HMS *Berkeley* in late June 1941 – she exchanged her stylish two-piece suit for a pair of trousers borrowed from captain Lt Cdr H. G. Walters so that she could have easy access across all decks and most areas of the battleship. Rosie's brief instance of cross-dressing and her 'mateship' with the crew was documented in a photograph that shows her posing proudly in her new

outfit while enjoying a 'tot of rum' (photograph, IWM catalogue number HU 65941).

21. A still frame from either Eileen Healey's or Micheline Rambaud's 'haircut' sequences was used on the cover of the *Paris Match*, no: 551, 31 October 1959 (Anon. 1959).
22. Micheline also filmed several scenes showing the women's personal hygiene and beautification routines. For instance, she included in her film images of a European and a Nepalese woman putting on lipstick while using a small hand mirror, while the voice over commentary traded apparent frivolity for the celebration of their survival skills: 'Que passe comme une faiblesse, mais que souvent a été notre force, notre féminité' ['What appeared to be a weakness, has often been our strength, our femininity']. Another scene filmed by her shows a Sherpani picking hair lice from a Nepalese man's head while he lay asleep next to her; this time, the voice over commentary leaves room for nuanced interpretations: 'Pourquoi pas . . . coquetterie!' ['Why not . . . coquetry!'].
23. Eileen Healey Diary, entry for Monday 12 October 1959. Eileen Healey files, Alpine Club Library.
24. Original French text: 'Sans être un film de gros bras avec des mollets poilus', interview with Micheline Rambaud published in *Quest-France*, 15 July 2013, <https://www.ouest-france.fr/pays-de-la-loire/challans-85300/micheline-rambaud-raconte-ce-voyage-sans-retour-odyssea-739545> (last accessed 3 August 2016).
25. Original French text: 'J'ai souhaité réaliser un film féminin attaché à la vie des femmes tout au long de la route. Il reste le reflet fidèle dans le temps et dans l'espace, de la fatigue à chaque pas, de notre joie de découverte, du désir d'arriver à notre montagne', ibid.
26. Both Eileen and Micheline remarked in their voice-over commentaries that several Sherpani demanded, and succeeded, in carrying heavier loads than those transported by the Sherpas, to secure a better payment.
27. This set of images subscribes to the visual rhetoric specific to early colonial amateur ethnographic records; one nevertheless still thriving today in well-meant advertisements such as 'Ingredients from afar', a testimonial by Susan Curtis, Neal's Yard Remedies and Natural Health Director and Ingredients Pioneer [*sic*], illustrated with an image of Nepalese women and children sitting on the ground against the backdrop of a mountain range. Curtis noted 'In Nepal, it was wonderful to meet the women who hand-harvest the nourishing dhatelo oil and chiuri butter we enrich our new Frankincense Intense Lift Cream with', in *Neal's Yard Remedies Catalogue*, Issue 3, Autumn 2017, pp. 12–13.
28. Eileen Healey's voice-over commentary included in the digital version of her amateur film, *Cho Oyu 1959*. A copy of the film is available at the Alpine Club Library, London. For a detailed report on each stage of the expedition see essays published by Margaret Darval ('First Phase', pp. 11–14), Eileen

Healey ('The Second Phase', pp. 14–18) and Dorothea Gravina ('The Last Phase', pp. 18–22) in *Ladies' Alpine Club Library Journal*, 1960, pp. 11–22.

29. Original French text: 'Un Sherpa pris dans une avalanche qui renter comme par miracle et dont il faut soigner ses mains gelées', Micheline Rambaud's voice-over commentary for her documentary, *Voyage sans retour* (FR., 1959/1960). A copy of the film is available at the Alpine Club Library, London.
30. Original French text: 'La moindre négligence expose à la catastrophe', Micheline Rambaud's voice-over commentary, ibid.
31. Original French text: 'Le peuple primitif du ciel sont rassemblé devant Dieu' and 'nous attendons les âmes qui aiment le sommet', ibid.
32. In his preface to *Lady Killer Peak*, Harper announced that his is a story 'of women's rebellion against man's natural assumptions of command decision, and of feminine rivalries that contributed to the loss of four lives', a story told 'by the only man to share the women's adventures'. Harper's sense of self-entitlement is as baffling as Micheline Rambaud's avoidance to include in her film direct references to the loss of four lives, and to the correct chronology of the expedition. For one of the more detailed reports on Claude Kogan's Cho Oyu expedition in 1959, see the special report published by *Paris Match* on 31 October 1959 (Anon. 1959), and Robert Daley's (1959) article 'The mountain is still the master'.
33. Eileen took colour photographs during her trip to Yugoslavia (27 March – 11 April 1953). See Eileen Healey Diaries, volume 18: 1953. Alpine Club Library, London, <http://www.alpine-club.org.uk/ac2/EH_diaries/EHD/EHD_18_1953.html> (last accessed 10 March 2017).
34. Similar visual rhetoric is found in Raymond Wilson's footage of 'setting camp at Baltal, and of trekking, porters and train horses across snowy peaks'; see Wilson-Pemberton Collection – Film 6, <http://www.s-asian.cam.ac.uk/archive/films/item/wilson-pemberton-collection-film-6/> (last accessed 25 April 2017).
35. Eileen Healey's voice-over commentary, *Cho Oyu Expedition 1959.*
36. Coxhead 1948a, magazine cover.
37. Kodacolor (lenticular process, 16mm film) and Kodachrome (16mm, integral tripack colour reversal film stock) see Spottiswoode (1969).
38. Attitude heuristics is commonly defined as the psychological process involving the use of positive or negative attitudes in establishing favourable or unfavourable (approach or avoidance) communication and relational strategies (see Gilovich et al. 2002).
39. The authors owe a great debt of gratitude to Jane Fish for her unstinting help and generous advice regarding Rosie Newman's film collections as well as background information about her film practice.
40. The author has also conducted a similar focus group with postgraduate students and junior research fellows during her seminar series, 'Visual Rhetoric of South Asian history', hosted annually by the Centre of South Asian Studies (CSAS), University of Cambridge. The feedback received

on this occasion was similar to that offered by the undergraduate students at the Department of Social Anthropology (University of Cambridge).

41. Hindsight heuristics or hindsight bias occurs when individuals, once aware of an outcome, overestimate their original foresight (Hertwig et al. 2003)
42. It is perhaps of no marginal relevance that the researcher who summarised the results of this focus group is a man.
43. Episode available on YouTube, at <https://www.youtube.com/watch?v=5yHdVLrUFi4> (last accessed 12 May 2016).
44. Rosie Newman is nevertheless credited in 'A World Away' with having 'captured some of the divisions within the Indian society that would lead to the Partition [of India]' – this voice-over commentary accompanies her scenes of signposts at an Indian train station denominating specific areas for access to water, or to rest areas allowing only Europeans, Hindus or Muslims respectively.
45. Rosie Newman's books include *Glimpses of India: The Story of the Film* (undated), *To the Land of the Pharaohs: The Story of the Film* (*c*.1937) *Britain at War: Narrative of a Film* (1942), *The France I Knew, the Story of the Film* (1943), *A Flying Visit to Yugoslavia, the Story of the Colour Film* (*c*.1956).
46. Representative heuristics is the psychological process during which an individual relies on similarity-driven assessments and judgements (see Gilovich et al. 2002; Aronson 2011).
47. Voice-over commentary, 'A World Away' episode, *The Thirties in Colour* documentary series, BBC, executive producer David Okuefuna, 2008.
48. Rosie Neman interviewed by David Kenten, 14 February 1980, for the TV production *A Bygone Special: Miss Rosie Newman – A Colour Supplement* (Anglia TV, 1980). Excerpt from interview rushes on three Nagra tapes; copies of the tapes and of the film are also held by the Imperial War Museum (IWM ref. MGH 1928; IWM Sound Archive ref. 13843/3).
49. See Stavridi Collection – Film 1, <http://www.s-asian.cam.ac.uk/archive/films/item/stavridi-collection-film-1/> (last accessed 2 May 2017); the Selkirk Collection (Acc. No. 196/163/004; Bristol Archives); and the Chisman/Keal Collection (Acc. No. 2006/005/010 Bristol Archives).
50. Raymond C. Wilson filmed at length his extensive tour of India which he undertook in the company of M. Pemberton between 1933 and 1934. While Mr Wilson filmed their journey, Mr Pemberton documented it in great detail in his travel journal. Mr Wilson's films and Mr Pemberton's diary are held by CSAS, University of Cambridge.
51. It is unclear whether Mr Pemberton referred to British Indian rupees or to local (Central Provinces) rupees.
52. Coxhead (1948b).
53. Judgement heuristics is the psychological process during which an individual employs a mental shortcut when attempting to understand, for instance, a concept, another person's behaviour, a social context or to solve a problem (see Gilovich et al. 2002; Crano and Prislin 2008).

54. Rosie Newman's large collection of amateur films deserves at least a comprehensive monograph. To date, Jane Fish, Senior Curator at the Imperial War Museum, London, has produced the only body of consolidated research dedicated to Newman's amateur films, alongside, since the mid-1990s, securing additional donations to this collection, including the gramophone plates Newman used during her public screenings and which Fish salvaged from a derelict garage owned by Bob Fennymore – Newman's former driver and projectionist.
55. Anon. (1977).
56. Similarly, Kevin Brownlow's amateur footage of the Irish Troubles recorded in the late 1960s were deemed 'unusable' by several film production companies since they did not show images of bombing, casualties or frontline action. Interview with Kevin Brownlow, London, March 2015 – November 2016 by Annamaria Motrescu-Mayes.
57. Anon. (194(6)).

CHAPTER 8

Reimagining Boundaries: Amateur Animations

> Don't give up . . . it's worth it for the magic and lasting pleasure animation can bring. (Graber 1982: 231)

For the amateur turned professional animator, Sheila Graber, cats and cartoons seem inseparable and part of the lasting pleasure of making films. As companions while she animates and as recurring characters, her feline figures are part of what Wells (1998: 122) calls an inner personal world made visible by animation. Their role in offering practical tips and reassurance to the amateur animator spanned decades: they enlivened an often earnest hobby literature and were reminders that even the committed amateur could be playful. Given their wider association with animation history, might we see also Graber's cats as an embodiment of the successful animator's skill in combining personal curiosity, ingenuity and patience? If, as Honess Roe (2013: 106) suggests, animation relies upon oblique and often metaphorical ways to evoke meaning and response, her notion of the genre's capacity to tap into memories and histories passed on through families and indeed whole cultures also seems pertinent to exploring female amateur animation. Given women's roles in curating cultural knowledge and family biographies, animated storytelling offers alternative ways of sharing historical experiences. The surrealist animator Jan Svankmajer, in his BBC broadcast *The Magic Art of Jan Svankmajer* in 1992, also suggests that animation helps to redefine the everyday (cited in Wells 1998). It invites viewers to question reality and challenge perceptions. Writing about the British animator, Joanna Quinn, Gomez (2010) speaks of 'the small details which fuel our everyday life' and anecdotes that provide her inspiration; Garcia (2010) similarly refers to how 'intimate routine moments' and 'fragments' of reality provide Quinn's 'raw material' and 'source of creative input'. As seen later, Graber draws much of her humour from familiar places and people. Animating thus holds a mirror to the live action discussed in this book and highlights how, in Roe's (2013: 22) words, animation's capacity to reach 'temporally, geographically, and psychologically' enables some women to explore aspects of their own lives and circumstances more freely.

National narratives of animation history have long privileged male agency and under-recognised women's contribution. As Britain's pioneering animators gain better visibility, it is appropriate to identify those women animators who made films alone, or with friends or family. For some women, those interests remained a leisure activity; for others animation brought paid employment. The cross-over between personal and professional activity arose partly from the flexible basis on which animating occurred and how studios outsourced to freelancers in a cottage industry fashion that continued for decades. Accordingly this chapter reveals closer links between professional and amateur activity than elsewhere in amateur visual practice.

As an experimental alternative to live-action format, for over eighty years, some women tried out different animating styles. From early on, Britain's hobby press promoted animation (Craven 2015: 28ff): as fulfilling particularly to the technically minded enthusiast who enjoyed constructing and modelling and later as an arena for avant-garde experimentalism that offered amateurs scope for imaginative invention away from professional comparisons. Much of that encouragement assumed a male readership and justified animating on grounds of its cinematic authenticity, scope for DIY skills and theoretical grasp of optics and mathematical calculations. Complicating animation's amateur credentials and constructing animation as technique-driven, were competing claims that anyone could animate and that it suited the solo hobbyist and club members working together (Malthouse 1939: 278; Wynn Jones 1958: 996; Alexander 1963: 228; Cleave 1971: 710; Noble undated). Graber's later contributions to *Movie Maker* reconnected amateur readers with animation: ably assisted by one of her many cats, drawn animation regained its place as self-expression that any filmmaker could try.[1]

Advocates of amateur animating invited filmmakers to experiment. Sometimes it became one style explored among many; for others it became the preferred way of working. Although considered by some commentators as more suited to the serious filmmaker than the dabbler, these women practitioners display the varied approaches found throughout amateur activity. They explored how to draw, paint, model or use ready-made everyday objects in creative ways. Animated drawings, objects and cut-outs provided ways to tell stories through frame by frame manipulation. Accessible raw materials became flexible resources for imaginative alternative realities and aesthetics. Animation could bring to life, miniature and hand-produced worlds in completely self-sustained ways but might also, as seen later, involve working with other people to rehearse, design, build, film, edit or add sound and dialogue.

Home animation may have had particular appeal for some women as it avoided camera use in public or the need to carry around equipment. It offered self-expression using new materials through socially valued crafting skills and attributes of precision and patience: the ability to assemble, shape, cut and paste. The influence of post-war proto-feminism and the growing challenges to orthodoxy and conventional ways of seeing the world brought by pop art and popular culture gradually opened bolder ways to explore idiosyncrasy, empathy and personal experience through animating. Pilling (1992: 5–7) identifies more women within the industry and art education as mid-century role models, which may have attracted women hobbyists to try animation too. New technologies replaced the complexities of adding synchronised sound and music and brought fresh possibilities to increasingly specialised amateurs who worked with hand-drawn components, three-dimensional models, puppetry and, later on, computer generated imagery (Graber 1992: 1–3; 2009). The visibility of women animators, particularly from the later 1970s onwards, broadened the genre's repertoire, reputation and outreach through education, media and popular culture. Home computer software gradually made it more feasible to devise and edit animations without having to dismantle or store analogue materials.[2] Changes in camera and editing equipment, particularly the increasing affordability of products designed for domestic and personal use, plus the ease of sharing digital files via online sources have further widened opportunities for amateur women animators.[3]

This chapter explores why and how animation attracted women from the early years of amateur filmmaking. It highlights individuals, the films they made and, where known, the context within which they produced and shared their films. Films and writings provide clues for interpreting different forms of animation and filmmakers' interests. Contact with practising animators informs how and why the magical power of animation continues to fascinate filmmakers, from relative beginners to seasoned practitioners, whose work now reaches international audiences. Examples reflect varied interests: some collaborations have been with partners, family or fellow members within a club setting; other women animate independently.

Interestingly, no evidence surfaced about Britain's amateur women filmmakers attempting animation within a colonial setting although some opportunities for work abroad persisted particularly during the 1960s.

Perhaps practical obstacles such as dust and the vagaries of weather, as noted by Chalke (2009: 241) when discussing the Grasshopper Group, might easily have disrupted even the most meticulously planned indoor stop-motion film production in a late colonial household. The mix of playful anarchy and creative imagining conducive to bringing inanimate objects and line drawings to life perhaps found little place in overseas domestic spaces that were still shaped as a protective buffer against the tensions of late imperialism. Perhaps other lingering class attitudes towards popular culture may also account for this absence within women's overseas filmmaking and this is briefly explored at the end of this chapter.

A Growing Presence

Britain's early amateur women filmmakers grew up within a society that witnessed a rapid rise in films using animated backgrounds, visual trickery and moving toys and puppets. Experiments in two- and three-dimensional animations occurred within the inventiveness surrounding early cinema and its moving picture precursors. Films by Birt Acres, George Méliès and other pioneering cinematographers brought alphabet letters, objects and toys to life. Animation's potential to simultaneously tell a story, convey a message and entertain ensured its swift adoption into advertising. From *c.*1899, Arthur Melbourne-Cooper made animations for the match company, Bryant and May. Shown at fairs and in music halls and cinemas, they demonstrated how animation could captivate an audience. Questioned by Gifford (1988; de Vries and Mul 2009) and others for their date and authenticity, Melbourne-Cooper's playful appeal to adults and children led to numerous productions before 1914.[4] One film, echoed by Thubron (see later), evokes a world of toys that come to life, as a young child falls asleep and enters a surreal but seemingly benign fantasy realm of silent clockwork creatures.[5] Another animation sought older audiences as shown by as its opening scene of a dancing girl puppet and an illicit embrace in a country lane.[6] As it evokes the dangers of car driving, it unsettles the seemingly rural idyll of Edwardian England and also foreshadows how animation would ultimately rival Punch and Judy shows.

Early animated cinema commercials targeted women's assumed interests. Animated sundae dishes and homely tea-trays promoted interval refreshments. Short animations advertised women's fashions, make-up, hair and health and built upon earlier gender-targeted marketing techniques pioneered by fashion, newsreels and department stores (McGrath

2012: 282; Hanssen 2009: 107; Uhlirova 2013: 137; Hammerton 2001). Garment, food and other household brand names marketed via simply animated advertisements offered products, shops and services to the modernising woman.[7] As psychologists and domestic advisors placed fresh emphasis on childhood (Urwin and Sharland 1992: 174; Thom 1992: 200) advertising particularly encouraged wives, mothers and aunts to purchase children's clothes, furnishing and also newly available film-inspired toys and furnishings for nursery and playroom. Animation thus joined other gendered flows of ideas and consumer goods that, according to Kidd and Nicholls (1999: 6), were redefining class, relationships and identities during the interwar years.

Animation soon impacted directly on amateur practice. Rapid innovations in animated line drawing became popular in the 1920s and imported characters became available on new formats. Home projection of cartoons rose although such characters as Felix the Cat, Betty Boop and Oswald the Lucky Rabbit lost their early popularity to Walt Disney's cartoons as sound and colour became established (Graber 2009: 66–7). Animations boosted watching home movies too: 'being able to see oneself up there with the stars' was part of the appeal, according to one filmmaker's elderly daughter, who remembered watching family films and hired cartoons on Sunday evenings and special occasions as a child in the 1930s.[8] Just as fashion mannequins had relocated objectified human forms from piers and peepshows into respectable feminised consumer settings (Evans 2005: 125–45), animated two- and three-dimensional characters gradually entered middle-class lives. Other screen characters crossed social barriers, spawned merchandising and prompted filmmaking too. The Hindleys, for example, filmed their young children encountering a Charlie Chaplin marionette during a visit to Blackpool promenade in *c.*1936.[9]

Animating appealed to lone workers including Dick Jobson in the Welsh Borders, and club members too, as filmmakers tried out visual trickery and playful subversion for comic or surreal effects.[10] As Lucy Fairbank and others discovered, animated titles with moving letters and objects created eye-catching openings to live action films. Animation took time and patience but when well done its technique and visual finesse could be impressive. Holiday films might start with a stop-motion sequence that involved the turning pages of a picture album or rotating souvenirs and other mementos or, even more simply, a suitcase gradually being packed and closed by unseen hands. Stylistically, animating could be a lone worker's alternative to the acted prologues created by filmmakers who worked together.[11]

The national revival of puppetry during the 1920s and opening of marionette theatres in London (Dixon, 2015) and elsewhere, prompted early appearances on television and also attracted the interests of early cine users.[12] Lotte Reiniger's unique cut-out silhouette animation encouraged shadow puppetry and, as Malthouse (1939: 278) enthused, had ancient oriental origins and avant-garde status even if described elsewhere as 'pretty pretty cut outs'.[13] *The Adventures of Prince Achmed* (1923–6) – widely acknowledged as the world's first full-length animation and produced long before Reiniger left Germany for London – preceded the first national amateur filmmaking competition that invited entries using cut-out techniques within short cartoon films (Anon. 1929e: 222). While Palfreyman (see note 13) regarded Reiniger as a 'goddess of the scissors', other writers believed that such 'craft' approaches avoided any need for drawing skills and identified silhouette films and shadow plays as a versatile medium (Marshall 1937: 585–7; Strasser 1936: 407–9). Influential upon Vera Linnecar's work with the Grasshopper Group in the 1950s, there may be other earlier examples of Reiniger's style.[14] Perhaps Reiniger's individuality was more akin to the avant-garde of continental Europe, yet even the cinematic innovation associated with Helen Biggar (Brownrigg and Main 2016), Violet Anderson (later Violet Neish) and other members of the Glasgow School of Art Kinecraft Society (GSAKS) during the 1930s did not attempt the same aesthetic delicacy.[15] Indeed the scenes of animated patterns, musical notation and drawing instruments produced by GSAKS and its contemporaries, form a distinctive body of visual experimentation that perhaps find their closest resonances with Margaret Tait's own rather isolated visual creativity and abstract experimentation in later decades (Neely 2009: 303–4).

For some pre-war cine users, simple stop-motion action that brought inanimate objects to life probably grew out of adult pleasure in making up stories or playing with children and their toys.[16] One such film was made to record the spontaneous delight of a grandchild on finding her birthday presents.[17] *Her Second Birthday* epitomises childhood pleasures in an English country garden as June discovers new toys in an apparently undirected record of imaginative play. She falls asleep and a stop-frame animated sequence subtitled 'Dreamland' next shows how the toys come to life and enjoy themselves playing and riding a tricycle. The film ends as June opens her eyes and looks directly into the camera lens as toys disappear from view (Figure 8.1).

K. Agnes Thubron (1934: 12–14) wrote that *Her Second Birthday* was first intended for family viewing. After the film was processed, its potential wider appeal prompted the grandparents to shoot additional scenes,

Figure 8.1 Still frame from K. Agnes Thubron, *Her Second Birthday.* (1932–3). © EAFA.

re-edit and enter it for a competition as they 'had long intended trying a stop action moving toy picture'. Thubron's commentary identified various difficulties: continuity, exposure 'as the sun appeared and disappeared behind clouds' and 'an inability to remember which leg or arm we had moved last time'. She offered practical advice too: 'Hat pins were stuck through the feet and into the lawn', and she recommended 'three or four frames of each movement' and 'drastic cutting'. Editing achieves more than the toys' 'magical disappearance'; June's 'waking . . . wonder was just a chance close-up cut in at the right spot, the "wonder" being more in the imagination of the audience than actually in the expression'. Thubron's words exemplify her agency and practical awareness of editing, lighting and composition.

Restricted Opportunities

During the 1940s, animation gained propaganda value and where cine use continued, amateur filming usually prioritised documentaries and recording families, although Strasser (1940: 433–4, 444) suggested improvisations based on Punch cartoons and cartoon strips. Exceptions include men with access to film: working with friends, George Wain animated the story of the willow pattern plate on film stock left over from producing wartime training films, and the hobby press occasionally reported that some post-war lone workers used stop-motion, model-making and visual effects to recreate specific military campaigns and manoeuvres on film (Lockwood 1955: 78).[18] Although Ace Movies gained fresh prominence from its creative post-war filmmaking, women's roles were probably restricted to acting as in the pre-war years (Dyson 2013: 135). In keeping with the club's emphasis on a collaborative studio-based culture, there are no individual film credits for *Marionettes* (finished in 1948 but mainly shot by 1938), a production that features life-size human puppets, but it seems likely that women helped with set, costume and prop design for this and other productions.

As cartoon techniques were diverted into wartime public information, training, and films and newsreels, women animators replaced male employees who joined the armed forces. They worked as inkers, drawers, in-betweeners or in other roles, but their personal scope was often limited and contracts were short term.[19] As with family and club productions, names of some women animators who moved between paid and unpaid work can be traced to this period although, as Jefferson (1985: 37) suggests, many more remain a shadowy presence and un-credited.[20] Working unpaid in a professional capacity and making films for pleasure are clearly different processes but in animation, even more than where personal film-making paralleled a day job in film production, the amateur/professional binary seems particularly porous.

Women's contributions to advertising, information and educational film production often lie buried within the narratives of larger companies and studios (Clark, 1983a: 6).[21] Joy Batchelor, well known for her creative partnership (and marriage) with John Halas (who also encouraged amateur animation) had roles in commissioning, studio management, design, story-telling, scene planning, scriptwriting and direction (Stewart 2015a: 24–31; Halas and Privett 1951). Despite her significant career, childcare responsibilities often distanced her from production work. Other women recruited directly from art school, including Vera Linnecar, Rosalie 'Wally' Crook and Liz Williams (aka Elizabeth Horn), were wartime animators at Halas and Batchelor, yet they also virtually disappeared from film credits for a mix of personal, company and other reasons (Stewart 2015b; Clark 1985: 24–7).[22] Ken Clark (1924–2009), a founder member of the amateur animation Grasshopper Group in the early 1950s, features in production photographs along with his wife Jean (née Griffiths) who remains less well known (Clark 1985: 24).[23] Within his British animation history, there are passing references to women's wartime and later contributions: 'Hoppy Hopkins and his wife sitting through Blitz raids "filling in cels"'; 'Laurie Price and a group of girl tracer/inkers [were] seconded to Technicolor Laboratories' and co-founder John Daborn's twin-sisters were 'press-ganged' into painting hundreds of cels for *The Battle of Wangapore* (1955) (Clark, 1982a, 1982b, 1982c; Chalke 2009: 246–8).[24]

Animation's post-war expansion brought new commercial and educational opportunities, boosted via widening availability of children's Saturday cinema clubs, television advertising and children's programmes but few women accessed creative openings. Ex-service personnel were recruited as at Gaumont-British Animation's (GBA) where Clark (1987: 25–7) again recalls 'String's girls' (Henry Stringer) 'learning to trace and paint'.[25] Eunice Macaulay (1923–2013) was born in Lancashire, served in the Women's Royal Naval Service (WRENS) and then moved from greeting card artwork to work on hand-colouring animations for GBA (Wise 2012). Although marriage meant moving to Scotland and then Canada for her husband's own film career development, she eventually returned to animation, working with the National Film Board of Canada. She received an Academy Award for her animations in *Special Delivery* (1978).

Networking, hard work and adaptability helped these mid-century women who combined personal and professional involvement in animation. Elizabeth Horn (aka Liz Williams) is another mid-twentieth century example: starting off with Halas and Batchelor in the early 1940s, she moved with Vera Linnecar on to Biographic Films where she teamed up with Nancy Hanna.[26] She later met her future husband, Richard (Dick) Horn at an early Grasshopper Group meeting, undertook some work in Canada, and through freelancing developed a strong profile and extensive output of independent and collaborative work with her husband and others (Clark 1985: 25). The combination of luck, determination and artistic skill enabled animators to develop careers despite the severe limitations on promotion in an industry dominated by men on both sides of the Atlantic.[27]

Chalke's (2009) charting of the Grasshopper Group's formative and unique role over almost three decades (*c*.1952–82) in British amateur animation is relevant here. First, the group's hybrid amateur status and identity offered creative opportunities unfettered by commercial concerns; second, it attracted experienced professionals and freelancers who contributed perspectives from workplace settings where women had already made contributions. Thus, although being male dominated in terms of membership and perhaps in its reliance on technical invention, the group was possibly more conducive to women's participation than some other newly emerging post-war cine clubs. Third, the Grasshopper Group brought together so-called lone workers, but as Clark's memories reveal, those male enthusiasts often had a partner who helped to promote amateur animation.[28] Thus, apart from animating, Ken Clark (1982a:7) and his wife Jean became the group's joint secretaries and printed its newsletter. Another couple, Stuart Wyn Jones, a prolific animator, and Hazel Swift (1961a, 1961b) had respective day jobs in commercial advertising and continuity but also contributed significantly to cine journalism (Clark, 1982a: 6).[29] Audrey Daborn (née Vayro), wife of founder member John Daborn, took part in *Two's Company*, an example of the club's experimental 'pixilated comedies' – a stop-motion frame by frame process of animating people rather than drawings or objects (Chalke 2009).[30] Margaret Turner worked on continuity for this film, and elsewhere there are references to women taking on varied roles in different projects (Daborn 1962: 356–7).

Grasshopper Group members showed that amateur animations could address contemporary societal concerns. Clark (1983b: 143) recalled how filmmakers Peter and Joan Foldes worked 'together for fifteen hours a day for months . . . in their London flat'. He wrote of how they made an 'artists' conception of the beginnings of life, and of 'man's eventual emergence . . . through evil, into sunshine'.[31] Their next film together evoked a post-nuclear apocalypse horror through animations. It gained BFI and National Film Theatre (NFT) screenings and commercial distribution in the US, despite (or perhaps due to) its criticism in the media.[32] Dorothy Roger's puppet animation also illustrated how, in less than a decade, the group's members pioneered with style, meaning and message.[33] Their experimentalism anticipated later developments in animation and built allegiances with such innovative groups as the all-women Leeds Animation Workshop.[34] Out of such vitality came new impetus for Britain's emerging amateur animators.

More affordable colour film and inventiveness in adding sound encouraged amateur activity. Inserted special effects and animated sequences remained typical of club productions, although notable male animators may be traced from the mid-1950s onwards, as seen in the work of Alan Cleave, Albert Noble and others.[35] Among lone workers, credits sometimes acknowledged women's input: in *Wire and Paper Animals* (1956), a young woman model-maker demonstrates prehistoric animals devised from different materials.[36] There is a female voice over, but whether the credit given to G. E. Higdon is for being narrator, demonstrator or model-maker is unclear. A later film shows a greater variety of materials, and credits the film's technical adviser, Miss I. P. Bewster, but again remains ambiguous about her precise role.[37] In Albert Noble's writing about animating household items he mentioned his wife's own short animations and recalled that she 'animated coins to tell how the decimal coins swept the old coins away'.[38] For some hobby press writers, reference to an 'animation widow' as a supportive assistant or fast-retreating partner from a film show suggests humour targeted at a male readership (Ranyard 1982: 11–13). Evidence of couples using animation and visual effects recur as seen within longer films by Betty and Cyril Ramsden and by Betty and Ian Lauder, another husband–wife partnership whose award-winning films also gained many Ten Best awards.[39] The Lauders (Lauder and Lauder 1962: 470) wrote about how they filmed together but they did not identify specific roles. Yet, to convey 'history is all around us', their use of models fitted in with current practice in animation and educational filmmaking.

Other couples worked on longer animations. May and Frank Webb were York-based filmmakers whose different interests prompted varied filmmaking opportunities (Norris Nicholson, 2015a: 211–13). *The Yellow Balloon* (1969) was a collaboration with an established puppeteer, Patrick Olsen, who wished to make a film about one of his locally popular string-operated characters, a lonely, elderly clown called Peedy. May directed the film, Frank assumed responsibility for photography and other friends assisted too. The resultant film captures the pathos of successive losses experienced by Peedy as he strives to have a balloon of his own.[40] Set to a piano accompaniment, the film combines gentle humour, sadness and an appreciation of young children's mischievousness and compassion. The plot is developed through live action sequences showing the balloon seller, children and rooftop views of the city and detailed shots of Peedy's head, hand and body movements. The turning pages of a book reveal credits and provide visual framing.

The film was made at a time when British children's television was awash with different kinds of manipulated puppets that became household names. Its historicism, however, seen in the Victorian clothes and cap for balloon seller and elsewhere amidst the contemporary clothes of other characters, perhaps hints nostalgically at a less complex world where acts of kindness occur, unaccompanied children roam streets without cars and, in a city without aerials on rooftops, stories still come from books. As much for adults as for children, the film involved many hours of individual and collaborative effort away from its makers' respective jobs as architect's modeller and camera shop owners. *Underwater Fantasy* (1970s), another well-shot collaboration by Olsen and the Webbs, started as a very short animation in *c.*1965 and refers to the Webb's diving interests.[41] The film featured sophisticated string puppetry and elaborate set design but lacked the multi-layered meaning of its predecessor.

Becoming Independent

As cine equipment evolved, more women were attracted by animation's versatility. Its increasing presence in film, advertising and on colour television, meant animation and its associated merchandising permeated popular culture. Animation's appeal to children and scope for hands-on learning also saw a new generation of filmmakers becoming involved. Some women took their Super 8 cameras into the classroom. Joyce Bolton, an infant teacher from Ilkley, West Yorkshire, made a short film with her infant class who drew and painted the imagery. Prompted by her husband's filmmaking, Joyce recognised the medium's classroom application and gained success with her first film, at the IAC Young Filmmakers' Competition and at SAFF.[42] Beryl Armstrong, a writer and filmmaker in Surrey, taught her young sons to make films, including short animations using stop-frame animation, table top models and synchronised sound.[43] Two Lancashire-based art teachers, Tony and Barbara Brindle (1978: 988–9; Anon. 1978c: 478), experimented with cut-out silhouette animation and shadow puppetry.[44] Other couples used cel animation, involving drawings first made on paper over a light box and then traced onto acetate. Over a thousand cels, using seven colours and thirty-six separate backgrounds and foregrounds, feature in *Pillage Idiot* (1976), a film that features Harold, 'the most fierce, most ruthless and most merciless Viking of all time'.[45] Made over twelve months, this award-winning production, built upon an earlier animated film and marked a couple's successful shift away from family films into animation.[46]

Prominent in the IAC and hobby press, Valrie Bristow Ellis (1938–2018) developed an 'over-riding passion' for animation.[47] Making animated films offered 'a tougher challenge and a more satisfying creative outlet'. As Head of Science at a girls' secondary school in Manchester, she ran media workshops for pupils and encouraged others for decades. She made award-winning animations on cine, video and digital formats. She was already a familiar entrant to the annual Ten Best competition when her irreverent *Genesis* (1980) gained commendation as 'the producer's best animated effort so far' (Rose and Cleave 1980: 654).[48] The cartoon spoof advertisement for a headache remedy played on Adam's boredom in the Garden of Eden; the critics liked Adam's 'evident self-satisfaction after being created which is a nice touch' and praised Ellis' use of colourful stylised drawings in 'an accomplished and entertaining little movie'. Its 'precision and . . . good sense of timing' and 'Miss Ellis' way of telling (the story)' drew praise. The 'operation' that creates Eve from an extracted rib in accordance with the biblical myth (Genesis 2:22), might also be a playful nod towards *Spare Rib*'s then emerging role as a magazine that championed the Women's Liberation Movement and second-wave feminism. The write-up suggests greater acceptance of women's filmmaking.[49] Venturing into abstract animation, Ellis experimented with revolving colours, shapes and patterns, in response to a popular song of the late 1960s.[50]

Changing social context, aesthetics and technologies assisted the emergence of adult-orientated animation. As the genre became, according to Jayne Pilling (2012: 4), more of a conduit for messages about bigger issues, animators tackled the concerns of the 1970s and 1980s: humankind's folly, insanity and survival in a world beset by greed, militarisation, inequalities and government bureaucracies. It became a means to engage through fantasy with the complexities of human experience and identity in freer abstract ways using caricature, exaggeration, parody and satire or humour. Its extension of fine line drawing in art school curricula sparked interest as students explored personal, social and women's issues. Joanna Fryer's *Make Up* (1978) is an animated line drawing that started as a three second experiment while Fryer was studying art at Goldsmith's College. Hailed in *Movie Maker* as a 'pleasing simple story told very definitely from the woman's angle', the film depicts how facial expressions change as the young woman puts on make-up and imagines a boyfriend's flamboyant arrival. His timid entry destroys the fantasy, glamour disappears and her face shows her contempt. Reportedly using 'felt-tipped pens, crayon, charcoal and water colour for the 700 odd drawings' and 'drawn entirely on paper before being photographed', Fryer's film illustrates fresh ways of expressing gender and identity (Anon. 1978a: 472; Anon. 1978b 481b).[51]

Mollie Butler typifies imaginative stop-motion animation from this late period of using Super 8 cine equipment.[52] Married, and with two sons, she was a member of both Mercury Movie Makers and also the IAC. She ran a film unit at Benton Park School in Leeds and made live action and fiction films before turning to animation.[53] *An Odd Ode* (1980) retells the story of what happens after a little girl called Peggy White eats a plum.[54] Butler used voice over and music and through coloured images and ink outlines

Figure 8.2 Still frame from Mollie Butler, *An Odd Ode* (1980). © EAFA.

she sketches Peggy's successive metamorphosis into a tree that supports a nest of fledglings, a child on a swing, and finally a festive Christmas tree (Figure 8.2).

Butler (1981: 11) produced another short film, *Magnum Opus* (1981) for the International Year of Disabled People (Figure 8.3).[55] It took almost four hours nightly over a six month period to produce more than a thousand drawings to accompany the recorded verse narrative. Here she creates a musical note ('a semi-breve with two left feet' and crutches) that suffers prejudice and ridicule before being accommodated within a more inclusive composition and welcomed back as a wheelchair using member in the conductor's score and concert. Simple outlines and partial colour show animation's capacity to evoke empathy in a short story of rejection, exclusion and rehabilitation. Evocative grey terrace streets and accents offer a distinctive northern character. *Bait Poem to Catch Girls* (1986–8) depicts a man living alone, his brief affair with a now grown-up girl from his past, sexual fantasy and a return to his bachelor

Figure 8.3 Still frame from Mollie Butler, *Magnum Opus* (1981). © EAFA.

existence. Butler accompanied the narrated verse with imagery of an unshaven man with his letters of rejection and the knock-kneed young woman with hairy legs who moves in for a while. An attendant dangling black spider, Arachne-like, weaves thoughts, wishes and times while a realistically drawn hand holds pencil and eraser, in a bedsit world of unfulfilled dreams (Figure 8.4).[56]

Butler promoted the educational value of filmmaking through productions and writing.[57] Her school films completed over many months evinces her school's support for cross-curricular learning. One of Butler's pupils later wrote about animation within the wider context of being at school.[58] Such encouragement, seen by Dyson (2015) as evidence of the 'democratisation of British amateur filmmaking', illustrates the creativity associated with educational film production at this time. In *Freak* (1988) an adolescent school girl daydreams about transforming into a punk rocker.[59] Set to a sound track by the late 1970s band GBH, the film mixes live action, stop-motion animation, photomontage, time-lapse photography and other special effects. Dress, adornment and body

Figure 8.4 Still frame from Mollie Butler, *Bait Poem to Catch Girls* (1986–8). © EAFA.

language symbolise the provocative sub-cultural youth identities associated with 1980s Britain. Fast intercutting shots present an alienating environment of brick, glass and concrete that disrupts the values of school life as much as looking at photos of punks instead of a textbook. The teenager's subversive metamorphosis fades as she resumes her uniformed classroom identity. Credited to Sharon Gadsdon, this award-winning film reinforces Butler's belief that 'Filmmaking gives the young person motivation, and imparts a sense of confidence and above all a sense of achievement' (Butler (1987: 11) (Figure 8.5).

Sheila Graber (b.1940) is an example of an amateur filmmaker who turned professional. According to Wells (in Graber 2009: 11) she is 'an unsung hero' who has dedicated herself to animation for almost fifty years. Her international reputation as an animator and teacher derive from her own pleasure in making films and 'also exploring the possibilities of others making their own films in their own way'.[60] The daughter of a master pilot on the River Tyne, she drew, painted and animated the movement

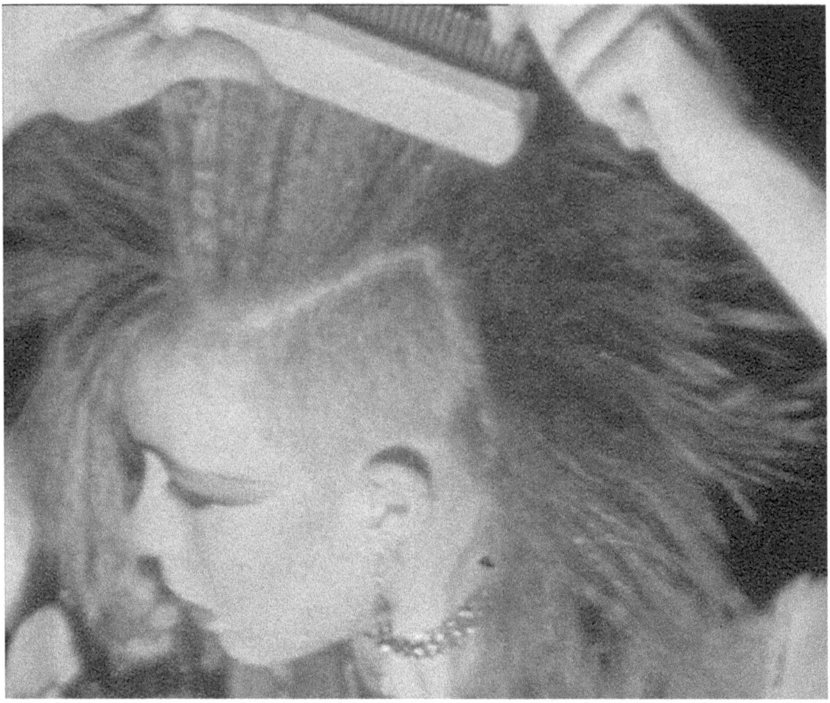

Figure 8.5 Still frame from Sharon Gadsdon, *Freak* (1988). © EAFA.

of people, boats and water from childhood. She was a secondary school art teacher for twenty years, during which time she ran an after school cine club and developed a Certificate of Secondary Education (CSE) in animation.

Graber purchased a Super 8 camera in 1970 for filming a summer holiday and experimented with single frame release processes to make a self-portrait on film. Numerous short projects using cut-outs, line drawing, plasticine, pastels, felt-tips and other materials followed over the next few years. She explored building her own sets and synchronising sound and image.[61] Graber innovated and improvised constantly: she worked with overlain acetate sheets or cels to reduce the overall amount of drawing necessary to convey movement and used a home-made light box and a rostrum devised from a tea trolley. Graber received a Ten Best award for *The Boy and the Cat* (1974), an animation inspired by her nephew and her pet cats having snowy adventures in her seaport

Figure 8.6 Still frame from Sheila Graber, *The Boy and the Cat* (1974). © EAFA.

home (Figure 8.6). The Tyneside bridges and shipyard cranes and her memorable characters – particularly those based upon her cats – recur and display a strong sense of place and domestic feel rooted in close observation. Her films express humour, insight, compassion and a lifetime of experience captured by what she describes as the 'magical mix of real and unreal moving images'. Other competition successes followed at home and abroad.[62]

Recognition of Graber's animations within the Ten Best awards prompted some disquiet. In 1976, she won three trophies in the same competition but she continued to teach full-time and make films 'for fun at night and weekends'.[63] Sound involved much ingenuity too although her use of recordings led to issues of copyright clearance later on. Teaching colleagues recorded live music for several films and precision stopwatch timing matched a separate sound track to image via a 'mime to playback' approach. Some animations started from familiar school songs or activities.[64] An animated history of transport stemmed from a strong sense of rhythm.[65] Animation brought different school subjects literally to life: one biology diagram used for years was shown to be wrong when a pupil attempted to animate the blood flow.[66] Art history lessons prompted witty experimentalism too as seen in *Four Views on Landscape* (1976), *Michelangelo* (1976) and the expressive use of chalks and pastels in *Face to Face* (1976). She began to address other audiences too.[67]

Graber's move to 16mm camera equipment brought broadcast quality and wider outreach at home and abroad via festivals and competitions. Meeting with Alison de Vere, another alumni from the Halas and Batchelor studio, prompted questioning of her work, reputation and the merits of working at a professional or amateur level.[68] Her technical experiments using ideas from literature, art and music continued, as seen in the dissolving drawings of *The Lady of Shallot* (1976).[69] Commissions led to other films and, by 1980, Graber had produced thirty films and gained recognition from her work being broadcast internationally. She produced a ten part television series based on Rudyard Kipling's *Just So Stories* and gave up secondary teaching to become a professional animator (Graber 1985: 34–5).[70]

Alongside her production company with Jen Miller, Graber continued to teach animation, write and contribute to the amateur film movement. She created an animation as part of the IAC's Golden Jubilee celebrations (1982) and remained a familiar figure to readers of the hobby press. She has enabled others to enjoy making films through running workshops, including filmmaking for people with special or additional needs. Moving from Super 8 to computer technologies transformed animation's outreach, in her words, 'as a means of communication not just for entertainment but for education and healing too', as seen by her many online resources for carers and people with hearing disabilities, for young offenders and in her innovative interactive guide to animation (Graber 2009). Almost fifty years on, her belief that anyone can create their own film is as strong as ever. As an advocate of amateur visual practice, and an example of a professional animator who champions the enthusiast, she is exceptional.

Coming of Age

No one else among Britain's professional women animators today so readily acknowledges her amateur beginnings as Sheila Graber. It is partly a result of timing. From the later 1950s onwards, funding initiatives offered opportunities for training and development that fostered creative growth spurts within a branch of Britain's film industry where there had long been more off-screen openings for women than in many other areas of the industry. As more women entered the workforce, there were jobs in the expanding television networks that included animation for children, education, public information, entertainment and advertising. Teaching offered a secure route too into employment where personal filmmaking interests could continue within a school setting or at home. New routes to pursue animation professionally opened via higher education's post-war expansion, and graduates in the 1970s and 1980s found opportunities in a fluid but vibrant mix of public, private and voluntary sector outlets. Greater participation in production teams, including all-female collaborations, offered paid openings, as at Channel 4 (Kitson, 2008: 40) and women directors provided role models too. Animation became a more viable career route, as shown by the proliferation of British and British-based women animators from this period including Alison Snowdon, Petra Freeman, Christine Roche, Candy Guard and Joanna Quinn (Wells et al. 2009).[71] Animations by, for and about women's issues gained greater public recognition at a time when the amateur movement faced uncertainty over its own survival as numbers from the pioneering generation dwindled and successive new technologies threatened its core identity. The hobby's perceived male dominance, despite the reliance upon women's participation at club and organisational levels, meant that some women newly attracted to animation chose not to align themselves closely with amateur activity even where it thrived nearby. One such instance was in Leeds, West Yorkshire.

Leeds Animation Workshop started in 1976 when a group of women came together to make a film about the need for pre-school childcare. According to its co-founder, Terry Wragg, they knew each other from women's groups, shared feminist principles and even though some were not parents, they saw free nurseries as central to the struggle for gender equality.[72] The success of their first film, *Who Needs Nurseries? We Do!*, led them to set up a production unit, run by and for women to tackle other current issues through film. 'We were consciously providing resources and tools and cultural materials for women's groups', Wragg recalls. They saw themselves as a collective, prepared to work unpaid but as paid up union members. Their nursery film gained from their contact with the political theatre group Red Ladder, then relocating to Leeds from London. This contributed an awareness of funding opportunities and a script devised by someone with understanding of teaching, animating and parenting. No one had a 16mm camera and all the initial hand-drawn and painting images, made at home, were taken to London for filming and processing.

Wragg recalls support from the Grasshopper Group and London film labs but generally much sexism and hostility 'in the world outside that room (where we met)'. Working cooperatively was challenging too as they gained the skills to work together and to produce their films at broadcast quality. Funded from regional arts and other organisations, they devised their projects in response to perceived needs. They found support and agency through networking among left-leaning groups of like-minded people in theatre and the arts, local union branches and political groups. They inspired others too: Leeds-based artist Joanna (Jo) Dunn discovered abstract animation accidentally through a friend's contact with the workshop (Pilling 1992: 39). Animation's capacity for bold, direct and subversive statements meant it became an effective and enduring vehicle for tackling the oppression of women, and minorities more broadly (Lant 1993: 161ff). As its remit expanded, the workshop gained recognition from mainstream media. Leeds Animation Workshop's survival underscores the founding belief that animation could help to make complex or sensitive issues more accessible to audiences, and at times offer an alternative point of view. Their work demonstrates how home-based professional production work by women could become sustainable without losing sight of its ideological roots.

Tina Fletcher's professionally co-produced puppet animation films also derive from a domestic setting (Toplis 1976; Fletcher 1984: 20; Hibbett 2010: 25–6). Telling stories using rod-operated puppets grew from a shared family hobby during the mid-1970s into a touring puppet theatre that visited schools, libraries and festivals. Funding-raising performances boosted their reputation: on behalf of the Venice in Peril appeal, for example, they toured a Venetian designed version of Wilde's *The Happy Prince* with the charity's chairman, John Julius Norwich, as the recorded narrator. Volunteer and professional involvement grew as touring expanded but much modelling, painting and recording still took place in the kitchen. Animation overcame the practical problem of rapid scene changes during work on a puppet script that involved flashbacks. From then on Fletcher combined live puppetry with animation to show cut-aways and changes in time and place. This approach evolved into making stop-motion puppet animation films, still home-based, although the puppetry and scene building increasingly relied upon professional input.

Two of Fletcher's Super 8 films gained grants, prompted her to use 16mm equipment and undergo further training. *The Burglar*, a 10 minute puppet animation film, won awards, and attracted interest from Channel 4 that led on to an ambitious un-commissioned project for a twelve-part series based on the *Simple Stories* that featured in the weekly satirical magazine, *Punch*, during the 1920s. The original project floundered but, in a reincarnated form, it was completed fourteen years later as *Willoughby Drive*. This thirteen-part series is a soap opera for puppets who live in a semi-rural suburban road of picturesque properties and where inquisitive neighbours query the bizarre events and characters that disrupt their self-contained everyday routines. It is a fantasy world, set loosely in 1950s Britain where coal fires, electric milk floats and telephone boxes still exist in a predominantly white society. Fletcher (undated) estimates the series took about forty-five hours per week over ten months per episode but maintains it is 'exhilarating and fun' being 'cocooned in this world of make believe'. She also highlights the hybridity of this as 'a labour of love' involving paid and unpaid labour as well as recycling and rebuilding models, sets, props, costumes and fitting different puppets heads to standardised bodies. 'Since the series was not commissioned for TV it was made very differently from most animation series, which are backed by a proper budget and with professional constraints.' As an independent and amateur filmmaker, she has autonomy: 'free of salaries, few deadlines, and absolute freedom'.

That wish to be inventive unites all these women animators and is seen in the final example. Jill Lampert, a retired teacher and active member of Sutton Coldfield Movie Makers since 2008, has made films for many years.[73] Like other older women filmmakers, she exemplifies the creative energy and drive that maintains female involvement in Britain's networks of voluntary group and organised clubs.[74] Part-time employment and semi-retirement offer greater freedom to be imaginative. Animation revisits pleasures from the past and sometimes involves her grandchildren. She traces her interest to childhood optical toys but only made her first animated film using video in 2002. Influenced by Tony Hart's 1970s shape-shifting character of Morph, Lampert's early projects used plasticine models: 'I had no computer at the time and the film was edited in camera insofar as it was edited at all . . . It was very short. Probably less than a minute.' Plasticine was a difficult medium: 'It was hard to keep the characters upright when they moved to a new position.'

The Little Shoemaker (2008) came next using a camcorder and was made as a video to music in response to her first club competition. Animation was ideal as Lampert did not yet know other club members. Song lyrics provided a storyline and her grandchildren helped with modelling. Using published instructions as tips and materials sourced via the internet, Lampert made and dressed her models, built her set and designed her props. 'Once I'd made the puppets, props and stage, I was ready to really plan the filming', she recalls. 'I took a lot of trouble to work out how many steps the characters would need to get across the stage and how that would fit with the music and so on.' She taught herself relevant computer skills and purchased editing software that had 'onion skins' so that she 'could see on the computer screen just how far the character had moved since the previous move'. Her reflections highlight the importance of 'finding effective solutions that worked and looked good' and the challenge of doing something well for its own sake:

> The whole thing took me about a month to make from start to finish. I can't say how many hours. I can say that I was working part time at the time, and I had family staying . . . so I would have just fitted it in when I could.

Locally, the film only came third but in larger competitions it gained praise and success. For Lampert, personal achievement came from giving pleasure to others: 'There is something heart-warming about the little models. They feel like real characters . . . This is animation just as I like it – magical.'

Conclusion

For almost a century, women's animations have offered scope for what Pilling (2012: 4) has called the 'unfettered imagination' – the opportunity to try something out, without any obligation to anyone else, in a self-sustained and self-contained way. Indeed, Pilling (2009: 8) suggests that, since the 1970s, personal animation has become one of the few areas of filmmaking in which women have made as strong a contribution as men. For amateur women animators, doing was what mattered, without the need for recognition, although that was a welcome bonus after a film was made. Admittedly their films' survival might suggest that many of the women gained a degree of success in their own eyes or when judged by others. Phillip Collins has also suggested that despite the notable achievements and cross-overs into professional activity, animation remained rather an esoteric peripheral form of amateur practice: 'for many men the cine camera was a status symbol'.[75] Women filmmakers were more interested in making a film than issues of status, he believes: 'If you spend £100.00 on an 8mm camera, the best way to demonstrate your brilliant choice was to go out in the public ream and film with it.' The amateur animator who worked alone attracted little attention, yet, until screening the film, the sense of fulfilment and creativity seem to have sustained many of the women discussed here.

Undoubtedly taking sole responsibility for a film from start to finish offered an independence unparalleled elsewhere in women's lives during many decades. For women, charged primarily with the continuous duties of childcare, homemaking and family responsibilities, working alone on animation offered agency within defined boundaries. Equally, many professional careers are surrounded by compromises within and beyond the workplace that reflect attitudes and practices still rooted in patriarchy and gender inequalities which deny self-realisation. For the professionals discussed here, the amateur world of make-believe is also a refuge that transcends everyday obligations and routines. Unlike much work in or beyond the home, spending unpaid time animating achieves a recognisable and more lasting outcome. Moreover, it is private and hidden, developing in a kitchen or bedroom until a chosen moment to share with others. Accountability is minimal, as long as it does not interfere with other roles and responsibilities. It is a reminder that as with much of women's amateur creativity, although it finds expression in wider social networks of exhibition, the processes of making that sustain artistic and crafting practices are often invisible and domestic.

A sense of fulfilment, maybe identity, also emerges from memories shared by different filmmakers. For some women, perhaps, escapism from personal, professional and wider issues may have influenced the wish to animate, even if the characters themselves have un-escapable situations or troubles. Although, as suggested earlier, much animation is grounded in the everyday, it also touches other layers of meaning, feeling and experience. Humour, traditionally often used against women, becomes a means to explore women's experience however gently. Other relationships recur: between older and younger people, teacher and pupil, or mother and grandmother with child or grandchild, or aunt and nephew. As a form of visual story-telling, women animators may offer changing messages but sustain age-old roles as transmitters of cultural meaning and cautionary tales about the everyday and less familiar worlds of growing up. Their animated stories, whether developed alone or with a partner, reveal aspects of themselves too in the choice of music, form and narrative as shown by the varied styles, themes and characters.[76]

Amateur animation, like much of amateur cinema, has not been overtly political although there have always been exceptions, including Ellis' collaboration on genetically modified crops.[77] Generally the targets tend to be more oblique, the messages more coded. The explicit flaunting of middle-aged sexuality, as in Joanna Quinn's raucous and voluptuous character Beryl and her Welsh factory co-workers, might not amuse some cine club audiences. Likewise, Quinn's exposure of British imperialism and animated political cartoon history, neglected even as an established animator, reveal the compromises between ideology and financial gain that separate her professional and more personal work.[78] Even at their most playful, the transgressive rule-breaking of early animated characters sometimes aroused distaste and displeasure. Seen as evidence of an imported American populism that was targeting cinema-going working class audiences of the interwar years, cartoon villains did nothing to alleviate the anxieties of class, taste and middle-brow aesthetics. Although Disney characters became household names, cartoons gained more limited entry into some homes, both in and beyond Britain, perhaps as a result of distribution systems as well as conservatism sustained in the expatriate homes of late colonialism. Thus, the filmmaking wife of a young civil servant posted overseas focused on live action films while abroad and only made animations after the young family's return to Britain.[79] From Armstrong's memoirs, there were so many unfamiliar subjects to focus on, animation only emerged as her own sons' filmmaking interests developed. Animation, moreover, needed a level of subversive irreverence and creative immersion that was untenable when managing a public-facing home and role abroad: joining together family film and live action reels was much more realistic given the technologies available mid-century. If, in the analogue era, women's animations were rather a minority practice, they seem to have been particularly inappropriate (or profoundly impractical), for those whose filmmaking role became part of their identity abroad.

Notes

1. Sheila Graber contributed short articles in cartoon style on animation in black and white and colour to many issues of *Movie Maker* between 1980 and 1983, including the colour cover for the Christmas issue, *Movie Maker*, December 1980.
2. Sheila Graber in conversation with author, 2016; Terry Wragg in conversation with the author, 1 May 2016.
3. Jill Lampert in conversation with the author, 24 September 2016.
4. Films attributed to the filmmaker Arthur Melbourne-Cooper may be viewed online at the East Anglian Film Archive. See also 'An Animated Dispute: Arthur Melbourne-Cooper and the birth of Film Animation', Norwich Film Festival, 2 December 2012, available at <http://www.norwichfilmfestival.co.uk/an-animated-dispute-arthur-melbourne-cooper-and-the-birth-of-film-animation> (last accessed 18 January 2018).
5. Arthur Melbourne-Cooper (1907) *A Dream of Toyland*, (5:3min, b/w, silent), EAFA no. 1893. Note this film has an alternative title, *Dreams of Toyland* (1908).
6. Arthur Melbourne-Cooper (1911) *Road Hogs in Toyland* (35mm, 5:06min, b/w, silent), EAFA no. 215265.

7. Fraserburgh Local Cinema Adverts (1931) *Fraserburgh Local Cinema Adverts* (5:00min, b/w, silent), NLS Id. 3534; see also animations produced by Colmans, Norwich, 1926: *Stopping the Rot* (2:44min, b/w, silent), EAFA no. 107; *The Happy Iron* (3:34min, b/w, silent), EAFA no. 103 features a modern young woman who, after sacking an incompetent laundry maid and her steam iron going on strike, finds effective ironing using Colman's rice starch in a cartoon that brims with contemporary visual references.
8. Sheelagh Simpson (daughter) and Peter Simpson (grandson) in correspondence with the author, August 2002.
9. John Hindley (*1933–6) *Hindley Family Scenes* (16mm, 13:50min, colour, b/w, silent), NWFA no. 3635.
10. See note 28 for further discussion of Richard (Dick) and his wife Pauline Jobson who was more interested in acting than making films (see Brownlow 1995).
11. See Chapter 2 for discussion of holiday films with scripted prologues made by Laurie and Stuart Day.
12. See for example, Alan H Pickard (1929) *Grand Prix Di Pozzo* (16mm, 20:53min, b/w, silent), YFA Id. 1956.
13. Attributed to Palfreyman, *The Financial Times* (1936) in Roe (2013: 189).
14. Vera Linnecar, Keith Learner and Bob Godfrey (1954) *Watch the Birdie* (16mm, 6:00min, colour, silent).
15. Helen Biggar, Violet Anderson and William J. MacLean worked with Norman McLaren as members of the GSAKS on *Camera Makes Whoopee* (1935) (16mm, 24:37min, b/w, silent), NLS Id. 1008. Biggar and McLaren worked together on *Hell Unltd* (1936). *Challenge to Fascism/Glasgow's May Day 1938* (1938) was Biggar's last film. Other non-realist films exploring visual forms include Glasgow Experimental Group (1935) *Marionettes* (16mm, 5:07min, b/w, silent), NLS Id. 3245; and Jean L. Gray (1938) *Witch Craft* (16mm, 3:36min, colour, silent), NLS Id. 1994.
16. See for example, A.G. Hinchliff and family (1938–9) *Tricks* (16mm, 7:2min, b/w, colour, silent), SASE Id. 8606.
17. K. Agnes and S. John Thubron (1932–3) *Her Second Birthday* (16mm, 5:31min, b/w, silent), EAFA no. 2684.
18. George Wain and Ernest Greenwood (*1937–46) *Old China* (16mm, 8:22min, b/w, colour, silent), NWFA no. 7130; George Wain and Ernest Greenwood (1936–51) 'Chinese Interlude' within *Family Scrapbook* (16mm, 15:46min, b/w, colour, silent), NWFA no. 4411. H. Lockwood reported from Blackpool ACA that 'War correspondent' (Mr H. H. Voss) involved no live actors in his combined live action filming and modelling of a task force landing on a Pacific atoll (filmed on South Shore, Blackpool).
19. Ken Clark, in his online history of British animation, identifies the in-betweener as someone (often a woman) who produces neat and accurate drawings between the key poses. These in-between drawings ensure continuity of movement within an animated sequence whether drawn traditionally or using computer software.

20. The anonymity and scale of women's largely invisible presence in Britain's mid-century animation industry is seen in Jefferson's interview with Maggy Clark: 'I started at Halas and Batchelor, like a little factory girl sitting there painting the white bits on the cels and somebody else did the red bits or whatever, and moved into tracing which is the next step – and progressed. A lot of people stay in paint and trace, they are housewives, they are people who have no further ambition than to earn pin money. If you aspire to something better then it seems like painting by numbers but it is perfectly O.K. as a job.'
21. Clark cites two couples, Bruce and Nina Woolfe and Reginald and Joan Jeffryes, who worked for Diagram Films, a unit that later supplied animation services for GB Instructional Films.
22. Clark's interview with Liz Horn identifies wartime experiences, the gender pay gap, changing opportunities from the late 1940s, overseas work, family commitments and an important career that deserves fuller attention.
23. Clark's article includes a photograph entitled 'A meeting of the Grasshopper Group (left to right) Bill Archer, Jean Clark, Ken Clark, Ron Clark, John Daborn and Dick Horn.'
24. The Grasshopper Group (1955) *The Battle of Wangapore* (16mm, 8min, colour, sound), available at <https://player.bfi.org.uk/free/film/watch-the-battle-of-wangapore-1955-online> (last accessed 21 May 2018)
25. J. Arthur Rank's plans to transform British animation and address children's interests also led to Mary Field being put in charge of the Children's Entertainment Films in 1943 (releasing through GB Instructional) and her subsequent commissioning of animated cartoons for showing at children's cinema shows on Saturday mornings.
26. Vera Linnecar, Keith Learner and Bob Godfrey (1954) *Watch the Birdie* (16mm, 6:00min, colour), available at <https://player.bfi.org.uk/free/film/watch-watch-the-birdie-1954-online> (last accessed 21 May 2018).
27. Craven (2015) identifies Sheila Graber as the only woman to have gained professional recognition. For other British-born animators whose work gained recognition in North America see also Shannon (2010); Tupper (2014) and the website, Amateur Cinema, available at <Amateurcinema.org> (last accessed 19 April 2018).
28. A Ten Best winner, *Driftwood and Seashell* (1956), is attributed to Dr Richard and Pauline Jobson (Chalke 2009: 256) although Dick (Richard) Jobson's tendency to work alone, is shown in Jeremy Sandford's interview, available at <http://www.JeremySandford.org.uk> (last accessed 21 January 2018).
29. Drawn directly onto film with Indian ink, *Short Spell* (1956) (35mm, 2:29min, b/w, silent), EAFA no. 3845 was one of Stuart Wynn Jones's earliest films before he moved to animated cel drawing. He worked with Stuart Halas and Joy Batchelor and later became a successful freelance animator.
30. *Two's Company* (1952), EAFA old catalogue.
31. Peter and Joan Foldes (1952) *Animated Genesis* (16mm, 22min, colour, sound). Made with support from the BFI Experimental Film Fund, this

co-written, animated and directed film highlights the difficulties in trying to trace the role of women even when associated with such a well-documented film unit as the Grasshopper Group: it is attributed to the Hungarian-born Peter Foldes in Bendazzi (2015: 179) and to Joan Foldes in Burton and Chibnall (2013: 34).

32. Peter and Joan Foldes (1956) *A Short Vision*, EAFA old catalogue.
33. Dorothy Roger (1959) *Spring is in the Air*, EAFA old catalogue.
34. Terry Wragg, founder member of Leeds Animation Workshop in conversation with the author, March 2016.
35. The upsurge of amateur animation during the 1950s–70s saw varied practice, writing and encouragement via competitions at local to international level. According to Ashby (1982: 19–21) almost seventy animated films were available by 1982 via the IAC film library. His listed couples include Tony and Barbara Brindle and John and Janice Watson, although films are not always attributed to both partners. Sheila Graber's films are included too. For a discussion of the significant contribution made by Alan Cleave, see Ian Craven (2015, particularly pp. 16–26); Albert Noble's early abstract stop-motion animation of objects is seen in *Red Type* (1961) (16mm, colour, sound, 125ft), EAFA no. 1052, and another film also involving a typewriter and warring typeface, *Black Face* (1963) (16mm, b/w, sound, 100ft), EAFA old catalogue.
36. Arthur Kingsbury (1956) *Wire and Paper Animals* (16mm, 10:00min, colour, sound), Bletchley Park College, EAFA old catalogue.
37. Arthur Kingsbury (with Miss I. P. Brewster as technical adviser) *Paper Masks and Models* (*c*.1957) Bletchley Park College, EAFA old catalogue.
38. Albert Noble (1965–8) *Button Ballet* (12:46min, colour, sound), EAFA no. 3154; Joan Noble *China River* (undated); *Drinking Glass* (*c*.2004), IAC List of films British International Amateur Film Festival (BIAFF) awards, 2004.
39. See Chapter 2 for further discussion of Betty and Cyril Ramsden. Film details for Betty and Ian Lauder are available online at East Anglia Film Archive, available at <http://www.eafa.org.uk> (last accessed 19 April 2018).
40. May and Frank Webb with Patrick Olsen (1969) *The Yellow Balloon* (16mm, 9:27min, colour, sound), YFA Id. 2289 and acquisition files.
41. May and Frank Webb with Patrick Olsen (1970s) *Underwater Fantasy* (16mm, 8:00 min, colour, sound), YFA Id. 2591.
42. Joyce Bolton (1963) *A Runaway Easter Egg* (8mm blown up to 16mm, colour, sound, 75ft), EAFA no. 4106; *The Enchanted Forest* (no details).
43. Beryl and Anthony Armstrong (1973) *One Frame at a Time* (Super 8mm, 5:15min, colour, sound), SASE Id. 1091.
44. See for example the couple's use of cut-outs and shadow puppets in *Silhouettes* (1973) (no details), *The Mermaid's Treasure* (1975) (Super 8mm, 5:54min, colour, 100ft), EAFA no. 4062 and *The Christmas Story* (1978) (Super 8, 2:55min, colour, sound, 65ft), EAFA no. 3972. All films received awards.

45. Janice and John Watson (1977) *Pillage Idiot* (16mm, colour, sound, 200ft), EAFA no. 1172.
46. Janice and John Watson (1975) *Precarious Potato* (Super 8, colour, sound, 35ft), EAFA no. 8107.
47. Between 1985 and 1988, Ellis contributed 'Val's View', a regular monthly page to *Amateur Film Maker* in which she wrote on animation on many occasions; Peter Donlan (1982), p. 25. See also, BIAFF Report 2004, IAC, <https://www.theiac.org.uk/eventsnew/biaff/biaff2004/movie2004report.html> (last accessed 21 May 2018).
48. *Genesis* (1980) (Super 8, 3:30min, colour, sound), EAFA no. 3365; Ten Best Gold Star 1980/IAC international film competition highly commended.
49. Peter Donlan, editor of the IAC's journal, *Amateur Film Maker*, was narrator on this film. Such involvement, over the years, by different established men within the movement or in other roles enabled some women's work to gain visibility. Most noteworthy perhaps was Alan Bennett being invited by Leeds Animation Workshop to narrate on one of their films, recalled as a turning point in the collective's own funding success, by Terry Wragg in conversation with the author, 1 May 2016.
50. Valrie Ellis (1982) *Windmills – My Style* (Super 8, 3:59min, colour, sound) was based on a 1968 song popularised by Noel Harrison, Dusty Springfield and many others, EAFA no. 4276; *Variations* (1979) (Super 8, 4:00min, colour, sound), EAFA old catalogue.
51. Joanna Fryer (1978) *Make Up* (Super 8, 2:40min, colour, sound), EAFA no. 3580.
52. Mollie Butler was the IAC's Youth Liaison officer in the mid-1980s and contributed numerous articles to *Amateur Film Maker*, usually on animation and special effects, in her regular feature for young filmmakers. For her shared interests with Valrie Ellis about 'our three favourite things': 'teaching, kids and animation', see Butler (1987: 11).
53. Mollie Butler (1973) *Locusts in Camera* (Super 8, 5:01min, colour, sound), EAFA no. 3553.
54. Mollie Butler (1980) *An Odd Ode* (Super 8, 1:21min, colour, sound), EAFA no. 3068.
55. Mollie Butler (1981) *Magnum Opus* (Super 8, 3:09min, colour, sound), EAFA no. 3575.
56. Mollie Butler (1986–8) *Bait Poem to Catch Girls* (Super 8, 2:01min, colour, sound), EAFA no. 3099.
57. Mollie Butler (1984) *Hand it to the Kids* (Super 8, 23:29min, colour, sound), EAFA no. 3392.
58. *Hand It to the Kids* (1984). See note 57. For another young filmmaker responding to her teacher as a role model and describing her involvement in film production at a secondary school, see Rossetti (1984: 21).
59. Sharon Gadsdon (1988) *Freak* (Super 8, 4:29min, colour, sound), IAC International Amateur Film and Video Festival Movie 88, Gold seal junior section, EAFA no. 3352.

60. Much of Sheila Graber's animation is available online as are additional resources associated with her 2009 book. Films, books, presentations, animation tutorials and other teaching materials are available at <https://www.youtube.com/user/sheilagraber> and <http://www.graber-miller.com> (both last accessed 19 April 2018). Some early work in the IAC library is also available online at the East Anglia Film Archive <http://www.eafa.org.uk> (last accessed 21 May 2018). Graber featured regularly in the hobby press during the 1970s and 1980s and designed a logo for the IAC's fiftieth anniversary (see Anon. 1982a: 11). Her early writing includes Graber (1974; 1976; 1983) and many line drawn articles on animation feature in *Movie Maker* during the 1980s. Since the writing of this chapter, more of Sheila Graber's early films have become available online at the North East Film Archive, via its shared website with the Yorkshire Film Archive, <http://www.yorkshirefilmarchive.com> (last accessed 21 May 2018).
61. *Puff the Magic Dragon* (1972) was an early example of Graber's hand-drawn and coloured animation.
62. Sheila Graber in conversation with the author, 2016.
63. Sheila Graber was profiled in *Movie Maker*'s Ten Best 'Meet the Winners' in successive years (1974–7).
64. Examples include *The Monarch and the Sea* (1975) (Super 8mm, 6:21min, colour, sound), EAFA no. 4070; and *The Twelve Days of Christmas* (1975) (Super 8mm, 4:05min, colour, sound), EAFA no. 3923.
65. Sheila Graber (1977) *Moving On* (16mm, 3:45min, colour, sound), EAFA no. 3634.
66. Sheila Graber in conversation with the author.
67. Sheila Graber (1976) *Four Views on Landscape* (16mm, 3:53min, colour, sound), EAFA no. 3349; *Michelangelo* (1976) (16mm, 3:23min, colour, sound), EAFA no. 3617; *Face to Face* (1976) (16mm, 1:59min, colour, sound), EAFA no. 3314; *Be a Good Neighbour* (1978) (16mm, 5:54min, colour, sound), EAFA no. 3105.
68. In her reflections on amateur and professional animation, Graber recalled that until she met Alison de Vere, 'I reckoned living in the frozen North and working from my dining-room table made me an Outsider.' The responses of other professional animators also enabled her to see animation more clearly: 'the real work is being done at ordinary tables by hard-working people from all walks of life with all sorts of training backgrounds . . . They envied the freedom I had as a lone worker to control everything from the initial idea to the mixed sound track. No clients to please, no deadlines to meet, except those self-imposed. Suddenly I found the roles reversed. To many full-time professional animators, the perfect animation studio would simply be a dining room table and freedom. So don't knock being an amateur: enjoy it and don't envy the professionals' (quoted from Graber 2009, Section 14 'Graber's guide 2'). See also Richard Taylor (2001).
69. Sheila Graber (1976) *The Lady of Shallot* (16mm, 5:13min, sound, colour, YouTube.

70. Sheila Graber, *Just So Stories* (ten videos), YouTube.
71. Alison Snowdon, Vera Neubauer, Petra Freeman, Christine Roche, Candy Guard, Joanna Dunn and Joanna Quinn were members of a new generation of highly individual female animators to emerge in the 1980s and 1990s.
72. Terry Wragg in conversation with the author, 1 May 2016; see also Ros (Rosalind) Delar (1973: 8–9) and the key demands of the Women's Liberation Movement as discussed in Barbara Caine (1997: 256, 312).
73. Jill Lampert in correspondence with the author, September 2016.
74. See also Chapter 2.
75. Author in conversation with Phillip Collins, IAC archivist, EAFA, 6–7 July 2016. See also longer discussion in Collins (2011, work in progress).
76. The final animations of Barry Lockwood, a member of Huddersfield Filmmakers' Club, were jointly made with his wife Wendy, shortly before he died, although this is not shown on the IAC website, and reveals that under-representation may still occur at the highest level within the amateur film movement.
77. Valrie Ellis, Brian Dunckley, William Davis and Garth Hope (2003) *Blowing in the Wind* (iMac using Adobe Premiere and Amiga 4000/030 using D Paint V).
78. Joanna Quinn (1993) *Britannia* (5min, colour, sound), YouTube, <https://www.youtube.com/watch?v=dKSLu2n7jL4> (last accessed 21 May 2018)
79. Beryl Armstrong. See Chapter 2.

Afterword

Presenting, analysing or comparing to amateur films made by over forty British women during most of the twentieth century remains nevertheless an initial survey of the vast and complex research sources and of their specific visual literacy. Their hobbyist practice was frequently an exercise in nuanced cultural and identity uphill battles, while creatively migrating from fixed, established social networks, and across personal rites of passage, towards self-empowering roles as producers of global culture. Whether teachers, homemakers, unmarried, middle or upper class, avid travellers or deeply anchored in remote communities, most British women who experimented with amateur filmmaking on film or video remain difficult to classify, both as psychological typologies and as women who chose to be behind a film camera in order to picture their identities in front of it – the images they filmed acting as their self-portraits. All done, fought for and expressed with polite and creative diligence in a 'man's' world and benefiting from a recently granted access to political entitlement. Importantly, their authorial and visual agency has translated more so than confirmed cultural assumptions about gender hierarchies and narratives. Many of their amateur films succeeded, directly or tangentially, voluntarily or accidentally, to break story-telling taboos and therefore the legacy of their diverse visual texts requires cross-disciplinary scrutiny. As they animated, recorded informally family scenes, and made documentaries, women amateur filmmakers were creating a corpus of visually mediated historical experience often against, or within, male-dominated master narratives. Patriarchal structures and assumptions shaped their everyday worlds for decades, even when they had agency and elements of autonomy within their personal lives. Today, their work, whether the simplest single cine reel with domestic scenes, or a carefully edited production, offers an uncharted theoretical territory. It was for these reasons that we chose to combine historical perspectives with experimenting with theories borrowed from visual and social anthropology, and with concepts such as autobiographical memory and the process of creating a storied self, when exploring some of the case studies discussed in this volume. Writing from complementary but contrasting perspectives, we hope that these women filmmakers' practices open fresh routes to the interpretation of amateur cinema.

The selected research corpus for this volume allows for rich explorations of interlocking themes within twentieth-century historical experience such as visual story-telling, memory and remembering patterns, adjustments to cultural changes at home and abroad, constructions of selfhood, and women's status within society. As discussed in this volume, women filmmakers' decisions and actions were part of modernising lifestyles that brought new means of relating to the past. Reminiscent of actuality cinema's social reportage, women's early camerawork displayed newfound agency as they chose not to pose with children but rather to objectify and depict their friends, families, neighbours and those people they encountered within the varied circles they inhabited. Their freedom as filmmakers was part of being in a world made smaller by faster and more convenient forms of travel that occurred, paradoxically, just as Britain's imperial grip was slipping. Their enduring enthusiasm for visual story-telling – demonstrated in live action and animation – continued through the century against geo-political and social change at different scales.

Evolving visual literacies surface through successive generations of women's amateur filmmaking as they experimented with the novelty of capturing movement. Their use of camera and sometimes subsequent editing of the footage indicate their fascination with sustained focus and the 'longer look' that appealed to the cine user. Many of them, just like Lucy Fairbanks, Kathleen Lockwood, Sheila Graber or Audrey Lewis, explored trick photography, early colour film stock, reversals, stop-motion, animation and slow motion techniques. From the earliest years of cinema, women were involved, primarily as performers but also, as seen in promotional literature, as the holders and possibly the users of cinematographic equipment. As their idiosyncratic visual practices developed, they defined themselves as amateurs who, for the most part, worked independently of Britain's later experimental film movements. Among the post-war generation, some women began to think of their practice as a non-commercial rather than non-professional alternative to mainstream cinema. During the 1970s, film became a tool for feminist activism, as seen by the rise of women-only filmmaking cooperatives; however, the record of women's domestic or home-based amateur filmmaking on video is still under-researched. Rising levels of women in paid employment, declining participation levels in all forms of organised leisure, and changing film technologies all impacted on numbers of amateur filmmakers during the 1980s. This study has also identified the rise of a digitally literate generation of club-based women practitioners who make and share award-winning films.

The life cycle of amateur filmmaking as an evolving hobby has been echoed by the changes in people's personal lives. Throughout this volume, we have explored how personal circumstances, geographies and lifestyles have intermeshed with filming opportunities. If being single offered early independence for some women in the first half of the last century, marriage also offered opportunities where some wives could reclaim personal autonomy via their own filmmaking even if a partner's work determined where they were able to film. As with the gender politics that underpin much of women's story-telling, other political concerns inform these narratives. For some filmmakers, undoubtedly the political moment was precisely the impetus to film, and their cine view as bystanders to the action is now particularly significant. No one considered here filmed a protester's placard (Brownrigg and Main 2016), though perhaps Rosie Newman's brief scene filmed at the Chawpatty beach in Bombay (Mumbai) in the early 1930s, or Wilma Gladstone's films of Ghana's independence celebrations in 1957 indicate more nuanced recordings of anti-imperial protests and emerging postcolonial national identities. Moreover, women amateur filmmakers were not untouched by wider issues, depending upon where they were, whether as the wife of a civil servant or missionary during a posting overseas, filming family life at home, or sharing picnics in the English countryside with Enoch Powell – one of the most controversial figures in Britain's post-war race relations history. Ideologies determined subjects and settings shot by upper middle class women wherever they were living in late imperial settings, in England's 'home counties', as aristocrats on their Scottish estates or during holidays abroad. Wars, economic crises, abdications, military threats and national service, industrial decline, unemployment, racial inequalities and social change were backdrops to these women's lived experiences and mirrors against which their visions of domesticity, travel and multi-layered identities may be set. Finally, whether filming somewhere in Cornwall, at Buckingham Palace, during political demonstrations or at their children's birthday parties, British women amateur filmmakers almost always acted as by default visual ethnographers, as social vectors of British national or expatriate ethos, and as independent mediators of gender emancipation and social commitment. Importantly, in their often unrecognised (even by themselves) role as culture and media makers, they promoted progressive visual literacies while acting as unique and valuable ambassadors between worlds, cultures, classes and often racial networks.

Each chapter has identified further issues to explore and addressed themes and theoretical perspectives that point to the potential for further cross-archival work that compares, complements, augments and ultimately challenges some of the ideas presented. An exploratory study of this kind cannot afford to be comprehensive or even fully representative. Moreover, space does not always allow for fuller discussions of some individuals mentioned only in passing. We are conscious too of the gaps and so we invite other scholars to join us in uncovering amateur visual practices that fully reflect Britain's trajectory towards an increasingly diverse society.

In spite of what might appear as an eclectic selection of case studies, this book is not a random collection of voices and visions: these British women's experiences and achievements as amateur filmmakers attest to their commitment, understanding and ways of being women at particular moments in Britain's recent past. Their visual practices hint not so much to a purely gendered way of seeing but how personal identities and inner meanings are also melded by wider processes of change. In recent years, several British film archives have started alert campaigns for collecting, restoring and promoting films made by women amateur filmmakers – media theorists, anthropologists and social scientists are equally committed to explore this new field of visual and identity 'staging of the self', and the ways in which women have used amateur filmmaking to create and communicate novel views on constructions of female selfhood (Doy 2005).

Selected Bibliography

Anon. (194(6)), 'One-Woman Film', *Daily Dispatch Manchester*, 18 March. Private papers of Miss Rosie Newman, IWM, 2 Microfilm Reels, Catalogue number: Documents.23389.

Aasman, Susan (2014), 'Saving Private Reels: archival practices and digital memories (formerly known as Home Movies) in the digital age', in Laura Rascaroli and Gwenda Young with Brian Monahan (eds) *Amateur Filmmaking. The Home Movie, the Archive, the Web*, London: Bloomsbury, pp. 245–56.

Alexander, Nathan (1963), 'Discover the world of animation', *Amateur Movie Maker* 6, 5, pp. 228–9.

Anon. (1928), 'Films by amateurs. New association with ambitious programme', *The Observer*, 18 November, p. 22.

Anon. (1929a), [Advertisement for Kodak], *Punch*, 27 March, p. 4.

Anon. (1929b), *Punch*, 18 December, pp. 4–5.

Anon. (1929c), 'Personalities – No. V. Frances Lascot', *Amateur Films*, 1, 6, p. 101.

Anon. (1929d), 'Why Aunt Agnes could use it', *Punch*, 7 August, p. 12.

Anon. (1929e), 'The National Convention', *Amateur Films*, 1, 10, p. 222.

Anon. (1931a) [Advertisement], *Punch*, 1 July, p. 3.

Anon. (1931b), 'The family album comes to life', *Punch*, 29 April, pp. 8, 18.

Anon. (1932), 'Individuals' films', *The Manchester Guardian*, 20 October, p. 11.

Anon. (1933), 'She was only a dope smuggler's daughter', *Home Movies Home Talkies*, pp. 89, 91.

Anon. (1936), 'In Manchester', *The Manchester Guardian*, 4 December, p. 13.

Anon. (1951), 'TV comes to the North. Holme Moss brings television to eleven million people', *Wireless and Electrical Trader*, 13 October.

Anon. (1954), 'Mr and Mrs Day represent Stoke on Trent region', *IAC News*, December, pp. 11–12.

Anon. (1957a), 'Amateur cine enthusiasts have their own theatre', *The Evening News*, (Edinburgh) 2 October.

Anon. (1957b), 'Making film in the home', *The Financial Times*, 17 September, p. 6.

Anon. (1959), 'La tragique expédition de Claude Kogan', *Paris Match*, no: 551, 31 October.

Anon. (1961), 'For women', *Cine Camera*, 2, 12, December, p. 42.

Anon. (1977), 'Rosie Newman's secret cine war', *Amateur Photographer,* Newsview, 2 February, p. 30.

Anon. (1978a), 'The Ten Best in detail: Joanna Fryer', *Movie Maker*, June, p. 472.

Anon. (1978b), 'Meet the producers', *Movie Maker*, June, p. 481.

Anon. (1978c), 'The Ten Best in detail: Tony and Barbara Brindle', *Movie Maker*, June, p. 478.

Anon. (1982a), Sheila Graber Jubilee cartoon, *Amateur Film Maker*, August, p. 11.

Anon. (1982b), 'Putting on style', *Amateur Film Maker*, 4, 4, August, p. 6.

Anon. (1988), 'Graber shows new movie', *Movie Maker*, May, p. 5.

Anon. (1997), 'Kathleen Lockwood. Obituary', *Holme Valley Express*, 27 June.

Armstrong, Beryl (1971), 'Filming the little railways', *Movie Maker*, 5, 7, July, pp. 446–8.

Armstrong, Beryl (1972), 'Editing with L-plates', *Movie Maker*, 6, 10, October, pp. 711, 714.

Armstrong, Beryl and Harry Walden (1972), 'Putting on a good show', *Movie Maker*, 6, 12, December, pp. 870–1.

Aronson, Elliot (2011), *The Social Animal*, New York: Worth Publishers.

Ashby, Bernard (1982), 'Animated films in the IAC film library', *Animator Magazine*, Autumn 2, pp. 19–21.

Barthes, Roland ([1980] 2000), *Camera Lucida*, London: Vintage Classics.

Bayne, Ralph (1982), 'The SERIAC story (South East Region of the IAC)', *Amateur Film Maker*, 4, 4, August, pp. 31–3.

Beaulieu, Michel S. and Ronald N. Harpelle (eds) (2005), *The Lady Lumberjack: An Annotated Collection of Dorothea Mitchell's Writings*, Thunder Bay, ON: Lakehead University Press.

Bell, Melanie and Melanie Williams (eds) (2009), *British Women's Cinema*, London: Routledge.

Belting, Hans (2014), *An Anthropology of Images: Picture, Medium, Body*, Princeton: Princeton University Press.

Bendazzi, Giannalberto (1994), *Cartoons: One Hundred Years of Cinema Animation*, Bloomington and London: Indiana University Press/John Wiley.

Bendazzi, Giannalberto (2015), *Animation: A World History*. Volume 2. Abingdon: Taylor & Francis.

Benjamin, Walter ([1936] 2008), *The Work of Art in the Age of Mechanical Reproduction*, London: Penguin. (Trans. J. A. Underwood.)

Berger, John with Mike Dibb, Sven Blomberg, Chris Fox and Richard Hollis (1972), *Ways of Seeing*, London: BBC/Penguin Books.

Bhabha, Homi K. (1984), 'Of mimicry and men: the ambivalence of colonial discourse', *October 28 Discipleship: A Special Issue on Psychoanalysis*, pp. 125–33.

Bloomfield, Elizabeth A. (2015), 'Gender role stereotyping and art interpretation', thesis, University of Iowa.

Bock, Gisella (1991), 'Challenging dichotomies: perspectives on women's history', in K. Offen, R. R. Pierson and J. Rendall (eds) *Writing Women's History*, London: Palgrave Macmillan, pp. 1–23.

Bourne, Stephen (2001), *Black in the British Frame: The Black Experience in Film and Television*, London: Continuum.

Bourne, Stephen ([2004] 2011), 'Atwell, (Una) Winifred (c.1913–1983)', *Oxford Dictionary of National Biography*, Oxford: Oxford University Press, <https://doi.org/10.1093/ref:odnb/58882> (last accessed 20 January 2018).

Brah, Avtar ([1996] 2003), 'Diaspora, border and transnational identities', in Reina Lewis and Sarah Mills (eds) *Feminist Postcolonial Theory: A Reader*, Edinburgh: Edinburgh University Press, pp. 613–34.

Brickell, Katherine and Bradley L. Garrett (2013), 'Geography, film and exploration: women and amateur filmmaking in the Himalayas', *Transactions of the Institute of British Geographers*, 38, 1, January, pp. 7–11.

Brindle, Tony and Barbara Brindle (1978), 'Animating the Christmas story', *Movie Maker*, December, pp. 988–9.

Britzman, Deborah P. (2006), 'Foreword', in Janet Alsup, *Teacher Identity Discourses: Negotiating Personal and Professional Spaces*, Urbana, IL: NCTE.

Brownlow, Kevin (1995), 'Obituaries: Pauline Murray', *The Independent*, 4 January, <http://www.independent.co.uk/news/people/obituaries-pauline-murray-1566531.html> (last accessed 18 January 2018).

Brownrigg, Jenny and Shona Main (2016), 'Helen Biggar, challenge to fascism: *Glasgow's May Day* (1938)', *MAP Magazine*, 1 May, <http://mapmagazine.co.uk/9910/challenge-fascism-glasgows-may-day-1938> (last accessed 20 January 2018).

Buckingham, David, Maria Pini and Rebekah Willett (2009), 'Take back the tube! The discursive construction of amateur film – and video-making', in David Buckingham and Rebekah Willett (eds) *Video Cultures: Media Technology and Everyday Creativity*, Basingstoke: Palgrave Macmillan, pp. 51–70.

Buckley, Cheryl and Hilary Fawcett (2002), *Fashioning the Feminine. Representation and Women's Fashion from the Fin de Siècle to the Present*, London and New York: I. B. Tauris.

Buettner, Elizabeth (2004), *Empire Families: Britons and Late Imperial India*, Oxford: Oxford University Press.

Burgess, Jean (2006), 'Hearing ordinary voices: cultural studies, vernacular creativity and digital storytelling', *Continuum: Journal of Media & Cultural Studies*, 20, 2, pp. 201–14.

Burghin, Victor, James Donald and Cora Kaplan (eds) (1986), *Formations of Fantasy*, London: Methuen.

Burton, Alan and Steve Chibnall (2013) *Historical Dictionary of British Cinema*, Lanham, MD: Scarecrow Press.

Bush, Barbara (1998), 'Britain's conscience on Africa: white women, race and imperial politics in interwar Britain', in Claire Midgley (ed.) *Gender and Imperialism*, Manchester: Manchester University Press, pp. 200–23.

Butler, Judith (1990), *Gender Trouble: Feminism and the Subversion of Identity*. New York and London: Routledge.

Butler, Mollie (1981), 'A cartoon of note', *Amateur Film Maker*, June, p. 11.

Butler, Mollie (1987), 'Make your skeletons dance', *Amateur Film Maker*, October, p. 11.

Caine, Barbara (1997), *English Feminism 1780–1980*, Oxford: Oxford University Press.

Callahan, Vicki (ed.) (2010), *Reclaiming the Archive: Feminism and Film History*, Detroit: Wayne State University Press.

Cannadine, David (2001), *Ornamentalism: How the British Saw Their Empire*, London: Allen Lane/Penguin.

Chadwick, Whitney (1996), *Women, Art, and Society*, 2nd edition, London: Thames & Hudson.

Chalfen, Richard (1987), *Snapshot Versions of Life*, Bowling Green, OH: Bowling Green State University Popular Press.

Chalke, Sheila (2009), 'Animated explorations: The Grasshopper Group 1953–1983', in Ian Craven (ed.) *Movies on Home Ground: Explorations in Amateur Cinema*, Newcastle-Upon-Tyne: Cambridge Scholars Publishing, pp. 238–69.

Chambers, Eddie, Amna Malik, Lucy Reynolds, Josephine Lanyon and Jane Connarty (eds) (2006), *Ghosting: The Role of the Archive within Contemporary Artists' Film and Video*, Bristol: Picture this Moving Image.

Chedgzoy, Kate (2007), *Women's Writing in the British Atlantic World: Memory, Place and History, 1550–1700*, Cambridge: Cambridge University Press.

Clark, Ken (1982a), 'The Grasshopper Group – part 1', *Animator Magazine* (originally published as *Animator's Newsletter*), Summer, 1, pp. 6–7.

Clark, Ken (1982b), 'The Grasshopper animators – part 2', *Animator Magazine*, Autumn, 2, p. 6.

Clark, Ken (1982c), 'The Grasshopper animators – part 3', *Animator Magazine*, Winter, 3, pp. 16–18.

Clark, Ken (1983a), 'The shadows move 1940s – part 3', *Animator Magazine*, Spring, 4, pp. 6–9.

Clark, Ken (1983b), 'Life cycle of the Grasshopper Group', *Movie Maker*, 17, 3, pp. 142–3.

Clark, Ken (1983c), 'The shadows move 1940s – part 3', *Animator Magazine*, Autumn, 6, pp. 15–19.

Clark, Ken (1985), 'Ken Clark chats with Dick and Elizabeth Horn', *Animator Magazine*, Spring, 12, pp. 24–7.

Clark, Ken (1987), 'Gaumont British Animation (GBA) – a great British achievement', *Animator Magazine*, Summer, 19, pp. 25–7.

Cleave, Alan (1971), 'Cartoon animation for everyone. Part I', *Movie Maker* 5, 11, p. 710–12.

Codell, Esmé Raji (2001), *Educating Esmé. Diary of a Teacher's First Year*, Chapel Hill, NC: Algonquin Books.

Cohler, Bertram J. and Thomas R. Cole (1996), 'Studying older lives: reciprocal acts of telling and listening', in Gary Kenyon, James E. Birren, Jan-Erik Ruth, Johannes J. F. Schroots and Torbjorn Svensson (eds) *Aging and Biography: Explorations in Adult Development*, New York: Springer, pp. 61–76.

Coles, Jan, Susan Phillips, Lyn Clearihan and Kymm Feldman (2011). 'Medical journal covers: an analysis of gendered images and how these influence best practice', *Australian Family Physician*, 40, 9, pp. 725–8.

Collins, Phillip (2011), *This Curious Little Sub-Culture. A History of the IAC and its Collection*, Norwich: East Anglian Film Archive (work in progress).

Compton, Margaret (2003a), 'Periodicals & pamphlets', *Film History*, 15, pp. 270–1.

Compton, Margaret (2003b), 'Small-gauge and amateur film bibliography', *Film History*, 15, 252–69.

Coxhead, Elizbeth (1948a), 'Historian in celluloid', *The Lady*, CXXVII, 3304, 17 June.

Coxhead, Elizbeth (1948b), 'Woman with a camera', *Liverpool Daily Post*, Thursday, 3 June.

C. R. (1938), 'A film society show', *The Manchester Guardian*, 7 December, p. 15.

Crano, William D. and Radmila Prislin (eds) (2008), *Attitudes and Attitude Change*, New York and London: Psychology Press.

Craven, Ian (2015), 'Eine Annäherung an den Avantgardismus? Amateuranimation und das Ringen mit der Technik' [Accommodating avant-gardism? Amateur animation and the struggle for technique'], in Siegfried Mattl, Carina Lesky, Vrääth Öhner and Ingo Zechner (eds) *Abenteuer Alltag. Zur Archäologie des Amateurfilms*, Vienna: Osterreichisches Filmmuseum und Synema Publikationen, pp. 28–42.

Curtis, Stanley J. and Myrtle E. Boultwood (1962), *An Introductory History of English Education since 1800*, London: University Tutorial Press.

Daborn, John (1962), 'Smoke with a twist', *Amateur Cine World*, 8 March, pp. 356–7.

Daily Express (1956), 'This is a 53-year-old Dorking housewife naming a 20,000ft. Peak "Daily Express"', *Daily Express*, 4 August.

Dake, Dennis M. (1995), 'Process issues in visual literacy', in Darrell G. Beauchamp, Roberts A. Braden and Robert E. Griffin (eds) *Imagery and Visual Literacy*, Blacksburg, VA: International Visual Literacy Association, pp. 1–23.

Daley, Robert (1959), 'The mountain is still the master', *The New York Times*, 29 October.

Davies, Gail (1998), 'Networks of nature: stories of natural history film making from the BBC', PhD thesis, University College London, <http://discovery.ucl.ac.uk/5188/1/5188.pdf> (last accessed 21 January 2018).

de Klerk, Nico (2013), '100 Years of image control: the case of J. C. Lamster's films for the Dutch Colonial Institute', *Journal of Early Visual Popular Culture*, 11, 4, pp. 312–21.

Del Plato, Joan (2002), *Multiple Wives, Multiple Pleasures: Representing the Harem, 1800–1875*, Vancouver: Fairleigh Dickinson University Press.

Delar, Ros (1973), 'Oppressed politics', *Red Rag*, pp. 8–9.

Derrida, Jacques ([1978] 2013), *La vérité en peinture*, Paris: Champs Essais.

de Vries, Tjitte and Ati Mul (2009), *'They Thought It Was a Marvel': Arthur Melbourne-Cooper (1874–1961), Pioneer of Puppet Animation*, Amsterdam: Pallas Publications.

Dixon Anthony, Aimee (2016), 'Early African American female filmmakers', in Melody Bridges and Cheryl Robson (eds) *Silent Women: Pioneers of Cinema*, Twickenham: Supernova, pp. 35–64.

Dixon, Michael (2015), *The British Puppet and Model Theatre Guild, 1925–2015*, London: Bob Books.

Donlan, Peter (1982), 'Who's who on IAC council: Valrie Bristow Ellis', *Amateur Film Maker*, August, p. 25.

Donovan, Josephine (2012), *Feminist Theory: The Intellectual Traditions*, 4th edition, London: Continuum.

Doy, Gen (2005), *Picturing the Self: Changing Views of the Subject in Visual Culture*, London: I. B. Tauris.

Dudding, Kathy (2007), 'Leaving home: from the lounge room to the cine lounge', *Illusions*, 39, pp. 4–8.

Dudding, Kathy (2010), 'Tracing the flaneuse: New Zealand/Aotearoa', paper presented at the 7th Orphan Film Symposium, New York, April, <https://sites.google.com/site/orphans7/home/tracing-the-flneuse> (last accessed 18 January 2018).

Duguid, Euan (2013), 'Women 94 clicks with archive flicks', *The View. South Lanarkshire Council*, June, p. 2, <www.southlanarkshire.gov.uk/download/downloads/id/7758/june_2013.pdf> (last accessed 18 January 2018).

Dunkley, Brian (1982), 'Did you know?', *Amateur Film Maker*, 4, 4, August p. 16.

Dyson, Francis (2013), 'Studio sensibilities. Occupying a distinguished but lonely place in the amateur movement: Ace Movies 1929–1964', in Ian Craven and Ryan Shand (eds) *Small-gauge Storytelling: Discovering the Amateur Fiction Film*, Edinburgh: Edinburgh University Press, pp. 125–43.

Dyson, Francis (2015), *TNA Project. Cataloguing of the Institute of Amateur Cinematographers Women Film-Makers' Films*, Norwich: East Anglian Film Archive.

Dyson, Francis (2012), 'Challenging the expectations of amateur film: Ace Movies and the Cine-club Film', paper presented at the Other Cinemas Screen Studies Conference 2012, University of Glasgow.

Easen, Sarah (undated), 'Mary Field (1896–1968)', British Film Institute, Screenonline, <http://www.screenonline.org.uk/people/id/581940/> (last accessed 19 January 2018).

Eco, Umberto (1992), *Interpretation and Overinterpretation*, ed. Stefan Collini, Cambridge: Cambridge University Press.

Eco, Umberto (1994), *Les limites de l'interprétation*, Paris: Le Livre de Poche.

Eliade, Mircea (1988), *Autobiography. Exile's Odyssey, Volume 2, 1937–1960*, Chicago: University of Chicago Press.

Elsaesser, Thomas (2009), 'Sonnen-Insulaner: on a Berlin island of memory', in Uta Staiger, Henriette Steiner and Andrew Webber (eds) *Memory Culture and the Contemporary City*, Basingstoke: Palgrave Macmillan, pp. 32–51.

Emberley, Julia V. (2007), *Defamiliarizing the Aboriginal: Cultural Practices and Decolonization in Canada*, Toronto, Buffalo and London: University of Toronto Press.

Enticknap, Leo (2005), *Moving Image Technology: from Zoetrope to Digital*, London: Wallflower.

Erens, Patricia (1991), *Issues in Feminist Film Criticism*, Chichester: John Wiley & Sons.

Ernst, Wolfgang (2013), *Digital Memory and the Archive*, Minneapolis and London: University of Minnesota Press.

Evans, Caroline (2005), 'Multiple, movement, model, mode: the mannequin parade 1900–1929', in Caroline Evans and Christopher Breward (eds) *Fashion and Modernity*, Oxford and New York: Berg, pp. 125–45.

Fayde, Iris (1951a), 'Just the job for the woman cine amateur', *Amateur Cine World*, 15, 8, December, pp. 805–6.

Fayde, Iris (1951b), 'When I directed a film', *Amateur Cine World*, 15, 7, November, pp. 636–8.

Fayde, Iris (1952a), 'A home of your own', photo caption, *Amateur Cine World*, 16, 1, May, p. 63.

Fayde, Iris (1952b), 'The feminine touch at the film show', *Amateur Cine World*, 15, 9, January, pp. 909–11.

Fayde, Iris (1952c), 'Women's pictures', *Amateur Cine World*, 16, 2, June, pp. 160–1.

Ferguson, Niall, (2014), *Empire: How Britain made the Modern World*, London: Penguin Books

Fish, Jane (1997), '". . . it looked more natural": Miss Rosie Newman's colour film of the Second World War', *Imperial War Museum Review*, 11, pp. 27–39.

Fisher, Mark (2016), 'Back to the rivers of blood: Enoch Powell returns to a divided Britain', *The Guardian*, 31 October.

Fletcher, Tina (1984), 'The kitchen as an puppet animation studio', *Animator Magazine*, Winter, 11, p. 20.

Fletcher, Tina (2007), 'The history of Willoughby Drive', <http://www.dolphinpuppetfilms.co.uk/> (last accessed 18 January 2018).

Fletcher, Tina (undated), 'How I came to animation and where it led me', Dope Sheet, *Animator Magazine* <http://www.dolphinpuppetfilms.co.uk/> (last accessed 18 January 2018).

Flusser, Vilem (2006), *Towards a Philosophy of Photography*, London: Reaktion Books.

Ford, Amanda (2015), 'The Decolonization of Christianity in Colonial Kenya', University of Arkansas, dissertation, <http://scholarworks.uark.edu/etd/1444> (last accessed 20 January 2018).

Forrester-Paton, Colin (2001), 'Obituary Wilma Gladstone M.B.E. (1914–2000)', *Scotland-Ghana Society*, Newsletter No.2, March.

Foster, Gwendolyn Audrey, Katrien Jacobs and Amy L. Unterburger (1998), *Women Motion Picture Producers and Directors*, Detroit and London: St James Press.

Foucault, Michel (1988), *The History of Sexuality: The Will to Knowledge*, Vol. 1, London: Penguin.

Fowkes Tobin, Beth (1999), *Picturing Imperial Power: Colonial Subjects in Eighteenth-Century British Painting*, Durham, NC: Duke University Press.

Fung, Richard (2008), 'Remaking home movies', in Karen L. Ishizuka and Patricia R. Zimmermann (eds) *Mining the Home Movies. Excavations in Histories and Memories*, Berkeley and Los Angeles: University of California Press, pp. 29–40.

Garber, Marjorie (2001), *Academic Instincts*, Princeton, NJ: Princeton University Press, pp. 9–11.

Garcia, M. Susana (2010), 'Joanna Quinn', in Juan Julia Igual et al. (eds) *Joanna Quinn. Art vs Animació, Exhibition catalogue*, 13 May–27 July, University of Valencia, International Cinema Jove Film Festival / National Media Museum, Bradford, UK.

Geppert, Dominik and Frank Lorenz Muller (2015) (eds) *Sites of Imperial Memory: Commemorating Colonial Rule in the Nineteenth and Twentieth Centuries*, Manchester: Manchester University Press.

Giardiello, Patricia (2014), *Pioneers in Early Childhood Education: The Roots and Legacies of Rachel and Margaret McMillan, Maria Montessori and Susan Isaacs*, Abingdon: Routledge.

Gifford, Denis (1988), *British Animated Films, 1895–1985: A Filmography*, Jefferson, NC: McFarland & Company.

Gilmour, Edwyn (1961), 'Mr Kingston's movie-workshop [reproduced image of "Mrs Movie-Maker"]', *Amateur Movie Maker*, July, p. 361.

Gilovich, Thomas, Dale Griffin and Daniel Kahneman (eds) (2002), *Heuristics and Biases: The Psychology of Intuitive Judgment*, Cambridge: Cambridge University Press.

Gledhill, Christine J. (ed.) (2012), *Gender Meets Genre in Postwar Cinemas*, Urbana, Chicago and Springfield: University of Illinois Press.

Gledhill, Christine and Julia Knight (eds) (2015), *Doing Women's Film History: Reframing Cinemas, Past and Future*, Champaign, IL: University of Illinois Press.

Goffman, Erving (1956), *The Presentation of Self in Everyday Life*, Second monograph, University of Edinburgh Social Sciences Research Centre.

Golding, Harry (1915), *The Wonder Book of Empire For Boys And Girls . . . With Fifteen Coloured Plates and Over Three Hundred Illustrations*, London: Ward, Lock & Company.

Gomez, Leonardo (2010), 'Joanna Quinn', in Juan Julia Igual et al. (eds) *Joanna Quinn. Art vs Animació, Exhibition Catalogue*, 13 May–27 July, University of Valencia, International Cinema Jove Film Festival / National Media Museum, Bradford, UK.

Graber, Sheila (1974), 'Animation. My way', *Movie Maker*, December, pp. 852–3.

Graber, Sheila (1976), 'Animator's progress', *Movie Maker*, October, pp. 692–4.

Graber, Sheila (1982), 'Sheila Graber on animation', *Movie Maker*, April, p. 231.

Graber, Sheila (1983), 'The films of Sheila Graber 1974 to 1977', *Animator Magazine*, Summer, 5, p. 29.

Graber, Sheila (1985), 'Sound and motion', *Movie Maker*, February, pp. 34–5.

Graber, Sheila (1992), 'From darkness to light or from Super 8 to Super-nova. Conversion to computer animation', *Animator Magazine*, Spring, 29, pp. 1–3.

Graber, Sheila (2009), *Animation: A Handy Guide*, London: A. & C. Black Publishers.

Graham Bower, Ursula (1950), *Naga Path*, London: John Murray.

Griffiths, Alison (2002), *Wondrous Difference. Cinema, Anthropology and Turn of the Century Visual Culture*, New York: Columbia University Press.

Griffiths, Morwenna (1995), *Feminisms and the Self: The Web of Identity*, London: Routledge.

Grimaldi, George (1934a), 'And this is what *The Manchester Guardian* said of the show', *IAC Bulletin*, 4, January, p. 28.

Grimaldi, George (1934b), 'Future honours for Miss Ruth Stuart', *IAC Bulletin*, 4, January, p. 29.

Halas, John and Bob Privett (1951), *How to Cartoon for Amateurs*, London and New York: Focal Press.

Halas, Vivien, with contributions by Clare Kitson, Brian Sibley, Jez Stewart, Jez Walker and Paul Wells (2014) *A Moving Image: Joy Batchelor, 1914–1991; Artist, Writer and Animator*, London: Southbank Publishing.

Halliday Josh and Louise Osborne (2015), 'Queen's Nazi salute footage raises pressure on royals to open archives', *The Guardian*, 20 July 2015, <https://www.theguardian.com/uk-news/2015/jul/19/queens-nazi-salute-video-pressure-mounts-on-royals-to-open-up-archives> (last accessed 10 September 2017).

Hammack, Phillip L. (2008), 'Narrative and the cultural psychology of identity', *Personality and Social Psychology Review*, 12, 3, August, pp. 222–47.

Hammerton, Jenny (2001), *'For Ladies Only?: Eve's Film Review: Pathé Cinemagazine, 1921–33*, Hastings: Projection Box.

Hanssen, Eirik Frisvold (2009), 'Symptoms of desire: colour, costume, and commodities in fashion newsreels of the 1910s and 1920s', *Film History*, 21, 2 pp. 107–21.

Harper, Stephen (1965), *Lady Killer Peak. A Lone Man's Story of Twelve Women on a Killer Mountain*, London: C. Nichols & Co.

Hawley, Steve (2009) 'The outsider: the films of George Higginson', in Steve Hawley (ed.) *Art School! Manchester School of Art since 1838. Contemporary Reflections*, Manchester: Manchester Metropolitan University, pp. 3–6.

Healey, Eileen (1960), 'Cho Oyu expedition, 1959', *Ladies' Alpine Club Journal*, pp. 14–18.

Heffer, Simon ([2004] 2008) 'Powell, (John) Enoch (1912–1998)', *Oxford Dictionary of National Biography*, Oxford University Press, <http://www.oxforddnb.com/view/article/69398> (last accessed 7 June 2017).

Hermans, Hubert J. M. and Harry J. G. Kempen (1993), *The Dialogical Self*, New York: Academic.

Hertwig, Ralph, Carola Fanselow and Ulrich Hoffrage (eds) (2003), 'Hindsight bias: how knowledge and heuristics affect our reconstruction of the past', *Memory*, July–September, 11, 4–5, pp. 357–77.

Hibbett, Brian (2010) 'A stroll down Willoughby Drive', *The Puppet Master*, Autumn, pp. 25–6.

Hinton, James (2002), *Women, Social Leadership, and the Second World War: Continuities of Class*, Oxford: Oxford University Press.

Hinxman, Margaret (1982), 'What has impressed me . . .', *Amateur Film Maker*, 4, 4, August, p. 6.

Hirsch, Marianne and Valerie Smith (2002), 'Feminism and cultural memory: an introduction', *Signs: Journal of Women in Culture and Society*, 28, 1, pp. 1–19.

Hirshler, Erica E. (2001), *A Studio of Her Own: Women Artists in Boston 1870–1940*, Boston: Museum of Fine Arts.

Hockenhull, Stella (2017), *British Women Film Directors in the New Millennium*, Basingstoke: Palgrave Macmillan.

Holden, Katherine (2007), *The Shadow of Marriage: Singleness in England, 1914–60*, Manchester: Manchester University Press.

Hölzl, Ingrid (2010), 'Moving stills; images that are no longer immobile', *Photographies*, 3, 1 pp. 99–108.

Honess Roe, Annabelle (2013), *Animated Documentary*, Basingstoke: Palgrave Macmillan.

Horn, Pamela (2015), *Country House Society. The Private Lives of England's Upper Class after the First World War*, Stroud: Amberley Publishing.

Howe, Maija (2014), 'The photographic hangover: reconsidering the aesthetics of the postwar 8mm home movie', in Laura Rascaroli and Gwenda Young with Brian Monahan (eds) *Amateur Filmmaking. The Home Movie, the Archive, the Web*, London: Bloomsbury, pp. 39–50.

Howe, Mark L. (2015), 'Memory development', in Lynn S. Liben and Ulrich Muller (eds) *Handbook of Child Psychology and Developmental Science, Vol. 2: Cognitive Processes*, Hoboken, NJ: Wiley, pp. 203–49.

Hughes, Kathryn (2015), 'Look again – the young Queen's Nazi salute tells another story', *The Guardian*, 19 July, <https://www.theguardian.com/commentisfree/2015/jul/19/queen-nazi-salute-images-movie> (last accessed 10 September 2017).

Hunter, Dan, Ramon Lobato, Megan Richardson and Julian Thomas (eds) (2013), *Amateur Media: Social, Cultural and Legal Perspectives*, London: Routledge.

Ishizuka, Karen L. and Patricia R. Zimmermann (eds) (2008), *Mining the Home Movie: Excavations in Histories and Memories*, Berkeley and London: University of California Press.

Jackson, Alan Arthur (1991), *The Middle Classes, 1900–1950*, Nairn: David St John Thomas.

Jefferson, David (1985), 'Trace and paint with Maggy Clark', *Animator Magazine*, Spring, 12, p. 37.

Johnston, Claire (1975), 'Women's cinema and counter-cinema', in Sue Thornham (ed.) *Feminist Film Theory: A Reader*, New York: New York University Press, pp. 31–40.

Jones, Angie and Jamie Oliff (2007), *Thinking Animation: Bridging the Gap between 2D and CG*, Boston: Thomson Course Technology.

Josselson, Ruthellen and Amia Lieblich (eds) (1993), *The Narrative Study of Lives*, Newbury Park, CA: Sage.

Kaplan, E. Ann (1983), *Women and Film: Both Sides of the Camera*, London and New York: Routledge.

Katelle, Alan (2000), *Home Movies: A History of the American Industry 1897–1979*, Nashua, NH: Transition Publishing.

Kay, Richard (2016), 'The Queen's private family album revealed: Candid footage taken by Her Majesty offers a fascinating insight into royal life - including pillow fights, toy cars and horsing around on her beloved yacht', *Mail Online*, 23 April, <http://www.dailymail.co.uk/news/article-3555139/Candid-footage-taken-Queen-offers-magical-insight-royals-pillow-fighting-horsing-holiday-sliding-deck-beloved-royal-yacht.html> (last accessed 3 May 2016).

Kerry, Matthew (2014), 'The changing face of the amateur holiday film in Britain as constructed by post-war *Amateur Cine World* 1945–51', *Historical Journal of Film, Radio and Television*, 34, 4, pp. 511–27.

Kidd, Alan and David Nicholls (eds) (1999), *Gender, Civic Culture and Consumerism: Middle-class Identity in Britain 1800–1940*, Manchester: Manchester University Press.

Kim, Elaine E. (2002), 'Knowing your place', in Helen Lee and Kerri Sakamoto (eds) *Like Mangoes in July: The Work of Richard Fung*, Toronto: Insomniac Press, <http://www.richardfung.ca/index.php?/writings/elaine-e-kim-2002/> (last accessed 20 January 2018).

Kitson, Clare (2008), *British Animation: The Channel 4 Factor*, Bloomington: Indiana University Press.

Knight, Julia (2000), 'Video', in Fiona Carson and Claire Pajaczkowska (eds) *Feminist Visual Culture*, Edinburgh: Edinburgh University Press, pp. 249–63.

Krasilovsky, Alexis (1997), *Women Behind the Camera: Conversations with Camerawomen*, Westport, CN, and London: Praeger.

Kuhn, Annette (1994), *Women's Pictures: Feminism and Cinema*, London: Verso.

Kynaston, David (2007), *Austerity Britain, Tales of a New Jerusalem, 1945–1951*, London: Bloomsbury.

Landzelius, M. (2004), 'The body', in James Duncan, Nuala C. Johnson and Richard H. Schein (eds) *A Companion to Cultural Geography*, Oxford: Blackwell, pp. 279–97.

Langford, Rachel (2007), 'How amateur films of French colonialism construct African space and place', paper presented at the Making Visual Histories:

Critical Perspectives on Amateur Film Practice Conference, Manchester Metropolitan University, 14 September.

Lant, Antonia (1993), 'Women's independent cinema in eighties Britain: the case of Leeds Animation Workshop', in Lester Friedman (ed.) *British Cinema and Thatcherism: Fires Were Started*, London: University College London, pp. 161–87.

Lant, Antonia and Ingrid Periz (eds) (2006), *Red Velvet Seat: Women's Writings on the First Fifty Years of Cinema*, London: Verso.

Lauder, Betty and Ian Lauder (1962), 'Eyam: review', *Amateur Cine World Weekly*, 29 March, p. 470.

Lauretis, Teresa de (1987), *Technologies of Gender: Essays on Theory, Film and Fiction*, Bloomington: Indiana University Press.

Lavaud, Laurent (1999), *L'image*, Paris: Flammarion.

Lawn, Martin (1987), 'What is the teacher's job? Work and welfare in elementary teaching, 1940–45', in Martin Lawn and Gerald Grace (eds) *Teachers: The Culture and Politics of Work*, London: Routledge, pp. 50–64.

Lawrence, Thomas Edward ([1926] 2014), *Seven Pillars of Wisdom*, Pickle Partners Publishing, Kindle edition.

Leadbeater, Charles and Paul Miller (2004), *The Pro-Am Revolution: How Enthusiasts are Changing our Economy and Society*, London: Demos.

Lerner, Gerda (1977), *The Female Experience: An American Documentary*, Indianapolis: Bobbs-Merrill.

Levine, Philippa (2004), *Gender and Empire*, Oxford: Oxford University Press.

Lewis, Jane (1984), *Women in England, 1870–1950: Sexual Divisions and Social Change*, Brighton: Wheatsheaf.

Liverpool Amateur Photographic Association Cine Group (1955), 'Club news', *Amateur Cine World*, September, p. 182.

Lockwood, H. (1955), 'Blackpool ACA (notes and news)', *Amateur Cine World*, 19, 1, p. 78.

Low, Rachael (1979a), *Documentary and Educational Films of the 1930s (History of British Film)*, London: Allen & Unwin.

Low, Rachael (1979b), *The History of British Film. Documentary and Educational Films of the 1930s*, London: Allen and Unwin.

Lowell, Thomas (1925), *With Lawrence in Arabia*, 16th edition, London: Hutchinson.

Lury, Karen (2013), 'The fragile magic of the home: amateur domestic comedies and the intimate geography of childhood', in Ian Craven and Ryan Shand (eds) *Small Gauge Storytelling: Discovering the Amateur Fiction Film*, Edinburgh: Edinburgh University Press, pp. 260–77.

Lury, Karen (2016), 'The Queen has two bodies: amateur film, civic culture and the rehearsal of monarchy', in M. Merck (ed.) *British Monarchy on Screen*, Manchester University Press: Manchester, pp. 225–42.

MacCannell, Dean (1973), 'Staged authenticity: arrangements of social space in tourist settings', *American Journal of Sociology*, 79, 3, November, pp. 589–603.

MacMillan, Margaret (1996), *Women of the Raj*, London: Thames & Hudson.

Malthouse, Gordon (1939),'Making a silhouette film', *Amateur Cine World*, 6, 6, pp. 278–82.

Margolis, Harriet, Alexis Krasilovsky and Julia Stein (2015), *Shooting Women: Behind the Camera, Around the World*, London: Intellect.

Marshall, J. F. (1937), 'Living lines: simple cartoon work for the amateur', *Amateur Cine World*, 3, 12, pp. 585–7.

McAdams, Dan P. ([1996] 2012), 'Personality, modernity, and the stories self: a contemporary framework for studying persons', in Kathleen D. Vohs and Roy F. Baumeister (eds) *Self and Identity, Vol. 1: Self-Concept and Self-Esteem*, Los Angeles, London and New Delhi: Sage, pp. 227–74.

McAdams, Dan P. (1985), *Power, Intimacy, and the Life Story: Personological Inquiries into Identity*, New York: Guilford.

McCabe, Janet (2004), *Feminist Film Studies: Writing the Woman into Cinema*, London: Wallflower.

McCann, Carole R. and Kim, Seung-kyung (2003), *Feminist Theory Reader: Local and Global Perspectives*, London: Routledge.

McGrath, Caitlin (2012), '"This splendid temple": watching movies in the Wanamaker department store', in Marta Braun, Charles Keil, Rob King, Paul Moore and Louis Pelletier (eds) *Beyond the Screen: Institutions, Networks, and Publics of Early Cinema*, Bloomington: Indiana University Press, pp. 282–6.

McKernan, Luke (1992), *Topical Budget: The Great British News Film*, London: BFI.

McKernan, Luke (2010), 'Amateur camerawoman, camera operator in the 1912–1913 Balkan War', Volume II, *Women and Silent British Cinema (W S B C) Women Film Pioneers Sourcebook*, <https://womenandsilentbritishcinema.wordpress.com/the-women/jessica-borthwick/> (last accessed 20 January 2018).

McKernan, Luke (undated), 'Topical budget: British identity and the Empire', Screenonline, <http://www.screenonline.org.uk/film/id/584643> (last accessed September 2016).

Mead, Margaret (1953), *The Study of Culture at a Distan*ce, Chicago: University of Chicago Press.

Mead, Margaret and Rhoda Metraux (eds) (1970), *A Way of Seeing*, New York: The McCall Publishing Co.

Millett, Kate (1973), *The Prostitution Papers*, Avon Books, Kindle edition.

Mills, Sara (1996), 'Gender and colonial space', *Gender, Place and Culture*, 3, 2, pp. 125–47.

Mohanty Talpade, C. (1984), 'Under western eyes: feminist scholarship and colonial discourses', *Boundary*, 2, 12/13, pp. 333–58.

Monahan, Barry, Laura Rascaroli and Gwenda Young (eds) (2014) *Saving Private Reels: Presentation, Appropriation and Re-contextualisation of the Amateur Moving Image*, London: Continuum.

Moore, Henrietta L. (1994), *A Passion for Difference. Essays in Anthropology and Gender*, Cambridge: Polity Press.

Morris, Jan (1978), *Farewell the Trumpets*, London: Faber & Faber.

Motrescu-Mayes, Annamaria (2005), 'British identities in amateur films from India and Australia, 1920–1940s', paper presented at British World Conference IV, University of Auckland, NZ.

Motrescu-Mayes, Annamaria (2007), 'Images of Empire: online amateur footage and the re-interpretation of British colonial identities', paper presented at Future Histories of the Moving Image Conference, University of Sunderland.

Motrescu-Mayes, Annamaria (2008a), 'Muted imperial identities: British amateur films from the 1920s–1940s', paper presented at Screen Studies Conference, University of Glasgow.

Motrescu-Mayes, Annamaria (2008b), 'Instances of trans-national Britishness in colonial amateur films: the British Raj', paper presented at Britishness, Identity, and Citizenship: the View from Abroad Conference, University of Huddersfield.

Motrescu-Mayes, Annamaria (2008c), 'British identities in amateur films from India and Australia, 1920s – 1940s', thesis, University of Bristol.

Motrescu-Mayes, Annamaria (2009a), 'Displaced Indian identities in early colonial amateur films', paper presented at Visual Empires Conference, University of Sheffield.

Motrescu-Mayes, Annamaria (2009b), 'Memsahibs' amateur films and British imperial agency in the 1930s', paper presented at Women, Gender and Political Spaces: Historical Perspectives - Women's History Network 18th Annual Conference, St Hilda's College, Oxford.

Motrescu-Mayes, Annamaria (2009c), 'Rare colour footage and unofficial testimonials to the Malayan Emergency', paper presented at Colour and the Moving Image: History, Theory, Aesthetics, Archive Conference, University of Bristol.

Motrescu-Mayes, Annamaria (2010a), 'Digital colonial amateur film collections and the study of imperial history', paper presented at World History and Digital Scholarship Conference, University of Cambridge.

Motrescu-Mayes, Annamaria (2010b), 'Private Australia: re-imagined nationhood in inter-war colonial home movies', *Journal of Australian Studies*, 34, 3, pp. 317–30.

Motrescu-Mayes, Annamaria (2011a), 'Rethinking colonial amateur cinema as a new source for the European imperial history curriculum', paper presented at Screen Studies Conference, University of Glasgow.

Motrescu-Mayes, Annamaria (2011b), 'Eroticizing the Empire: voyeurs, imperial fetishes and colonial amateur films', paper presented at The Erotic–Exploring Critical Issues Conference, Prague, Czech Republic.

Motrescu-Mayes, Annamaria (2011c), 'Imperial narratives displaced by subaltern Indian identities in early amateur films', *Journal of Early Popular Visual Culture*, 9, 2, pp. 107–21.

Motrescu-Mayes, Annamaria (2011d), 'Uncharted Masonic identities in British colonial amateur films, 1920–1940', paper presented at Freemasonry and Empire Conference, Canonbury Masonic Research Centre, London.

Motrescu-Mayes, Annamaria (2011e), 'Locating imaginary cartographies of the 1911 Coronation Durbar in colonial amateur photographs and films', paper presented at the Staging Empire – New Perspectives on the 1911 Coronation Durbar Conference, University of Manchester.

Motrescu-Mayes, Annamaria (2012a), 'Imperial imagination and colonial cities in inter-war amateur films', paper presented at Invisible Cités Coloniales Conférence, Université de Strasbourg, France.

Motrescu-Mayes, Annamaria (2012b), 'Amateur films and the silent migration of female colonial identities', paper presented at the Screen Studies Conference, University of Glasgow, 30 June.

Motrescu-Mayes, Annamaria (2012c), '"Cross-genre" home movies, religious narratives and British imperial studies', paper presented at the NECS Conference: Time Networks: Screen Media and Memory, New University of Lisbon and the University of Coimbra, 21 June.

Motrescu-Mayes, Annamaria (2012d), '"Stimulating Empire consciousness" with colonial amateur films', paper presented at Reflections on the Study of Amateur Cinema Symposium, University of Glasgow, 24 April.

Motrescu-Mayes, Annamaria (2013), 'Women, personal films and colonial intimacies', *Close Up: Film and Media Studies*, 1, 2, pp. 37–49.

Motrescu-Mayes, Annamaria (2014a), 'Uncensored imperial politics in British home movies from 1920s-1950s', in Laura Rascaroli, Gwenda Young, with Barry Monahan (eds) *Amateur Filmmaking. The Home Movie, the Archive, the Web*, London and New York: Bloomsbury Academic, pp. 95–107.

Motrescu-Mayes, Annamaria (2014b), 'Personal films in the digital space', a guest-edited special issue of *New Cinemas: Journal of Contemporary Film*, 11, 2–3.

Motrescu-Mayes, Annamaria (2014c), 'Growing-up in the Empire: amateur films of the "never home"', paper presented at the Children and Nontheatrical Media: From Film to Video Conference, University of Glasgow, 11 April.

Motrescu-Mayes, Annamaria (2014d), 'Amateur media, open-ended memory, and visual constructions of Tamil identities', paper presented at the Visual Anthropology and Contemporary South Asian History Conference, University of Cambridge, 5 April.

Motrescu-Mayes, Annamaria (2014e), 'Imperial imagination and colonial cities in inter-war amateur films', in A. Choné, F. Granchamp-Florentino and C. Repussard (eds) *(In)visibles cités coloniales. Stratégies de domination et de résistance de la fin du XIXe siècle à nos jours*, Paris: Orizons, pp. 103–14.

Motrescu-Mayes, Annamaria (2015), 'Britische Frauen mit imperialer Mission und ihre Amateurfilme', in Siegfried Mattl, Carina Lesky, Vrääth Ohner and Ingo Rechner (eds) *Abenteuer Alltag. Zur Archäologie des Amateurfilms*, Vienna: Osterreichisches Eilmuseum, Synema, pp. 172–82.

Mulvey, Laura (1975), 'Visual pleasure and narrative cinema', *Screen*, 16, 3 pp. 6–18.

National Film Preservation Foundation (2004), *The Film Preservation Guide. The Basics for Archives, Libraries, and Museums*. National Film Preservation Foundation, USA.

Neely, Sarah (2009), '"Ploughing a lonely furrow": Margaret Tait and professional filmmaking practices in 1950s Scotland', in Ian Craven (ed.), *Movies on Home Ground: Explorations in Amateur Cinema*, Newcastle-Upon-Tyne: Cambridge Scholars Publishing, pp. 301–22.

Neely, Sarah (2014), 'My heart beat for the wilderness': Isobel Wylie Hutchison, Jenny Gilbertson, Margaret Tait and other twentieth-century Scottish women filmmakers', in MacKenzie Scott and Anna Westerståhl Stenport (eds) *Films on Ice: Cinemas of the Arctic*, Edinburgh: Edinburgh University Press, pp. 302–12.

Nelson, Jimmy (2015), *Before They Pass Away*, Kempen, Germany: teNeues Media.

Neumann, M. (2001), 'Home movies on Freud's couch: an exploration of spontaneous performance, gender, and latent meanings in amateur films', Northeast Historic Film's Symposium, <http://www.oldfilm.org/nhfWeb/ed/essays/NeumannEssay2001.htm> (last accessed June 2010).

Newman, Rosie (undated), *Glimpses of India: The Story of the Film*, London: The Athenaum Press.

Newman, Rosie (*c*.1937), *To the Land of the Pharaohs: The Story of the Film*, R. Newman; IWM catalogue number LBY 86/801.

Newman, Rosie (1942), *Britain at War: Narrative of a Film*, London: Maxlove Publishing.

Newman, Rosie (1943), *The France I Knew: The Story of the Film*, London: Chiswick Press.

Newman, Rose (*c*.1956) *A Flying Visit to Yugoslavia, the Story of the Colour Film*, London: Wm Carling & Co.

Nicholson, Virginia (2008), *Singled Out: How Two Million Women Survived without Men after the First World War*, Oxford: Oxford University Press.

Niemeyer, Katharina (ed.) (2014), *Media and Nostalgia: Yearning for the Past, Present and Future*, Basingstoke: Palgrave Macmillan.

Noble, Albert (undated) 'AnimatioN animates any mate!', <http://www.theiac.org.uk/film/learn/animation/animation-animates.html> (last accessed 18 January 2018).

Nochlin, Linda (1999), *Representing Women*, London: Thames & Hudson.

Nora, Pierre (1989), 'Between memory and history: les lieux de mémoire', *Representations*, No. 26, Special Issue: *Memory and Counter-Memory*, Spring, pp. 7–24.

Norris Nicholson, Heather (2002a), 'Picturing the past: archival film and historical landscape change', *Landscapes* 3, 1, pp. 81–100.

Norris Nicholson, Heather (2002b), 'Telling travellers' tales: framing the world in home movies, c.1935 – 1967', in Tim Cresswell and Deborah Dixon (eds) *Engaging Film: Geographies of Mobility and Identity*, Lanham, MD: Rowman & Littlefield, pp. 47–68.

Norris Nicholson, Heather (2003), 'British holiday films of the Mediterranean. At home and abroad with home movies, c. 1925 –1936', *Film History*, 15, 2, pp. 102–16.

Norris Nicholson, Heather (2004), 'At home and abroad with cine enthusiasts: regional amateur filmmaking and visualising the Mediterranean, c.1928–1962', *Geo Journal* 59, 4, pp. 323–33.

Norris Nicholson, Heather (2006a), 'Sites of meaning: picturing Mediterranean and other landscapes in British home movies, c. 1928–1965', in Martin Lefebvre (ed.) *Landscape and Film*, London: Routledge, pp. 167–88.

Norris Nicholson, Heather (2006b), 'Through the Balkan states: home movies as travel texts and tourism histories', *Tourist Studies*, 6, 1 pp. 13–36.

Norris Nicholson, Heather (2009a), 'Floating hotels: cruise holidays and amateur film-making in the inter-war period', in David Clarke, Marcus Doel and Valerie Crawford Pfannhauser (eds) *Moving Pictures/Stopping Places: Hotels & Motels on Film*, Lanham, MD: Rowman & Littlefield, pp. 49–71.

Norris Nicholson, Heather (2009b), 'Framing the view: holiday recording and Britain's amateur film movement c.1925–1950' in Ian Craven (ed.) *Movies on Home Ground: Explorations in Amateur Cinema*, Cambridge: Cambridge Scholars Press, pp. 93–127.

Norris Nicholson, Heather (2009c), 'Journeys into seeing: amateur film and British tourism encounters in Russia, c.1932', *New Readings*, 10, pp. 57–71, <http://www.cardiff.ac.uk/euros/resources/newreadings/volume10/Norris%20Nicholson.pdf.> (last accessed 20 January 2018).

Norris Nicholson, Heather (2012a), *Amateur Film: Meaning and Practice, c. 1927–77*, Manchester: Manchester University Press.

Norris Nicholson, Heather (2012b), 'Seeing differently – women's amateur film practice in Britain's cine era', paper presented at the Screen Studies Conference, University of Glasgow, 30 June.

Norris Nicholson, Heather (2012c), 'Manchester's moving memories: tales from Moss Side and Hulme: archive film and community history-making', in Sonia Kmec and Vivian Thill (eds) *Tourists and Nomads: Amateur Images of Migration*, Magsburg: Jonas-Verlag, pp. 137–46.

Norris Nicholson, Heather (2013a), 'Cultural relations and comfortable curiosity: Manchester's cold war tourism in archive film', unpublished paper, Centre for Visual and Oral History Research, University of Huddersfield.

Norris Nicholson, Heather (2013b), 'Looking beyond the moving moments: adaptation, digitisation and amateur film footage as visual histories', in Laurence Raw and Defne Ersun Tutan (eds) *The Adaptation of History: Essays on Ways of Telling the Past*, Jefferson, NC: McFarland, pp. 196–206.

Norris Nicholson, Heather (2014), '"Legends, romance and the intelligent knowledge of history": story-telling on film and imagining the past', in Katherine Morey (ed.) *Bringing History to Life through Film. The Art of Cinematic Storytelling*, Lanham, MD: Rowman & Littlefield, pp. 89–109.

Norris Nicholson, Heather (2015a), 'Das Alltagsleben und andere Geschichten: Visuelle Praktiken britischer Amateur-Filmemacherinnenin' ['Everyday life and other stories: the visual practices of Britain's amateur women filmmakers – some preliminary findings'], in Siegfried Mattl, Carina Lesky, Vrääth Öhner and Ingo Zechner (eds) *Abenteuer Alltag. Zur Archäologie des Amateurfilms*, Vienna: Osterreichisches Filmmuseum und Synema Publikationen, pp. 199–217.

Norris Nicholson, Heather (2015b) 'Living on location: amateur creativity and negotiating a sense of place in Yorkshire', in Ian Franklin, Kirsten Skoog and Hugh Chignell (eds) *Regional Aesthetics: Mapping UK Media Cultures*, Basingstoke: Palgrave Macmillan, pp. 17–34.

Norris Nicholson, Heather (2017), 'Mediating northern identities', in Ewa Mazierski (ed.) *Heading North: The North of England in Film and Television*, Basingstoke: Palgrave Macmillan, pp. 73–92.

Odin, Roger (1995), *Le film de famille, usage privé, usage public*, Paris: Méridiens-Klincksieck.

Oram, Alison M. (1996), 'Women teachers in state schools in England and Wales 1900–1939: the development of feminist allegiance and political strategies', thesis, University of London.

O'Sullivan, M. (2000), 'Amateur Australian women film-makers of the 1930s and 1940s', *Metro Magazine*, 123, pp. 20–4.

Pasternak, Gil (2015), 'Taking snapshots, living the picture: the Kodak company's making of photographic biography', *Journal Life Writing*, 12, 4, pp. 431–46.

Pengelly, Kathleen (1961a), 'At the hairdressers', *Cine Cinema*, 2, 9, September p. 9.

Pengelly, Kathleen (1961b), 'Filming fireworks', *Cine Camera*, 2, 11, November pp. 14–15.

Penley, Constance (ed.) (1988), *Feminism and Film Theory*, London: Methuen and British Film Institute.

Phelan, Peggy (1993), *Unmarked: The Politics of Performance*, London: Routledge.

Phythian, D. M. (1958), 'Round the world record', *Amateur Movie Maker*, 1, 4, January, pp. 33–4.

Pilling, Jayne (ed.) (1992), *Women and Animation: A Compendium*, London: British Film Institute.

Pilling, Jayne (2009), *Animation 2D and Beyond*, Crans-Pres-Celigny: Rotovision.

Pilling, Jayne (2011), *A Reader in Animation Studies*, Bloomington and London: Indiana University Press/John Libbey, pp. 54–6.

Pilling, Jayne (ed.) (2012), *Animating the Unconscious. Desire, Sexuality and Animation*, London: Wallflower.

Pinder, Matt (2015), 'BBC 1 Scotland's home movies. The amateur filmmakers whose home movies help tell the story of 20th century Scotland', BBC 1 Scotland, 3 August, <http://www.bbc.co.uk/programmes/p02ypzfj> (last accessed 20 January 2018).

Powell, Dilys (1950), 'A considerable advance', *Amateur Cine World*, 14, 1, May pp. 33–4.

Pratt, A. E. (1948), Letter to the editor of *The Lady*, 18 June 1948. Private papers of Miss Rosie Newman, IWM, 2 Microfilm Reels, Catalogue number: Documents.23389.

Pratt, Mary Louise (1992), *Travel Writing and Transculturation*, London: Routledge.

Procida, Mary A. (2002), *Married to the Empire: Gender, Politics and Imperialism in India, 1883–1947*, New York: Manchester University Press.

Rambaud, Micheline (2015), 'Micheline Rambaud raconte la première expédition féminine en Himalaya', Rencontres, *Le magazine de la Fédération Française de la Montagne et de l'Escalade*, FFME IMAG, 7 December 2015.

Ranyard, Les (1982), 'Cutting the cost of cel animation', *Animator Magazine*, Autumn 2, pp. 11–13.

Rascaroli, Laura, Gwenda Young and Brian Monahan (eds) (2014), *Amateur Filmmaking: The Home Movie, the Archive, the Web*, London: Bloomsbury.

Reekie, Duncan (2003), 'Not art: an action history of British underground cinema', thesis, University of Plymouth.

Rock, Paul (2013), *Deviant Behaviour*, London: Routledge.

Rose, Tony (1957), 'We visit a cinema in an attic', *Amateur Movie Maker*, 1, 3, December pp. 30–1.

Rose, Tony (1958), 'Bad show at Bad Ems', *Amateur Movie Maker*, 1, 15, December p. 615.

Rose, Tony (1962), 'Women!', *Amateur Cine World Weekly*, 4 January, p. 11.

Rose, Tony (1968), 'Other people's movies', *Movie Maker*, 2, 9, September, p. 597.

Rose, Tony (1969a), 'Salute to the winners', *Movie Maker*, 3, 8, August, p. 508.

Rose, Tony (1969b), 'All done by electricity. Francis and Edith Williams. Other people's films', *Movie Maker*, 3, 8, August, p. 509.

Rose, Tony (1971), 'Other people's pictures', *Movie Maker*, 5, 3, March, p. 153.

Rose, Tony (1981), 'Making movies out of school', *Movie Maker*, 15, 2, pp. 105–6.

Rose, Tony and Alan Cleave (1980), '*Movie Maker* Ten Best competition results', *Movie Maker*, 14, 4, p. 654.

Ross, Kerry (2015), *Photography for Everyone. The Cultural Lives of Cameras and Consumers in Early Twentieth-Century Japan*, Palo Alto: Stanford University Press.

Rossetti, Lindsey (1984) 'How I made my first animated film', *Amateur Film Maker*, August, p. 21.

Rouch, Jean (1978), 'On the vicissitudes of the self: the possessed dancer, the magician, the sorcerer, the filmmaker, and the ethnographer', *Studies in Visual Communication*, 5, 1, Fall, pp. 2–8.

Rugg, Linda Haverty (2004), *Picturing Ourselves: Photography and Autobiography*, Chicago: University of Chicago Press.

Russell, Barrie (2004), 'Perspective: the Anne Robinson of Woodrush School; freelance writer and fellow Welford resident Barrie Russell looks at the life and work of one Britain's top amateur film makers – still going strong at 84', The Free Library, Birmingham Post & Mail Ltd, <https://www.thefreelibrary.com/Perspective%3a+The+Anne+Robinson+of+Woodrush+School%3b+Freelance+writer. . .-a0118661901> (last accessed 19 January 2018).

Said, Edward, (1979), *Orientalism*, New York: Vintage.

Sandford, Jeremy (undated), 'The Warp (Dick Jobson)', Jeremy Sandford Fan Club Archives, available at <http://www.JeremySandford.org.uk> (last accessed 18 January 2018).

Sandford, Jeremy (2008), 'A film show, Saturday, January 05, 2008', blog, Radnorian, <http://tredelyn.blogspot.co.uk/2008/01/> (last accessed 18 January 2018).

Schneider, Alexandra (2013), 'The tripod paradox and amateur film archaeology', paper presented at the Amateur Film Archaeologies Conference, Austrian Film Museum/Ludwig Institute, Vienna, 21–3 March.

Scholes, F. C. (1939), 'Making a film of school life', *Amateur Cine World*, 6, 4, p. 184.

Shannon, Sonya (2010), '10 noteworthy women animators. Women in animation: female animators who made history', *Artwarestudios*, 21 October, <http://www.artwarestudios.com/image-culture/10-noteworthy-women-animators/> (last accessed 18 January 2018).

Shepherd, Anna (2014), *Helen Unlimited: A Little Biggar*, Ryde, Isle of Wight: Billie Love Historical Collection.

Shone, Rev. Alan (1961), 'What every woman should know about cine', *Amateur Cine World Weekly*, 16 November, p. 787.

Shone, Rev. Alan (1962), 'Men can be dim too', letter, *Amateur Cine World Weekly*, 4 January, p. 8.

Showalter, Elaine (1986), 'Toward a feminist poetics', in Elaine Showalter (ed.) *The New Feminist Criticism: Essays on Women, Literature and Theory*, London: Virago, pp. 125–43.

Sinfield, Alan (1997), *Literature, Politics, and Culture in Post-war Britain*, London: Athlone Press.

Smith, Kathleen M. (1961), 'Insult to women', letter, *Amateur Cine World Weekly*, 14 December, p. 956.

Smith, Paul (1988), *Discerning the Subject*, Minneapolis: University of Minnesota Press.

Smith, Sidonie (1993), *Subjectivity, Identity and the Body: Women's Autobiographical Practices in the Twentieth Century*, Bloomington: Indiana University Press.

Smith, Sidonie and Julia Watson (eds) (1998), *Women, Autobiography, Theory: A Reader*, Madison: University of Wisconsin Press.

Spence, Jo and Patricia Holland (eds) (1991), *Family Snaps: The Meaning of Domestic Photography*, London: Virago.

Spencer, Stephanie (2005), *Gender, Women and Work in Britain in the 1950s*, Basingstoke: Palgrave Macmillan.

Spottiswoode, Raymond (1969), *The Focal Encyclopaedia of Film and Television Techniques*, London: Focal Press.

Stevenson, Mary (1982), 'Northwest frontiers', *Amateur Film Maker*, 4, 4, August, pp. 31–2.

Stewart, Gerald Pakenham (undated), *The Rough and the Smooth: an Autobiography, 1870–1947*, unpublished, 237pp, 3 boxes, Centre of South Asian Studies.

Stewart, Jez (2015a), ' A life in pictures (Halas and Batchelor)', *Sight and Sound*, 25, 8, pp. 24–31.

Stewart, Jez (2015b), 'The mystery of the disappearing women', 11 June, <http://halasbatchelor75.co.uk/where-did-they-go/> (last accessed 18 January 2018).

Stoker, Ann Laura (2002), *Carnal Knowledge and Imperial Power*, Berkeley: University of California Press.

Strasser, Alex (1936), 'Shadow plays for the Christmas film show', *Amateur Cine World* 3, 9, pp. 407–9.

Strasser, Alex (1940), 'Wartime plots for filming', *Amateur Cine World*, 6, 10, pp. 433–4, 444.

Stuart, Ruth (1934), 'How I made it: Egypt and back by Imperial Airways', *IAC Bulletin*, 4, January, pp. 7, 9.

Swanson, Dwight (2003), 'Inventing amateur film: Marion Norris Gleason, Eastman Kodak and the Rochester scene, 1921–1932', *Film History*, 15, 2, pp. 126–36.

Swift, Hazel (1961a), 'The continuity girl', a three part series, *Amateur Cine World Weekly*, 3 August, pp. 174–5, 200.

Swift, Hazel (1961b), 'The continuity girl', *Amateur Cine World Weekly*, 24 August, pp. 294–5.

Swift, Hazel (1961c), 'The continuity girl', *Amateur Cine World Weekly*, 28 September, pp. 482–3.

Swift, Hazel (1961d), 'They went that away', *Amateur Cine World Weekly*, 24 August, pp. 294–5.

Taylor, Astra (2014), *The People's Platform: Taking Back Power and Culture in the Digital Age*, London: Fourth Estate.

Taylor, Richard (2001), 'Alison de Vere. Obituary', *The Guardian*, 15 January, <https://www.theguardian.com/news/2001/jan/15/guardianobituaries> (last accessed 18 January 2018).

Tepperman, Charles (2014), *Amateur Cinema: The Rise of North American Moviemaking, 1923–1960*, Berkeley: University of California Press.

Thane, Pat (2010), 'Women and political participation in England, 1918–1970: what difference did the vote make?', in Patricia Thane and Esther Breitenbach (eds) *Women and Citizenship in Britain and Ireland in the Twentieth Century*, London: Continuum, pp. 11–28.

Thom, Deborah (1992), 'Wishes, anxieties, play, and gestures: child guidance in inter-war England', in Roger Cooter (ed.) *In the Name of the Child: Health and Welfare, 1880–1940*, London: Routledge, pp. 200–19.

Thompson, Lara (2010), 'Monochrome now: digital black and white cinema and the photographic past', *Screening the Past*, 29, <http://www.screeningthepast.com/2015/01/monochrome-now-digital-black-and-white-cinema-and-the-photographic-past/> (last accessed 29 January 2018).

Thompson, Sharon (2009), 'Our cameras, our lives: lesbian home movies, c. 1935 – 1999', paper presented at Ways of Watching, 10th Annual Northeast Historic Film Summer Symposium, 24–5 July, <http://oldfilm.org/content/2009-symposium> (last accessed 18 January 2018).

Thomson, Alistair and Alexander Freund (eds) (2011), *Oral History and Photography*, New York: Palgrave Macmillan.

Thubron, K. Agnes (1934), 'How I made it: *Her Second Birthday*', *IAC Bulletin*, 4, January, pp. 12–14.

Todd, Selina (2005), *Young Women, Work and Family in England*, Oxford: Oxford University Press.

Toplis, Elisabeth (1976), 'Family group brings magic of puppet heroes and villains', *Guernsey Evening Press and Star*, 15 April.

Townsend, Derek (1961), 'Mr and Mrs Movie-Maker. Exercise with scissors', *Amateur Movie Maker*, November, 4, 11, pp. 562–3.

Treneman, Anne (2016), 'What shadows at Birmingham Rep', *The Times*, 3 November, <https://www.thetimes.co.uk/article/theatre-what-shadows-at-birmingham-rep-klzjzdj7q> (last accessed 29 January 2018).

Tupper, Carrie (2014), 'A history of women in animation: mothers of a medium', *The MarySue*, 4 June, <https://www.themarysue.com/history-women-in-animation/> (last accessed 18 January 2018).

Turner, Michael (2015), *Eltham Palace. English Heritage Guidebooks*, London: English Heritage.

Uhlirova, Marketa (2013), '100 years of the fashion film: frameworks and histories', *Fashion Theory: The Journal of Dress, Body & Culture*, 17, 2 pp. 137–58.

Urbach, Karina (2015), 'Behind the infant Queen's gesture lies a dark history of aristocratic Nazi links', *The Guardian*, 19 July 2015, <https://www.theguardian.com/commentisfree/2015/jul/19/nazi-hitler-royal-family> (last accessed 10 September 2017).

Urry, John (1990), *The Tourist Gaze: Leisure and Travel in Contemporary Societies*, London: Sage.

Urwin, Cathy and Elaine Sharland (1992), 'From bodies to minds in childcare literature: advice to parents in inter-war Britain', in Roger Cooter (ed.) *In the Name of the Child: Health and Welfare, 1880–1940*, London: Routledge, pp. 174–99.

Valentine, Elizabeth R. (2006), *Beatrice Edgell: Pioneer Woman Psychologist*, New York: Nova Science Publishers.

van Baal, J. (1963), 'The cult of the bull-roarer in Australia and Southern New Guinea', *Bijdragen Tot De Taal-, Land- En Volkenkunde [Journal of the Humanities and Social Sciences of Southeast Asia]*, 119, 2, pp. 201–14.

Vicinus, Martha (1985), *Independent Women: Work and Community for Single Women, 1850–1920*, London: Virago.

Wade, Anne R. (undated), 'Biography of Isobel Wylie Hutchinson', National Library of Scotland, <http://movingimage.nls.uk/biography/10018> (last accessed 20 January 2018).

Wade, Anne R. (2004), 'Gilbertson, Jenny Isabel (1902–1990)', *Oxford Dictionary of National Biography*, <http://www.oxforddnb.com/index/101068740/Jenny-Gilbertson> (last accessed 19 January 2018).

Wade, John (2004), *Cine Cameras*, Risborough: Shire Publications.

Wagner, Gillian (1979), *Barnardo*, London: Weidenfeld & Nicolson.

Wagner, Gillian (1982), *Children of the Empire*, London: Weidenfeld & Nicolson.

Wagner, Gillian (*c*.2004), *Chair of Barnardo's and Many Other Charities*, interview, London: National Portrait Gallery, <http://www.npg.org.uk/assets/files/pdf/displays/interviews/Interview_GillianWagner.pdf> (last accessed 20 January 2018).

Wain, George (1951), *How to Film as an Amateur*, London: Focal Press.

Walden, Harry (1982), 'The hobby of a lifetime', *Amateur Film Maker*, 4, 4, August, pp. 29–30.

Webster, Wendy (1998), *Imagining Home: Gender, 'Race' and National Identity, 1945–1964*, London: University College London Press.

Wells, Paul (1998) *Understanding Animation*, Abingdon: Routledge.

Wells, Paul (2009), 'Introduction', in Sheila Graber, *Animation: A Handy Guide*, London: A. & C. Black Publishers.

Wells, Paul with Joanna Quinn and Les Mills (2009), *Drawing for Animation*, La Vergne: Ava Publishing/Ingram Publisher Services.

West, Nancy Martha (2000), *Kodak and the Lens of Nostalgia*, Charlottesville: University of Virginia Press.

White, Hayden (1978), *Tropics of Discourse: Essays in Cultural Criticism*, Baltimore: Johns Hopkins University Press.

Williams, A. Susan (2000), *Ladies of Influence: Women of the Elite in Interwar Britain*, London: Allen Lane/Penguin Press.

Winchester, Clarence (ed.) (1933), *The World Film Encyclopedia: A Universal Screen Guide*, London: The Amalgamated Press.

Wise, Wyndham (2012), 'Eunice Macaulay', *The Canadian Encyclopaedia* online, <http://www.thecanadianencyclopedia.ca/en/article/eunice-macaulay/> (last accessed 19 January 2018).

Wood, Leslie (1950), 'Party spirit; Maidenhead's Scientific Film Society's presentation of the Ten Best', *Amateur Cine World*, 13, 10, February, p. 886.

Woollacott, Angela (2006), *Gender and Empire*, London: Palgrave Macmillan.

Wynn Jones, Stuart (1958) 'Anyone can a-n-i-m-a-t-e! This does mean you!', *Amateur Cine World*, 21, 10, pp. 996–7.

Yzer, Marco C. and Brian G. Southwell (2008), 'New communication technologies, old questions', *American Behavioural Scientist*, 52, pp. 8–20, <https://pdfs.semanticscholar.org/e531/d5c0d05c6c9219c8a9080ade37beceaa25fa.pdf> (last accessed 29 January 2018).

Zalmanovich, Tal (2009), '"Woman pioneer of Empire": the making of a female colonial celebrity', *Postcolonial Studies*, 12, 2, pp. 193–210.

Zimmermann, Patricia (1995), *Reel Families: A Social History of Amateur Film*, Bloomington: Indiana University Press, pp. 61–2.

Zimmermann, Patricia (1996), 'Geographies of desire: cartographies of gender, race, nation and empire in amateur film', *Film History*, 8, pp. 85–98.

Zimmermann, Patricia (2008), 'Morphing history into histories: from amateur film to the archive of the future', in Karen L. Ishizuka and Patricia R. Zimmermann (eds) *Mining the Home Movie. Excavations in Histories and Memories*, Berkeley, Los Angeles and London: University of California Press, pp. 275–88.

Index

CPSIA information can be obtained
at www.ICGtesting.com
Printed in the USA
JSHW020453280920
8208JS00001B/13

9 781474 474337